"This book is about a vital but neglected aspect of game-based learning: emotionally imbuing participants with motivation and meaning through aesthetic experiences. Like the vision of games it espouses, Dickey weaves a seamless, elegant, and complete exposition of design principles for aesthetic learning."
—**Chris Dede**, Wirth Professor in Learning Technologies, Harvard University, USA

"A useful, in-depth examination of how aesthetics contribute to the growing complexity of gaming, filling another niche in the rapidly developing world of gaming scholarship. Michele Dickey examines how aesthetics are used in a number of different ways and via differing critical lenses in order to give a comprehensive, well-informed picture of how they inform game-based design and learning. By studying the ways that aesthetics function within different game genres, as well as providing useful directions to using aesthetics within educational game design, this book provides an informative, solid guide to critical and practical applications of aesthetics in gaming."
—**Esther MacCallum-Stewart**, Digital Cultures Research Centre, University of the West of England, UK

Aesthetics and Design for Game-based Learning

Aesthetics and Design for Game-based Learning provides learning designers with insight into how the different elements that comprise game aesthetics can inform the design of game-based learning. Regardless of the cognitive complexities involved, games are essentially entertainment media, and aesthetics play a large role in how they are experienced. Yet, too often, the role of aesthetics in the research about game-based learning has been relegated to a surface discussion of graphics or neglected altogether.

Aesthetics and Design for Game-based Learning begins by addressing the broad context of game aesthetics, then addresses specific elements, with chapters focusing on:

- player positioning
- game mechanics
- narrative design
- environment design
- character design.

Each chapter includes research and guidelines for design, and a conclusion addresses aesthetics in the research of game-based learning.

Michele D. Dickey is a Professor of Instructional Design and Technology at Miami University of Ohio, USA. She is currently Program Coordinator for the graduate programs in Educational Technology and Instructional Design and Technology. In addition to research, she has also authored the 3D immersive game-based environment *Murder on Grimm Isle*.

DIGITAL GAMES AND LEARNING

Series Editors Sara de Freitas and Paul Maharg

Online Gaming and Playful Organization by Harald Warmelink

Aesthetics and Design for Game-based Learning by Michele D. Dickey

Aesthetics and Design for Game-based Learning

Michele D. Dickey

NEW YORK AND LONDON

First published 2015
by Routledge
711 Third Avenue, New York, NY 10017

and by Routledge
2 Park Square, Milton Park, Abingdon, Oxon OX14 4RN

Routledge is an imprint of the Taylor & Francis Group, an informa business

© 2015 Taylor & Francis

The right of Michele D. Dickey to be identified as author of this work has been asserted by her in accordance with sections 77 and 78 of the Copyright, Designs and Patents Act 1988.

All rights reserved. No part of this book may be reprinted or reproduced or utilised in any form or by any electronic, mechanical, or other means, now known or hereafter invented, including photocopying and recording, or in any information storage or retrieval system, without permission in writing from the publishers.

Trademark notice: Product or corporate names may be trademarks or registered trademarks, and are used only for identification and explanation without intent to infringe.

Library of Congress Cataloging-in-Publication Data
Dickey, Michele D.
  Aesthetics and design for game-based learning / by Michele D. Dickey.
    pages cm. — (Digital games and learning)
  Includes bibliographical references and index.
  1. Educational games—Design and construction.   2. Simulation games in education—Design and construction.   I. Title.
  LB1029.G3D52 2015
  371.33′7—dc23
  2014034272

ISBN: 978-0-415-72094-6 (hbk)
ISBN: 978-0-415-72096-0 (pbk)
ISBN: 978-1-315-86666-6 (ebk)

Typeset in Minion
by Apex CoVantage, LLC

Contents

	Illustrations	ix
	Digital Games and Learning: Series Introduction	xi
	Sara de Freitas and Paul Maharg	
	Acknowledgments	xiii
1	Aesthetics, Experiences and Games	1
2	Aesthetics and Game Genres	13
3	Aesthetics and Player Perspective	41
4	Aesthetics and Narrative Design	57
5	Aesthetics and Character Design	81
6	Aesthetics and Environment Design	103
7	Aesthetics and Game Mechanics	125
8	Aesthetics, Inquiry and Research	141
	Index	153

Illustrations

Figures

3.1	Freytag's pyramid of dramatic structure	49
4.1	The three-act story structure	59
4.2	The hero's journey	65
4.3	Episodic long-form narrative	69
4.4	Serial long-form narrative	69
5.1	Squash and stretch	96

Tables

5.1	An outline of the affective domain and associated functions	83
5.2	Character types and roles	90
7.1	Core game mechanics and constructive learning	129
7.2	Game mechanics and cognition	130
7.3	Categorizing small quests by knowledge domains	134

Digital Games and Learning
Series Introduction

SARA DE FREITAS AND PAUL MAHARG

While clearly the use of games for supporting education is not new, the use of digital games is comparatively recent. With the emergence of web-based services, increased broadband and the growth of online communities, the use of digital games presents us with a unique set of engaging tools and techniques, based upon game mechanics such as competition, narrative, missions and quests.

Increasingly, games are being seen not as a technology but as a cultural form with its own genres, be they casual games played by everyone, serious games played to learn and engage, or gamification, whereby game elements are used to reach new audiences. Games offer us new toolsets that can be used effectively in activities as wide-ranging as therapy, awareness-raising or marketing, as well as more conventional curricula. The versatility of digital games to be applied to any problem or challenge has gained games new cultural status that they did not have previously. Digital educational games seek to inform, educate and motivate learners and to extend the range of our ability to learn in classrooms by making the world our classroom and by putting social interaction rather than curriculum objectives at the center of the learner's experience.

Game science is evolving too, and game mechanics are just beginning to transform education, how it is produced and how learning is assessed, with real potential for providing just-in-time learning and supporting hard-to-reach learner groups. However, the growth and spread of digital games in educational contexts are still relatively in their infancy, and the best methods for developing, assessing and deploying these approaches are also in their earliest stages of advancement. This book series thus aims, primarily, to bring existing game theory and practices together to support the ongoing development of game science as a sub-disciplinary and cross-disciplinary academic body of evidence, as a methodology of investigation, and as a set of tools, approaches, methods and frameworks for learning.

While game science has the power to transcend normal silos of disciplines, the academic communities in different disciplines and in different continents have had too few opportunities to work as an interdiscipline, in part because the field is so new and research has been taking place in such diverse disciplinary, sectoral and international contexts. This book series therefore specifically aims to

xii • Digital Games and Learning

build bridges between diverse research, teaching, policy and learner communities and is inspired by the next generation of young researchers currently completing their early studies in the field. Toward this end, the series brings together leading theorists, thinkers and practitioners into a community of practice around the key themes and issues of digital games and learning. These theorists come from areas as diverse as health and well-being, business and innovation, education, computer science and engineering, to name a few. Their perspectives include views from professional practice as well as from theoretical perspectives.

It is important not to underestimate the scale of the work ahead in this new field, but it is also important to recognize the power of these new tools beyond our current understanding of what they can do or will do in the future. Games will always be a central part of early-stage learning, but now the capability of games to save lives, to inform citizens and to contribute positive outcomes socially is just beginning to be understood. We have always understood the power of games to entertain; this series shows us scientifically how the power of play can be harnessed for more profound purposes and more altruistic reasons in new forms of sustainable and scalable education. *Digital Games and Learning* will explore the lineaments of the new learning and will reveal how and in what contexts that learning will take shape.

Professor Sara de Freitas
Coventry University, Coventry, UK

Professor Paul Maharg
The Australian National University, Canberra, Australia

June 2013

Acknowledgments

I would like to thank my family for all of their support during the writing process. I would also like to express my gratitude to my family, friends and students who share my love of games and endure my lack of skills. In particular, I would like to thank Andy Trick and Lucas Frazier for their insight into games and gameplay.

1
Aesthetics, Experiences and Games

Seeing what appears obvious is not always easy.

Elliot Eisner, 1998

Introduction

Within the broad realm of education and training, there has been much proselytizing about the impact of educational games and game-based learning to revolutionize teaching and learning. Digital games have long been viewed by educators and instructional designers as a model for interactive design. Games entertain by engaging and challenging players in environments that require players to strategize, plan, synthesize, analyze and evaluate. They induce the types of higher-order thinking skills that are the goals of current education. Regardless of the cognitive complexities evoked, games are essentially entertainment media and, as such, aesthetics play a large role in how they are realized and experienced. Yet far too often, the role of aesthetics in the research about game-based learning is relegated to a surface discussion of graphics, or the topic is neglected altogether. The aesthetics in popular games are much more than graphics; they are central to how a game is experienced and felt, and play an important role in conjuring and supporting the cognitive complexity of games. As such, they need to become a vital part of the research and design of game-based learning.

Aesthetic Experiences

Within the diverse field of education and central to most discussions about aesthetics is Dewey's (1934) discourse about aesthetic experiences. Dewey maintains that an experience occurs when the material experience is fulfilled or is consummated:

> [W]e have an experience when the material experienced runs its course to fulfillment. Then and then only is it integrated within and demarcated in the general stream of experience from other experiences. A piece of work is finished in a way that is satisfactory; a problem receives its solution; a

2 • Aesthetics, Experiences and Games

game is played through; a situation, whether that of eating a meal, playing a game of chess, carrying on a conversation, writing a book, or taking part in a political campaign, is so rounded out that its close is a consummation and not a cessation. Such an experience is a whole and carries with it its own individualizing quality and self-sufficiency. It is an experience.

(p. 37)

Experiences are memorable in the sense that they are recalled as standing out from events, activities and feelings that came before and came after. Aesthetic experiences are heightened and meaningful experiences in which each phase flows into the next seamlessly from one part of the phase to the other. The term "flow" does not imply that elements are without pause or that the phases are the same. Dewey uses the example of a play to illustrate that the phases are different, yet flow together. Each part or phase may be distinct, but flows into the next without seams, gaps or voids. Aesthetic experiences also have a sense of unity of the parts to the whole. It is that unity that allows the experience to be named or recalled as something complete and separate. The unity of the flow of parts or phases makes the experience a single entity: "an experience." The unity of *an* experience is not exclusively emotional, practical or intellectual, but is determined by a single, pervasive quality. Aesthetic experiences also have a conclusion that is a consummation of the flow of phases or elements. Culminations are more than a mere cessation, but instead are marked with a sense of anticipation of the culmination of all that went before.

Works of art and games in various forms provide examples of aesthetic experiences because the different aspects of games construct a unity of elements that flow from one part to the next, culminating in a consummation. With an aesthetic experience, there is a connection between each element and what went before and after. In contrast, the non-aesthetic lies within a polar progression of a loose succession or a strictly mechanical connection of parts. Because much of our everyday experiences fall within this progression, aesthetic experiences stand out from the norm.

According to Dewey (1934), emotion plays a large role in distinguishing an aesthetic experience. Dewey maintains that aesthetic experiences are emotional because emotions are attached to the events within the experience. Emotions are not separate, but instead arise from the experience and are "qualifications of a drama and they change as the drama develops" (p. 43). Emotion is what binds the parts into the whole that impacts how we perceive the experience. Emotions are what constitute unity in an aesthetic experience. As Dewey maintains:

Emotion is the moving and cementing force. It selects what is congruous and dyes what is selected with its color, thereby giving qualitative unity to materials externally disparate and dissimilar. It thus provides unity in and through the varied parts of an experience.

(p. 44)

Key aspects of Dewey's description of aesthetic experiences include the following:

- Memorable: distinguishable and stand out from what went before and after
- Flow: events, phases, parts flow seamlessly to a holistic whole
- Unity (bound with emotion): unity in the parts is constructed through the emotions experienced
- Consummation: a culmination of the events leads to a consummation

Within Dewey's chapter about experiences, one of the first examples of experiences he provides is games and playing chess. He casually lists these among several other examples to exemplify experiences that are individual with self-sufficiency that culminate in a type of consummation. Games are a fitting example of what Dewey delineates as aesthetic experiences. Although Dewey first published his foundational work, *Art as Experience*, in 1934, many of the key aspects of his characterization of aesthetic experiences are also key aspects of contemporary digital games. Elements such as flow, unity and consummation are, to varying degrees, aspects of contemporary game design and as such provide an innovative model for creating experiences.

The Value of Aesthetic Experiences for Learning

The roots of the field of instructional/learning design are grounded in science-based traditions of behaviorist and cognitivist perspectives, yet it is also a design discipline and as such it is a discipline in which the central act is to plan and create. Harris and Walling (2013) argue that despite the science-based traditions of the field, the work of the learning designer is "composed of both art and science." While cognition is central to learning, learning experiences also include cultural, emotional and social qualities (Wilson, 2005). As Parrish (2009) argues, learning designers are also "in the business of creating refined and intensified forms of experience" (p. 514), even if we typically avoid talking about their aesthetic qualities. At the core of learning design is the act of design and as such is essentially creative and innovative in nature. We know from a wide variety of sources that aesthetics influence interactions (Norman, 2004; McArthur, 1982; Miller, Veletsianos & Hooper, 2006; Tractinsky, Katz & Ikar, 2000). What is aesthetically pleasing impacts our emotions and, in turn, our behavior.[1] Yet too often, the topic of aesthetics is relegated to the fringes of learning design. Much of the focus of traditional instructional design has been on systematic design that focuses almost exclusively on cognition. The role of aesthetics is often a side note relegated to a discussion of principles of graphic design for the design of visual materials. In an era in which the needs of education and the educated workforce are rapidly shifting from learners who are receptive and programmable to learners who are creative and innovative problem-solvers, it is the whole learner that needs to be central to the learning experience (Harris & Walling, 2013; Kay, 2010). The arts in

4 • Aesthetics, Experiences and Games

various forms provide guidance on how to create immersive, memorable, cohesive experiences. As Eisner (1998) contends, "creative thinking—is not characterized by conformity to a predetermined standard" (p. 103).

Ironically, despite the need for more holistic approaches to learning design, there is value in aligning learning design with science. Wilson (2005)[2] provides a compelling discussion of the polarity between science and design in the field of learning design. Wilson briefly outlines the emergence of the "learning sciences" and how within academia the term "learning sciences" affords more prestige because of the perception of science-based fields as more rigorous disciplines. Unfortunately, too often these attitudes are embraced by the field of instructional/learning design. Being aligned with "science" affords more prestige, potential of power, and most certainly funding. Beyond concerns of reputation, the fields of psychology and cognitive science and other related fields are central to learning design, and this book is not meant to imply otherwise, but rather the goal is to value and reconcile aesthetics with science-based approaches to learning design.

Aesthetics and Learning Design

The field of instructional/learning design has been primarily focused on cognition and the science of learning; however, Parrish (2005, 2009) attempts to address this disparity by drawing upon Dewey's (1934) explication of aesthetic experiences. According to Dewey, there is a type of "dynamic organization" to experiences that fosters growth through the duration of the inception, development and fulfillment. These roughly correspond to Aristotle's foundation of dramatic structure of beginning, middle and end (exposition, climax and dénouement). Parrish (2009) integrates Dewey's *experience* by outlining aesthetic principles for instructional design in an attempt to reconcile the duel natures of learning design. Parrish's principles include:

> Principle 1: Learning experiences have beginnings, middles and endings.
> Principle 2: Learners are the protagonists of their own learning experiences.
> Principle 3: Learning activity, not subject matter, establishes the theme of instruction.
> Principle 4: Context contributes to immersion in the instructional situation.
> Principle 5: Instructors and instructional designers are authors, supporting characters and model protagonists.

Among Parrish's (2009) principles are narrative arcs, immersion, first-person protagonist, theme, context (environment) and roles. All of these elements are aspects of games and game-based learning. Understanding the differing aesthetics that contribute to games and game design can both inform game-based learning and also hold relevance for interactive educational media, distance learning and traditional classroom-based practices.

Aesthetics and Game-based Learning

Games have long been part of the spectrum of educational media and instructional design, but due to limitations of technology and the necessity of programming skills, there were relatively small groups of researchers conducting research about the design of digital games for teaching and learning. However, as technology improved and became more accessible, digital games became more sophisticated and began to cultivate a larger and more diverse population of players. The growing popularity of games has helped spark greater interest in the use of games for teaching and learning. In the late 1990s and early 2000s, educational researchers such as Bruckman (2000), Dede (2003), Gee (2003), Prensky (2001), Rieber (1996) and Squire (2003) ushered in a new era of research into the educational use of games and the burgeoning field of game-based learning.

Much has been written about the potential of games for teaching and learning in both the design of educational games and the implementation of "off-the-shelf." This growing body of work initially focused on the potential of digital games to transform learning and reshape learning environments; however, research to support these claims is limited and only beginning to emerge (Barab & Dede, 2007; de Freitas & Neumann, 2009; Jamaludin, Chee & Ho, 2009; Ketelhut, Dede, Clarke & Nelson, 2007; Kim, Park & Baek, 2009; Papastergiou, 2009; Squire & Jan, 2007; Annetta, Minogue, Holmes & Cheng, 2009; Tuzun, Yilmaz-Soylu, Karakus, Inal & Kizilkaya, 2009). Most of the research that contributes to our knowledge about educational games and game-based learning relies upon science-based methodologies to document, describe and investigate what are essentially dynamic aesthetic experiences. Science-based modes of inquiry are certainly important for the design and research into games and game-based learning; however, the foundation of digital games, like other forms of educational media such as educational films and television, was primarily established as an entertainment media. Entertainment media and many forms of fine and performing arts are meant to be felt, sensed and experienced. Aesthetics are at the core of the arts and artistic media, yet too often science, as the prevailing mode of inquiry, misses the impact and influence of the aesthetics. Science-based methodologies provide a means for gathering and analyzing data, but they do not allow for the designer/ technologist to "get inside" the experience. Often, in research about game-based learning, the role of aesthetics is reduced to some minor notion of graphics or color. Yet, it is the neglected elements of aesthetics that may impact cognition and learning.

The purpose of this book is to explore how aesthetics function in gameplay and to address how differing aesthetics from diverse fields can inform the design of game-based learning. Games involve more than cognitive rules, actions and procedures; they also provide sensory and embodied experiences. Understanding how aesthetics function in the overall gameplay experience is an important step in the effective design of game-based learning. However,

6 • Aesthetics, Experiences and Games

just as the aesthetics vary among different literary genres and film genres, aesthetics function differently in varying types of gameplay, and understanding those differences provides key insight into the development of game-based learning that is cognitively engaging on many levels. The goal of this book is twofold; the first goal is to provide insight into how aesthetics function in different types of games and the different elements that comprise gameplay aesthetics. The second goal is to address how the function of different aesthetics informs the design of game-based learning.

Aesthetics in Games

Any discussion about aesthetics should include a definition of aesthetics; however, defining aesthetics is not an easy task and may rapidly digress into a philosophical discussion about beauty, art and the meaning of art. Although, in itself, that is an interesting discussion, it is not one that advances the goal of this book. Therefore, in an attempt to remain focused on the topic and within scope of this book, the definition(s) of aesthetics will be focused on how aesthetics are discussed within the field of game design. There are three main ways in which aesthetics are typically addressed in the field of game design: (1) art design (graphics, color, animation, video, etc.), (2) interactive design, and (3) games as art.

Aesthetics and Art Design

The term "aesthetics" is often used in text about game design to refer to the art design in games. In some of the earliest digital games, visual representation was limited to text (*The Colossal Cave Adventure*); however, advancements in computers, computer graphics and the advent of consoles allowed designers to integrate graphics, sound, animation and video. These forms were not only appropriated from other types of media, but also within the context of a game formed their own unique aesthetic. As the technology developed, so did the capabilities of adding richer and more dynamic art design. Narrative design, 3D animation, character design and immersive environments are now part of the complex aesthetic that constructs the gameplay environment and impacts how the player feels, senses and experiences a game. Hunicke, LeBlanc and Zubek (2004) devised the MDA framework as a means to approach design and research of games. The MDA framework delineates between three main areas of game design: mechanics, dynamics and aesthetics. Within the realm of aesthetics, Hunicke, LeBlanc and Zubek (2004) define aesthetics as the type of experiences evoked in different games (i.e., discovery, fantasy, fellowship). In later work, LeBlanc (2006) argues that the aesthetics provide the "emotional content" of a game and are responsible for evoking the emotional responses that players have when they play. LeBlanc contends that a game's aesthetic emerges from the game's dynamics (behavior) and how the behavior of the game evokes responses from the player.

Aesthetics and Interactive Design

Beyond the dynamics of art design, other game designers and theorists focus on the interactive elements of games in their definitions of game aesthetics. Mortensen (2009) addresses the aesthetics of immersion and interactivity and how the game structure (genre and mechanics) and interface design, along with the narrative and visual design, support both the immersion of the player in the experience and the interactivity between the game and the player. Similarly, veteran game designer and theorist Chris Crawford (2003) maintains that interactivity is the essence of a digital game. Crawford stresses the importance of a game aesthetic that is *process intensive* vs. *data intensive* because it promotes more organic interaction. Myers (1990a) also defines game aesthetics as being the result of interactivity. According to Myers, "A computer game 'aesthetic' cannot be based solely on game content but must consider player-game relationships as well" (1990b, p. 290).

Games as Art

Finally, the term "aesthetics" is also used in reference to games as an artistic medium. Theorists and designers have discussed the importance of cultivating the aesthetic of games—not just art games, but games as art (Crawford, 1984, 2003; Aarseth, 1997; Costikyan, 2002; Rollings & Adams, 2003; Mortensen, 2009). Costikyan's seminal discussion about games as art argues for the need to cultivate an aesthetic unique to the medium. These arguments have been echoed and championed by theorists and designers who argue that although games incorporate aesthetics from literature, film and animation, games are essentially interactive environments that share commonalities with existing mediums, but nonetheless are a unique medium and not to be compared or held to standards of other mediums.

Chapter Overview

The aesthetics of game art, interface design, interactive design and even games as art are all important elements when discussing aesthetics and game design; however, those brief discussions reveal little about how aesthetics function in gameplay or how they inform the design of game-based learning—which is the central tenet of this book. To that end, the focus of this book is on the intersection of aesthetics in games and the various sources and resources for creating and infusing aesthetics for game-based learning. The purpose of this chapter is to provide the foundation for why aesthetics are important for learning and to provide an overview of how they are discussed in relation to contemporary games. Chapter 2 provides an overview of how aesthetics function in different game genres. Chapters 3–7 provide in-depth exploration of different elements that encompass game aesthetics. Each chapter includes guidance for integrating these different elements into game-based learning and learning design. Finally, Chapter 8 concludes with a discussion of connoisseurship and criticism, and methods for

8 • Aesthetics, Experiences and Games

inquiry about the design of game-based learning and as a means for addressing aesthetics in research and education about game-based learning.

Chapter 1: Aesthetics, Experiences and Games

The purpose of this chapter is to present a discussion about Dewey's description of aesthetic experiences and to present an argument as to the importance of aesthetics in learning design and the relevance of aesthetics for the design of game-based learning. Following is an overview of how aesthetics are viewed in the realm of games and game design.

Chapter 2: Aesthetics and Game Genres

The purpose of this chapter is to address the differing aesthetics in various types of game genres. This chapter includes an analysis of the role of aesthetics in each of the following game genres: adventure games, role-playing games (along with Massively Multiplayer Online Role-playing Games), action games, simulations and strategy games, and virtual worlds. Included in each analysis is an outline of key aspects of aesthetic design for the genre. Following each outline is a review of research about the educational integration and/or design related to the aesthetics of each genre in the application of game-based learning.

Chapter 3: Aesthetics and Player Perspective

The focus of this chapter is on the different elements that construct player positioning in games. Player positioning is constructed by different elements in games: mechanics (camera view and movement), narrative, embodiment and immersion. This chapter begins with a discussion of the classic modes of player positioning in different games, both graphical and text-based. This section is followed by a discussion of how narrative perspective and point of view contributes to player perspective. This discussion is followed by a short analysis of how character design affordances and constraints foster embodiment. Following this analysis is a discussion of immersion through the lenses of two differing dramatic aesthetics (Aristotelian and Brechtian) and the educational implications of player perspective for the design of game-based learning.

Chapter 4: Aesthetics and Narrative Design

The purpose of this chapter is to provide a discussion of the aesthetics of narrative design in games and to provide strategies for incorporating aesthetics of narrative design for game-based learning. This chapter begins with an overview of narrative in games, followed by three analyses of narrative structures found in games: the three-act story structure, quest and long-form narrative. Within each analysis is a discussion of strategies used to integrate narrative within games, followed by a discussion of the educational implications related to each narrative structure. This chapter concludes with guidelines for developing and integrating narrative for game-based learning. Much of this chapter is based on my research in games and narrative. It includes updated and expanded work from several journal articles.

Chapter 5: Aesthetics and Character Design

The purpose of this chapter is to provide a discussion about the role and design of characters in games and game-based learning. The chapter begins with an overview of the affective domain and emotional intelligence, followed by a review of research about the integration and design of characters (pedagogical agents) for learning. The next section focuses on methods for character design from such fields as literature, game design and theater. This section is followed by a review of methods and strategies for visual design. The final section includes guidance and strategies for developing compelling characters (pedagogical agents) for game-based learning.

Chapter 6: Aesthetics and Environment Design

The purpose of this chapter is to provide a discussion of different sources of environmental design that can provide guidance and insight into the design of environments for game-based learning. This chapter begins with the field of game design and a heuristic of game elements that shape the game space. The focus of this section is on Adams' (2014) outline of game dimensions and includes a discussion of the relevance Adams' outline of game dimensions provides for learning design and game-based learning. This section is followed by a discussion of experience design in storied spaces, evocative places and narrative environments. This discussion focuses on how differing aesthetics in physical spaces such as museums, cathedrals, casinos and amusement parks can educate, influence behavior and evoke emotions. Following this section is an overview of research about the educational use of virtual space (for game-like learning) and research about virtual world design. Included in this discussion is a heuristic for the integration of architectural elements to aid in navigation and wayfinding for game-based virtual environments.

Chapter 7: Aesthetics and Game Mechanics

This chapter begins with an overview of game mechanics, followed by a discussion of core mechanics and strategies for mapping core mechanics with elements of constructivist learning environments. This section is followed by an outline of common secondary mechanics and a discussion of the types of cognition, based on Bloom's taxonomy, they foster. Following is a discussion of game mechanics in different genres (adventure game puzzles, RPG small quests, arcade/shooter-style mechanics and construction mechanics) and how they foster cognition.

10 • Aesthetics, Experiences and Games

Chapter 8: Aesthetics, Inquiry and Research

The purpose of this chapter is to discuss modes of inquiry into game-based learning that present alternatives to science-based methods of inquiry: connoisseurship and criticism. The chapter begins with a discussion of connoisseurship. This section is followed by a discussion of educational criticism for game-based learning. The chapter concludes with a short discussion of qualitative criticism as a means of integrating arts-based and science-based modes of inquiry.

Notes

1. Two great examples of how aesthetics can impact behavior can be found online at Volkswagen's initiative, Thefuntheory.com (http://www.thefuntheory.com/). The *Piano Staircase* and *The World's Deepest Bin* are great examples of how aesthetic experiences can impact behavior.
2. Wilson (2005) provides a compelling framework for integrating aesthetics in learning design.

References

Aarseth, E. J. (1997). *Cybertext: Perspectives on ergodic literature*. Baltimore, MD: Johns Hopkins University Press.

Adams, E. (2014). *Fundamentals of game design* (3rd ed.). Indianapolis, IN: New Riders.

Annetta, L. A., Minogue, J., Holmes, S. Y., & Cheng, M. T. (2009). Investigating the impact of video games on high school students' engagement and learning about genetics. *Computers & Education*, 53, 74–85.

Barab, S. A., & Dede, C. (2007). Games and immersive participatory simulations for science education: An emerging type of curricula. *Journal of Science Education and Technology*, 16(1), 1–3.

Bruckman, A. (2000). Situated support for learning: Storm's weekend with Rachael. *Journal of the Learning Sciences*, 9(3), 329–372.

Costikyan, G. (2002). I have no words & I must design. Toward a critical vocabulary for games. In F. Mäyrä (Ed.), *Computer Games and Digital Cultures Conference Proceedings. Studies in Information Sciences* (pp. 9–33). Tampere, Finland: Tampere University Press.

Crawford, C. (1984). *The art of computer game design*. Amazon Digital Services.

Crawford, C. (2003). *Chris Crawford on game design*. Indianapolis, IN: Peachpit Press.

Dede, C. (2003). Multi-user virtual environments. *EDUCAUSE Review*, 38(3), 60–61.

de Freitas, S., & Neumann, T. (2009). The use of "exploratory learning" for supporting immersive learning in virtual environments. *Computers & Education*, 52, 343–352.

Dewey, J. (1934). *Art as experience*. New York, NY: The Berkley Publishing Group.

Eisner, E. W. (1998). *The enlightened eye: Qualitative inquiry and the enhancement of educational practice*. Upper Saddle River, NJ: Merrill.

Gee, J. P. (2003). *What video games have to teach us about learning and literacy*. New York, NY: Palgrave/Macmillan.

Harris, P., & Walling, D. R. (2013). The learning designer: Merging art and science with educational technology. *TechTrends*, 57(5), 35–41.

Hunicke, R., LeBlanc, M., Zubek, R. (2004). MDA: A formal approach to game design and game research. Retrieved November 9, 2014, from http://www.cs.northwestern.edu/~hunicke/MDA.pdf

Jamaludin, A., Chee, Y. S., & Ho, C. M. L. (2009). Fostering argumentative knowledge construction through enactive role play in Second Life. *Computers & Education*, 53, 317–329.

Kay, K. (2010). 21st century skills: Why they matter, what they are, and how we get them. In J. Bellanca & R. Brandt (Eds.), *21st century skills: Rethinking how students learn* (pp. xxiii–xxxi). Bloomington, IN: Select Tree Press.

Ketelhut, D. J., Dede, C., Clarke, J., & Nelson, B. (2007). Studying situated learning in a multi-user virtual environment. In E. Baker, J. Dickieson, W. Wulfeck & H. O'Neil (Eds.), *Assessment of problem solving using simulations* (pp. 37–58). New York, NY: Lawrence Erlbaum Associates.

Kim, B., Park, H., & Baek, Y. (2009). Not just fun, but serious strategies: Using meta-cognitive strategies in game-based learning. *Computers & Education*, 52(4), 800–810.

LeBlanc, M. (2006). Tools for creating dynamic game dynamics. In K. Salen & E. Zimmerman (Eds.), *The game design reader* (pp. 438–459). Cambridge, MA: The MIT Press.

McArthur, L. Z. (1982). Judging a book by its cover: A cognitive analysis of the relationship between physical appearance and stereotyping. In A. H. Hastorf & A. M. Isen (Eds.), *Cognitive social psychology* (pp. 149–211). New York, NY: Elsevier.

Miller, C., Veletsianos, G., & Hooper, S. (2006). Demystifying aesthetics: An exploration of emotional design. In *Proceedings of the 2006 Computers and Advanced Technology in Education (CATE)* conference, October 4–6, 2006, Lima, Peru.

Mortensen, T. E. (2009). *Perceiving play: The art and study of computer games*. New York, NY: Peter Lang Press.

Myers, D. (1990a). Chris Crawford and computer game aesthetics. *Journal of Popular Culture*, 24(2), 17–28.

Myers, D. (1990b). Computer game genres. *Play & Culture*, 3(4), 286–301.

Norman, D. (2004). *Emotional design: Why we love (or hate) everyday things*. New York, NY: Basic Books.

Papastergiou, M. (2009). Digital game-based learning in high school computer science education: Impact on educational effectiveness and student motivation. *Computers & Education*, 52(1), 1–12.

Parrish, P. E. (2005). Embracing the aesthetics of instructional design. The *International Visual Literacy Conference*. Trinity College, Dublin, Ireland, October 2005.

Parrish, P. E. (2009). Aesthetic principles for instructional design. *Educational Technology Research and Development*, 57(4), 511–528.

Prensky, M. (2001). *Digital game-based learning*. New York, NY: McGraw-Hill.

Rieber, L. P. (1996). Seriously considering play: Designing interactive learning environments based on the blending of microworlds, simulations, and games. *Educational Technology Research & Development*, 44(2), 43–58.

Rollings, A., & Adams, E. (2003). *Andrew Rollings and Ernest Adams on game design*. Boston, MA: New Riders.

Squire, K. (2003). Video games in education. *International Journal of Intelligent Simulations and Gaming*, 2(1), 49–62.

Squire, K. D., & Jan, M. (2007). Mad City Mystery: Developing scientific argumentation skills with a place-based augmented reality game on handheld computers. *Journal of Science Education and Technology*, 16(1) 5–29.

Tractinsky, N., Katz, A., & Ikar, D. (2000). What is beautiful is usable. *Interacting with Computers*, 13, 127–145.

Tüzün, H., Yılmaz-Soylu, M., Karakuş, T., Inal, Y., & Kızılkaya, G. (2009). The effects of computer games on primary school students' achievement and motivation in geography learning. *Computers & Education*, 52(1), 68–77.

Wilson, B. G. (2005). Broadening our foundation for instructional design: Four pillars of practice. *Educational Technology*, 45(2), 10–15.

2
Aesthetics and Game Genres

Introduction

The purpose of this chapter is to present some of the more popular game genres and address the role of aesthetics in each genre. This chapter includes an analysis of the role of aesthetics in each of the following game genres: adventure games, role-playing games (along with Massively Multiplayer Online Role-playing Games), action games, simulations and strategy games, and virtual worlds. Included in each analysis is an outline of key aspects of aesthetic design for the genre. Following each outline is a review of research about the educational integration and/or design related to the aesthetics of each genre in the application of game-based learning.

Adventure Games

Background

Among one of the oldest genres of digital games is the adventure game. The roots of adventure games can be traced to text-based interactive fiction/adventure games such as *The Colossal Cave Adventure* (Hafner & Lyon, 1996; Levy, 1984). Adventure games are interactive stories that place the player in the central role of a character within that story. The purpose of gameplay is to advance the plot through exploration and solving challenges. Adventure games, unlike other game genres, do not include competition, combat or time management.[1] Storytelling is central to adventure games. The conflict within the game is a function of the narrative. The types of challenges players typically encounter include different types of puzzles. Solving a puzzle will often unlock a new area of the game and trigger the presentation of some aspect of the story to advance the game.

The earliest adventure games were text-based environments in which the player (cast in the leading role) used text commands to explore text-based *rooms* or *locations*. Within those rooms, players encountered characters, objects and doors and openings. The player used text commands to interact with the environment, manipulate objects and interact with characters. At the time when adventure games first emerged, computers were text-based environments that required the use of commands to operate. Users with DOS or UNIX systems were accustomed to environments and actions constructed entirely of text. In that era,

13

14 • Aesthetics and Game Genres

most users were adept at using different command words to accomplish various computer functions. Text-based adventures were well suited to the constraints and skills of the time.

With the advent of computers with graphic capabilities, adventure games developed into graphical games in which players could "point and click" within a graphical environment. This convention has continued in contemporary adventure games. Among the earliest is the legendary game *Myst*, an ethereal adventure with exotic locales. The game consisted of various scenes in which players clicked on specific objects to manipulate and explore. Within this style, the point of view or player perspective was predefined—typically, a mise-en-scène wide view of a scene. This convention still exists in some contemporary casual adventure games.

Narrative

Central to the adventure game genre is the story. The story typically centers on a character put in the position of having to uncover a mystery or overcome some challenging conflict. The character typically has to explore different locations, spaces or rooms throughout the duration of the story. While exploring different locations, the character encounters obstacles and puzzles that must be solved to both advance the plot and unlock new rooms or spaces.

Character

Adventure games are typically designed to be single-player games in which the player is cast in the leading role of the protagonist in the story. The player may encounter characters within a scene and interact with those non-player characters (NPC) by clicking on the character and choosing from selections of predefined dialogue. Although most adventure games are single-player games, social environments such as discussion groups and blogs have emerged devoted to games such as the *Nancy Drew* series, in which fans interact with other fans and offer advice. These form a type of social environment that complements the game and fulfills some needs for social interaction, although the games remain single-player games.

Environment and Perspective

Adventure games typically consist of a series of related rooms or spaces that the player must explore. The game space may be as seemingly simple as a series of pre-rendered scenes of rooms or spaces that the player enters and exits by clicking on the right, left, top and bottom of a frame, or the game space may be a real-time 3D environment in which the player moves the character through the setting. Both styles have advantages and disadvantages. The pre-rendered scenes are in some respects easier to construct inasmuch as only those aspects of the environment that will appear in the game need to be created. The visual design can be controlled more easily with lighting and shadows supporting the mood and tone. Because the scenes are pre-rendered, they can contain a great deal of detail that is difficult to duplicate in real-time rendered scenes without skillful texture mapping. However, pre-rendered games tend to be less immersive experiences.

The player perspective may be first-person (typical with pre-rendered scenes), first-person real-time or third-person real-time. The first-person perspective in pre-rendered scenes places the player outside of the staged scene and looking in, much like a theatrical performance. In a real-time rendered environment, the player perspective may also be first-person, but the difference is that the player has more choice of movement within the scene, rather than being external. The camera moves with the player, and the player encounters the setting as the character encounters it. There is also the option of third-person perspective in real-time rendered adventure games. In third-person perspective, the player is able to view the character being played, but typically from behind and over the shoulder. This allows the player to see the main character and, depending upon the visual design and animation of the character, perhaps also get a stronger sense of the character from the visual design.

The game space can be as simple as a series of related rooms or spaces, or a complex multilevel environment. Typically, within the adventure game genre, most locales are not readily accessible at the start of the game, but become accessible as the player solves challenges and unlocks new locales.

Challenges/Mechanics

There are a variety of challenges within adventure games, but the predominant type of challenge are puzzles. There is a wide variety of puzzle types, but the most common include the following:

1. Inventory manipulation
2. Dialogue-based puzzles
3. Mazes
4. Environment puzzles
5. Locks
6. Jigsaw puzzles
7. Slider puzzles
8. Audio puzzles
9. Combination puzzles

Adams (2014) and Schell's (2008) respective work provides some general guidelines for puzzle design in adventure games. First and foremost, the solution to a puzzle should not be random and rely solely on trial and error (Adams, 2014; Graft, 2013). Clues to solving a puzzle should exist within the environment the player has encountered. The goal of a puzzle should be easily understood by looking at or interacting with the puzzle (Adams, 2014; Schell, 2008). For example, piano

16 • Aesthetics and Game Genres

keys would imply the solution may be a sequence of music or a series of notes. Puzzles should be solvable within the context of the game and not require players to look outside the game for solutions (Adams, 2014; Schell, 2008). In other words, the solution to the puzzle should exist in the game itself and not require players to consult resources outside of the game to gain knowledge to solve puzzles.[2] Finally, puzzles should increase in difficulty throughout the game (Schell, 2008). Puzzles and puzzle types encountered at the end of the game should be more difficult than puzzles encountered earlier in the game.

Character

There are two main methods of character movement throughout a scene: *point and click* and *direct control*. In *point and click* games, players can view their character and move their character by clicking somewhere within the game space. The character then walks to that location. For areas that are inaccessible, the character may state aloud, "I can't go there," or the character may move as close as possible to the location and stop. The advantage of this method is that setting does not have to be fully developed; only areas that the character is able to move within have to be developed. The player can also see the character and get a sense of the character. In contrast, with the *direct control* method, the player controls the character with a mouse or key commands (WASD, a common configuration of arrow keys). With direct control, the player has more control over the character and typically has the option of viewing the environment through first-person ("sees" what the character "sees") or third-person (over the shoulder of the character).

Objects

In addition to manipulating and moving the character, players also interact with objects within adventure games. Typically, only key objects within a scene are interactive. There are different methods for signifying object interaction. The simplest is when the player merely clicks on everything in the attempt to uncover the interactive objects. This can be tiresome for players. Another method is to highlight interactive objects either permanently through use of color, lighting or effects, or dynamically, such as when the player moves a mouse over an interactive object or moves the character near the object.

Interface

Most adventure games include some form of inventory (often located at the bottom of the screen, separated from the main scene). The inventory is often consistent with the main theme of the game (a forensic bag for collecting evidence of a crime or a backpack for an explorer). Interactive objects typically are added to the inventory as the player's character encounters the objects. In addition to inventories, some adventure games include journals, notebooks or scrapbooks that provide documentation about what the player's character has already encountered, and a list of goals (both long-term and short-term). Long-term goals are typically related to the goal of the game (e.g., solve the crime), whereas short-term goals may provide a type of scaffolding to help guide the player (find a shovel to remove debris blocking a door).

Platforms

Adventure games are more commonly associated with computers, but there are also console and mobile versions. A popular form of adventure game often found in mobile gaming are casual *hidden object* adventure games in which players are often required to find a list of objects hidden within a scene to advance the storyline.

Adventure Games, Aesthetics and Learning

As one of the oldest of game genres, there have been many initiatives to both develop and integrate adventure games for teaching and learning. However, research and even discussion about the design aspects of adventure games is somewhat limited, and much of the early research focused on Malone's (1981) groundbreaking studies into intrinsic motivation and games (Baltra, 1990; Quinn, 1991). Some of the earliest studies argue that adventure games provide an instructional design model for creating computer-based problem-solving environments (Sherwood, 1991; Curtis & Lawson, 2002). Despite the limited discussion, there are findings that provide insight into the design and integration of adventure games for education. Baltra (1990) argued that the very design of text-based adventure games supports communication and fluency for English language learners. Cavallari, Jedberg and Harper's (1992) study was among the first in the field of education to outline the following characteristics of adventure games:

- Environment: realism or fantasy and the rules governing the environments
- Context: the setting, such as an island or cave
- Plot: the story
- Theme: moral thread (good vs. evil)
- Characters
- Objects
- Text: dialogue and game commands
- Graphics
- Sound: sound effects and speech
- Animation: animated sequences (presumably cut scenes)
- User interface: features that allow the player to communicate with the computer

18 • Aesthetics and Game Genres

Cavallari et al.'s list of characteristics also includes broad guidelines for the application of the characteristics for educational design, which include recommendations such as:

- Understand the culture and motivation of the characters.
- Maintain consistency with the rules of the environment.
- Maintain awareness of cultural conventions within the environment and with the objects and how that might impact learners from different cultural backgrounds.

Another insightful early investigation into the design of educational adventure games is Quinn's (1991) development of an educational adventure game using *HyperCard* as the authoring system. Quinn's recommendations include both aesthetic concerns of narrative design as well as cognitive aspects of interface design. He advocates the importance of embedding problems (challenges) so that they are intrinsic to both the learning activity and the story. Quinn addresses the difficulty of embedding learning activities into the storyline and character by stating that it is difficult to "construct problems that contain the desired structure and are also believable" (Quinn, 1991, p. 239). This is a key hindrance to the design of any game for learning. Quinn also addresses the need for information that learners may need to complete different problems and advocates providing options for taking notes. He also contends that students' notes may not always be sufficient for every student, but that students may need to rely on other strategies (which in itself is a subject of study). Quinn also provides insight into the interface design, stating that the interface should support the learning activity and reflect the way the user thinks about the activity.

Ju and Wagner (1997) also investigated the structure of adventure games and the suitability of this genre for learning. They formulated a model for the architecture of adventure games that included:

- The story: the plot, setting, characters, objects, tasks, place and time
- Development approach: the visual representation of the characters and setting
- Implementation: the technical details and game mechanics

According to Ju and Wagner (1997), the game story should be revealed as a series of events that help support the goal of the game. Although they do not provide much specific information about the design of educational adventure games, they do note key challenges for design that include finding methods to ensure that learners remember what they have learned during the game activity rather than merely remembering aspects of the game such as characters and the appeal of the interface.

Beyond Quinn (1991) and Ju and Wagner (1997), there have been several initiatives into developing models for creating educational adventure games. Amory, Naicker, Vincent and Adams (1999) and Amory (2001) mapped game elements with pedagogical dimensions of learning to inform the design of the Game Object Model (GOM). GOM is loosely based on object-oriented programming with nested objects and functions. The elements related to aesthetics (nested within the elements space) include fun, graphics, sounds and technology, and those nested within the actor's space include drama, interaction and gestures. With subsequent development of social games, Amory presented GOMII, which both expands upon the pedagogical dimensions and also extends the game space and outline of aesthetic elements to include role models, emotive backstory and game rhythm (Amory, 2001, 2007). In the initial application of GOM, which was used to inform the development of the adventure game *Zadarh*, a game designed to address "misconceptions held by biology students," Amory identified some of the challenges of perspective, space design and graphics.

Moreno-Ger, Martínez-Ortiz and Fernández-Manjón (2005), noting some of the challenges for developing educational games, developed an authoring environment for creating educational adventure games. <e-Game>, and later <e-Adventure>, provide an authoring tool kit for educators to create their own educational *point-and-click* adventure games without having to rely on programming skills (Torrente, Moreno-Ger, Fernández-Manjón & Sierra, 2008; Torrente, del Blanco, Marchiori, Moreno-Ger & Fernández-Manjón, 2010). The authoring tool kit allows educators to upload their own components; however, as Moreno-Ger, Burgos, Martínez-Ortiz, Sierra and Fernández-Manjón (2008, p. 2538) note, "the burden of creating a compelling story that will provide the fun-factor still lies in the writers of the game" and further state that it is "perfectly possible to use the game design and still create a boring and non-motivational story."

Both Sedano, Leendertz, Vinni, Sutinen and Ellis (2013) and Adams, Mayer, MacNamara, Koenig and Wainess' (2012) respective research to some degree addresses issues of story/narrative in adventure-style games, but with very different findings. Adams et al. (2012) reported finding that narrative did not improve learning, whereas Sedano et al. (2013) found that fantasy/narrative was a central factor that triggered affective and cognitive engagement. Though the findings vary, in both cases, researchers noted the importance of more research for understanding the impact of narrative/fantasy.

One interesting approach to developing engaging narratives/story proposed by Manero, Fernández-Vara and Fernández-Manjón (2013) draws upon Laurel's (1993) supposition of computers as theater. Manero et al. (2013) outlined their efforts of applying Constantin Stanislavski's "The Method" as a means of looking at the development of conflict within the narrative. Part of the Stanislavski acting method requires actors to focus on the characters' objectives and the types of conflict their characters encounter. Manero et al. (2013) outline the following different types of conflicts characters may encounter:

- Intersubjective: a conflict between characters with opposing objectives
- Environmental: a conflict in which the environment prevents the objective
- Intimate: a conflict in which the action carries inner consequences

20 • Aesthetics and Game Genres

What is noteworthy about Manero et al.'s approach is the emergence of a framework for developing compelling characters within the narrative.

Adventure games are a genre well suited for closed narratives or even open narratives (Dede, Nelson, Ketelhut, Clarke & Bowman, 2004; Dickey, 2011b, 2011c) but where the story drives the gameplay or provides the impetus for the learning objectives:

- Problem or conflict framed as a story
- Learner plays the main role in solving or exploring the problem
- Learner interacts within objects (elements) that help uncover the story
- Clues should be embedded to provide scaffolding to help learners with problem-solving

Role-playing Games (RPG) and Massively Multiplayer Online Role-playing Games (MMORPG)

Background

Role-playing games, or RPGs as they are more commonly known, are an older form of digital games. The roots of RPGs originated in social tabletop games such as *Dungeon and Dragons*. In tabletop games, players create unique characters, explore dungeons, overcome obstacles and gather treasure. In tabletop RPGs, typically, one player acts as the *Dungeon Master* or *Game Master* (GM) who sets up the game, plays other roles and acts as an arbiter for the games. Much of the game relies upon rolling dice to determine the outcome of actions.

Central to tabletop RPGs is collaborative role-playing among players. Tabletop games rely little on graphical displays, but instead on the imagination of the players, group storytelling and the ability of players to improvise in their roles. With the advent of computers, digital versions of RPGs began to emerge in the late 1970s and early 1980s (Barton, 2007). In the late 1970s, Roy Trubshaw and Richard Bartle developed the first computer multiuser game-like environment, Multi-user Domain or Multi-user Dungeon (MUD). Subsequent MUDs adapted some conventions of tabletop RPGs (along with adventure games) to become role-playing adventures (Bartle, 1990).

In the 1980s and beyond, computer RPGs adopted many of the conventions of tabletop RPGs (along with aspects of adventure games and action games) to form the basis of contemporary RPGs. Typically, within RPGs, players begin by creating unique characters; however, unlike other game genres, in RPGs, players are not assigned a role to play, but instead define their own role through the character they create.

Narrative and Environment

Narrative plays a significant role in RPGs, though storyline is not as tightly constructed as in adventure games. Storylines typically focus on some overarching goal in which the player's character plays an integral part (e.g., saving the world or at least a kingdom). Storylines typically require players to explore new locales where they encounter various non-player characters (NPCs). During their travels, players undertake various quests to earn money, gain experience and enhance their skills and reputation, all the while moving toward the central goal. As players traverse and complete quests, the storyline progresses (along with twists and turns in the plotline). Depending upon the extent of the narrative, these quests may be a simple one-stage quest (defeat five enemies), or they may be more complex and require the player to complete several small quests to completely uncover the narrative (e.g., collect several herbs, then find an herbalist to mix the herbs and create a poultice to cure an illness). Both the selection and the successful completion of quests advance gameplay and reinforce the player's role in the overarching narrative.

During gameplay, the player's characters also develop and enhance their skills, accumulate weapons and develop more strength in order to become more powerful and to succeed in the final confrontation. What is different about narrative in RPGs is that, unlike adventure games, the narrative may differ from player to player depending upon the unique characteristics of each player's character. This adds to the replay-ability of a game. The environment in RPGs tends to be a series of locations within a larger world. As the player explores and journeys through an area, the player engages in gameplay. Often, as the player completes the various goals for a location, more of the narrative storyline is exposed, which in turn leads the player to a new section of the environment.

Character

Typically, players are presented with a variety of base characters from which to select. Players customize their characters by choosing from a selection of attributes. The types of attributes most commonly found in RPGs include race, gender (male/female), class, skills and appearance. In many RPGs, players first select a race for their character from a selection of races. Common races found in western fantasy RPGs might include *humans, elves, trolls, dwarves* and *gnomes*. To varying degrees, some of a player's character appearance may be determined by their selection of race. In RPGs, a player can also select the moral code for a player, such as good, evil or neutral. In some RPGs, the moral code is set by the player's actions and choices during the game. Players also typically select a gender for their characters.[3] Gender selection in RPGs impacts only the appearance of a character and does not impact other characteristics such as strength, power or speed. Class refers to the player's specialized skill set. Common classes found in western fantasy RPGs include *warriors, healers, spell casters, thieves* and *hunters*. Typically, the selection of class affords characters strengths in some areas and weaknesses in others. For example, a spell caster (priest, mage, shaman or magician) may be very powerful in the use of magic but lack skills or power using a sword. Typically, most RPGs allow players to develop their character's skills in various areas, although sometimes this is limited or determined based on class (physical, mental, moral and social). Players also

22 • Aesthetics and Game Genres

have some control over their character's appearance and can often select height, weight, body shape, facial features, hair color and style, along with other physical adornments. The individual combination of attributes, skills and traits are what make each character unique. Throughout gameplay, players continually enhance their character's skills and attributes.

Gameplay and Mechanics

Exploration is a central focus of most RPGs. As a player's character journeys through various locations, the character interacts with NPCs, finds various objects and resources, and overcomes challenges. During interactions, players engage in small quests offered by NPCs. They also typically find objects to sell or craft into other objects, engage in combat, undertake training and find ways to solve problems. Those various actions typically result in players gaining more experience points (XP). As the character gains experience points, the character becomes more powerful. In addition to pursuing the main quest, most RPGs also have provisions for side quests—which temporarily take the character off the course of the main quest. However, side quests can benefit the character by exposing the player to new resources and to other small quests to help build experience and enhance the player's character. Typically, there is some type of reward for completing side quests. The rewards may be in the form of items, power, new skills, financial compensation, advanced knowledge, advanced access or other gains. Often, players have a choice of the type of reward they may select.

Inventory

As a character completes quests, finds (or steals) objects and *loots* from fallen enemies, the player's character accumulates objects that are placed in the inventory. Most RPGs have some type of inventory system—such as a bag(s), knapsack or chest. Often, RPGs allow players to have a traveling inventory as well as a chest or bank at some type of home base. This allows players to store more objects but carry only what their characters need. Typically, most inventories have limits on the amount of goods a character can carry. Often, RPGs have some type of economic system that allows characters to sell unwanted objects for gold (or some other type of remuneration). Limits on inventory space also force players to make choices about what to keep and what to discard.

Leveling

Typically, for various actions, a player's character gains experience and becomes more powerful during gameplay. The power of a character is typically chronicled as levels—the higher the level, the more powerful the character. Experience is gained by defeating enemies, overcoming challenges and completing quests.

Perspective

Player perspective differs from game to game. Some are basic third-person over-the-shoulder view, while others are first-person direct control. Yet others allow players to toggle between first- and third-person. Regardless of the methods of character control and viewpoint, the player plays the game as the character and interacts with NPCs as the character.

Interfaces

Interfaces in RPGs tend to be more complex than in adventure games. Typically, there are different types of window interfaces: combat, inventory, quest logs and maps. Often, games will have options to allow players to toggle between interfaces and overlay windows.

MMORPGs

Background

A Massively Multiplayer Online Role-playing Game (MMORPG) is a persistent, networked, interactive, narrative environment in which players collaborate, strategize, plan and interact with objects, resources and other players within a multi-modal environment. The roots of MMORPG were strongly influenced by the development of RPGs and MUDs. An MMORPG varies from other types of gameplay inasmuch as there is typically no end to the game. There is no final victory or loss condition, but rather the game continues to evolve and players continue to evolve their character (and/or develop new characters to play).[4]

The core of MMORPG design is a narrative interactive environment. In various game genres, such as single-player RPGs and adventure games, the game centers on the narrative of a single storyline that is typically linear in nature. In both of these genres, the storyline stops when the player stops playing and resumes when the player begins again. In contrast, MMORPGs are networked, persistent, communal environments. Because they are multiplayer, networked environments, gameplay continues even when a player logs off. Within the MMORPG genre, there typically is no one single storyline for players to uncover, but rather the gameplay experience is an environment. Embedded within the environment are thousands of short narrative storylines. These short narratives are usually embedded in the environment in the form of NPCs posing a short narrative tale in which they request the aid or assistance of the player's character. What is different about the quest structure in MMORPGs is that some quests may be accomplished by individual players, while others require the organized efforts of several players. Because the central design of most MMORPGs is communal gameplay, the underlying design of MMORPGs provides incentives for collaboration (Taylor, 2009). Players must work with other players to complete many quests. This requires players to form relationships with other players (friends and guilds). Social play may involve as

24 • Aesthetics and Game Genres

little as two to three players for small "quests" or 40 or more players collaboratively playing to accomplish a quest. Other aspects of social gameplay include trading, buying and selling goods (made by individual "characters") and hiring characters for assistance (charms, spells and lock picking). As a result, it is in a player's best interest to develop relationships with other players and foster a reputation of being a good collaborative player.

Narrative and Environment

Most MMORPGs tend to have a broader storyline than single-player RPGs. Typically, MMORPGs have an overarching narrative and a central conflict (e.g., two groups are fighting for control over a kingdom). The player's character determines which type of role the player will have in this overarching narrative. In most game genres, the player is often cast in the lead role of the protagonist; in contrast, characters in MMORPGs begin the game as low-level members of "rank and file." During gameplay, one of the goals is to advance the character by enhancing skills and attributes (Rollings & Adams, 2003). Like RPGs, small quests also form the basis of gameplay.

Narrative in MMORPGs is not merely a storyline, but instead MMORPGs are persistent, networked narrative spaces in which other players contribute to a player's narrative. Typically, a chat tool allows players to communicate with other players during the gameplay experience. Narratives emerge that are parallel and embedded in the narrative landscape of the interactive gameplay environment, but are player contributions and not those of the game designers.

The narrative design of an MMORPG is a design model that fosters exploration. Players continually explore various regions to find both quest givers (NPCs) and objects related to completing a small quest. There is often no "one way" to complete a small quest, but rather players must balance the skills and attributes of their characters against the demands of the quest and plan strategically to accomplish most quests. Additionally, players must make critical choices about whether the rewards are worth the investment required to complete a small quest. Because MMORPGs are narrative environments, the environments are often vast, and it may take players a great deal of time to "travel" from region to region. Players often make critical choices about the most economical way to complete a variety of small quests in the most travel-efficient way.

Small quests are usually framed as short narrative tales. As players move through the environment, they encounter various NPCs requesting their aid or assistance. The request for assistance is usually framed as a small quest (e.g., deliver a package, find a lost book, escort an ally). Players may opt to select and complete or reject the small quest. Typically, within the environment are many small quests from which players may select. Upon the successful completion of a small quest, a player's character is rewarded. This allows players to continually enhance their character's attributes and skills. Rather than the focus of gameplay being on uncovering one major narrative storyline, the environment is a network of narrative spaces (Jenkins, 2002) in which the player interacts and, even in limited ways, helps shape.

The focus of gameplay in RPGs is the narrative adventure, both uncovering the storyline and developing a character to progress. The focus of gameplay in MMORPGs is on character development. In both RPGs and MMORPGs, players move their characters through the narrative environment and select and complete quests. Typically, there is some type of reward for completing a small quest and, additionally, during the process of completing a quest, players' characters accumulate points and other rewards as well. The rewards may be in the form of items, power, new skills, financial compensation, advanced knowledge, advanced access or other gains. Often, players have a choice in the type of reward, as well as input into the ongoing development of their characters.

Character

Similar to RPGs, character design and management is essential to MMORPGs, with players creating unique characters by selecting from an array of options.

Gameplay and Mechanics

A key aspect within the MMORPG environment is character management. In the course of gameplay, players continually have to make choices about enhancing their character's skills and primary and secondary attributes. Skills might include such actions as combat skills, healing powers and casting abilities. Primary attributes might include such features as strength, agility, intelligence and stamina. Players typically also have the option of adding various adornments to their characters as they progress. Adornments might include clothing, armor, shields and protection spells. Secondary skills are often predicated on the combination of traits, skills, primary attributes and adornments. For example, depending upon the game, healing powers (the amount of healing a character can provide) might be determined by such elements as armor and protective spells, along with a character's intelligence. The choice of skills, attributes and adornments impacts how a player's character advances in the game. When collaborating with other players, a player's skills, attributes and adornments often indicate the potential contribution a player may provide when participating in collaborative events, which in turn may impact the type and amounts of invitations to collaborate with other players.

Leveling

Like RPGs, a player's character gains experience and becomes more powerful during the course of gameplay. The power of a character is typically chronicled as levels—the higher the level, the more powerful the character. Experience is gained by defeating enemies, overcoming challenges and completing quests.

26 • Aesthetics and Game Genres

However, unlike RPGs, MMORPGs are social environments, and communal and collaborative gameplay is part of the experience. Many collaborative quests require players to attain a specific level in order to participate. This helps motivate players to "level up" their characters to participate.

Perspective

Just as with RPGs, player perspective differs from game to game. Typically, most allow players to toggle between first- and third-person. Regardless of the methods of character control and viewpoint, the player plays the game as the character and interacts with NPCs as the character.

Interface

Interfaces in MMORPGs tend to be more complex than in adventure games. They are similar to RPGs in the different types of window interfaces: combat, inventory, quest logs and maps. However, MMORPG interfaces also include provisions for chat and to track the health or other vital information about other characters during group gameplay. Because of the amount of information, typically, there are provisions to allow players to toggle between interfaces and overlay windows.

Role-playing Games, Aesthetics and Learning

Most of the research about role-playing and education centers on the use of role-playing games for teaching and learning. Although much of the research is about the use of role-playing or integrating role-playing game strategies in the classroom, some of the research yields insight for design and aesthetics for game-based learning. Papargyris and Poulymenakou (2005) investigated the learning potential of two MMORPGs. Their findings revealed that the social and anonymous affordances of MMORPGs support different types of learning and community building. Similarly, Steinkuehler (2006) addresses the impact of game discourse in fostering game communities both online and beyond the parameters of a game. Rankin, Gold and Gooch (2006) studied the integration of the popular MMORPG *EverQuest 2* (EQ2) for language learning. While their findings provide insight about using EQ2 as a tool for language learning, their findings also provide insight into aspects of design. They found that character development was motivational for learners and that communication opportunities provide opportunities for developing conversational skills. Ang, Zaphiris and Mahmood (2006) studied the impact of cognitive load processing with three subjects in an MMORPG and found aspects of the design that resulted in cognitive overloads. Chen, Lien, Annetta and Lu (2010) found that the use of their role-playing game, *FORmosaHope* (FH), improved learners' sense of cultural identity through interaction with the game environment and characters within the game. Jang and Ryu (2011) studied the development of leadership skills of MMORPG players and how they translated into real-world situations. In a study I conducted with students, I found that aspects of the design of MMORPGs provided incentives for collaboration, but that not all qualities displayed or developed in the game translated to the classroom (Dickey, 2011a).

Of the limited research about the integrating of RPGs/MMORPGs, there are some very loose themes that emerge which include characters, environment and communication. This is consistent with many of the findings in research about the design of educational RPG/MMORPGs. Carbonaro et al. (2006) identified one of the key challenges of developing educational games as the need for programming skills. They address strategies to aid educators not adept in programming to adapt the RPG *Neverwinter Nights* as a platform for educational games. Childress and Braswell (2006) used *Second Life* as an MMORPG for educational activities and outlined spaces created for socializing. Sancho, Moreno-Ger, Fuentes-Fernández and Fernández-Manjón (2009) provide insight into the design of RPGs for learning. They outline their e-learning framework, *NUCLEO*, for socio-constructive design. What is insightful about their work is that they capitalize on one of the key characteristics of MMORPGs—collaborative tasks—and integrate them into their design. To succeed in some activities, students must collaborate with other students within their team. Collaborative small quests are key aspects of MMORPG design that are meant to foster social gameplay, and integrating that element into an MMORPG learning environment provides incentives for collaborative and social learning that are fundamental to a constructivist perspective of learning. Sancho et al. (2009) also provide insight into developing roles (like classes) for players based on the needs of the narrative. Mathevet et al. (2007) provide a review of their role-playing game, *BUTORSTAR*, an RPG to help players understand the dynamics of socio-ecosystems. They offer insight into the process of developing roles that needed to be balanced with differing attributes. They also provide insight into how they dealt with issues of the design in the game environment and needing to balance realism with a level of simplicity to help the learner. Finally, their work also addresses issues of character conflict and resolution and aspects of emotional states of characters. Similarly, Watcharasukarn, Krumdieck, Green and Dantas' (2011) study about their game-based survey tool, *Travel Activity Constraint Adaptation Simulation (TACA SIM)*, is based on design aspects of role-playing games. They address the need to include provisions for character development and maintenance as strategy to motivate players.

Of the limited work directly related to the design of educational RPGs/ MMORPGs, Villalta et al. (2011) outline guidelines they developed during the process of creating a Classroom Multiplayer Presential Game (CMPG). Included in the guidelines are mechanics linked to learning objectives, clear narrative and collaboration. Simpson and Elias (2011) present a review of their work integrating RPG gameplay into classroom activities. Although they relied on aspects of tabletop gameplay (dice), they found that role-playing and character development helped support their learners in gaining insight from different perspectives as characters resonated with students.

28 • Aesthetics and Game Genres

Central to RPG/MMORPG is character design and management in an environment that includes challenge. As a genre for game-based learning, RPGs/MMORPGs should feature:

- Activities in which transformation is part of the learning goal and the learner has input and choice in the process
- Activities in which the learners must balance attributes with those of other learners to complete tasks
- Activities in which the environment provides a framework for different types of interaction
- Activities in which differing strategies can be employed to find solutions

Action Games

Background

The roots of action games can be traced back to some of the earliest computer and arcade games in the late 1970s and early 1980s. The earliest action games were among the first digital arcade games. Games such as *Space Invaders*, *Asteroids* and *Pac-Man* altered the landscape of arcades previously dominated by pinball machines by providing a new type of gameplay. Action games are games in which speed, reaction time and eye-hand coordination play a central role in the genre. Action games are most commonly noted as being "quick twitch" games—in which the ability to react quickly is of primary importance in gameplay. Subgenres of action games include platformers (and side-scrollers), fighting games and shooter games.

Narrative and Environment

Often, narrative plays a limited role in action games. It often may be a complex mystery, or it may serve as a simple framework to situate the gameplay (aliens attacking Earth). In many action games, the environment consists of a series of levels, and the environment of each level is linear in nature—designed for the player to traverse one way. However, newer games allow for players to negotiate their own path through different levels.

Character

Within action games, the player typically controls the main character, who serves as the protagonist in the game. The player engages in combat, collects objects and avoids or overcomes obstacles. Players must manipulate the character through the environment, combat and defend themselves against enemies and collect and manipulate objects. Character development is typically limited to gaining points to become more powerful. In some games, power points can be spent for temporary increases of power (power-ups). Typically, a character has a number of *lives*, which are reprieves from death that allow the player to resurrect the character when the character has been killed. In some games, the character may resurrect at the spot the character died, whereas in other games, a character is resurrected at a checkpoint.[5] Often, in action games, players may earn more "lives" as the game progresses. When the character runs out of "lives," the game ends.

Gameplay and Mechanics

According to Adams (2014), the mechanics of action games include character lives, energy, collectables, power-ups and time limits. Most action games provide players' characters with a limited number of lives. Another aspect of game mechanics is *energy* or *health* reserves. Throughout the environment, players may encounter objects or elements that allow the character to replenish health. Central to gameplay is the management of energy/health resources against the depletion of those resources during combat. Collectables are bonuses the player might obtain during a level. Collectables do not negatively impact a player for not collecting them, but typically there is a benefit or bonus for collecting. Often, the risk is commensurate to the reward. Power-ups are the rewards earned for progression. Often, they are awarded upon completing a level. Sometimes they are permanent (for the duration of the game), and in other games they may be limited to the current life of the character or level the character is playing. Time and speed play a central role in action games. Often, players must complete a level within a specified amount of time or they must complete a task within an allotted amount of time.

Levels

Typically, action games comprise different levels beginning with the easiest to more advanced. Levels may be theme-related, and within each level are various challenges such as enemies to defeat and obstacles to avoid. The enemies and obstacles are typically related to the theme of the level. Typically, most levels require players to defeat waves of enemies and overcome obstacles before encountering the *boss* for the level. The boss is typically the most powerful enemy for a level. Often, action games have an increasing progression of bosses at the end of each level, and a final or *big boss* that must be defeated to *win* the game. Most levels have similar types of challenges that allow players to build upon their skills. Some levels may include shortcuts to other levels, wildcard enemies (powerful and designed to distract) and hidden treasure.

Perspective

Player perspective varies from game to game with action games. Some games are single-screen 2D environments (Pac-Man), others may be 2D scrollers (side or up and down), and yet others are immersive 3D environments with third-person or first-person perspective.

30 • Aesthetics and Game Genres

Interfaces

Because so much of gameplay depends upon speed and fast manipulation, the interface of action games tends to be simple and limited to the immediate needs of the player. Information such as energy/health, time and access to power-ups are of primary importance.

Action Games, Aesthetics and Learning

Much of the research about learning and action games is within the field of cognitive science. Action games are games in which physical dexterity, speed and perception play a large role in the gameplay. Green and Bavelier (2003) found that, in a comparison of performance between non-gamers and action gamers, action gamers had an improved range of visual skills, including enhanced attention capacity, greater number of visual items that can be apprehended, and enhanced capacity of visual attention and spatial distribution. In a later study, Green and Bavelier (2006) found that action gamers exhibited enhanced attentional resources in both peripheral and central vision. Achtman, Green and Bavelier (2008) note the differences in information processing and spatial recognition among different types of action games. They identified the types of visual processing related to the design of different action games, including first-person shooter games, racing games, visuo-motor games (*Tetris*), simulations (*SimCity*) and card games. Dye, Green and Bavelier (2009) maintain that playing action games reduces perceptual reaction time without sacrificing errors. There are a variety of other studies addressing how playing action games increases brain plasticity (Green & Bavelier, 2012), improves attention abilities for children with dyslexia (Franceschini et al., 2013) and enhances peripheral vision and cognitive abilities (Oei & Patternson, 2013).

While these findings are insightful, there are some counterarguments that perhaps action gamers perform well in some areas of visual processing and cognition not because they play action games, but because people with enhanced skills in spatial recognition and fast response times are attracted to action games because those are the types of skills that are required in action games (Boot, Blakely & Simons, 2011). What is relevant about this entire body of research for this chapter is what it conveys in terms of the aesthetics of action games and what that means for the design of game-based learning. Action games require visual acuity, attention to periphery, rapid decisions and quick actions. They are games in which visual design plays an important role. The aesthetic is not one of narrative design or compelling characters, but one in which the visual environment (color, textures and sound) drive the aesthetics. In terms of game-based learning, the environment design plays an important role in creating action games for learning.

Action games are games in which quick speed and rapid response are key aspects of gameplay. Certainly, different styles within the overarching genre require

Aesthetics and Game Genres • **31**

players to analyze and strategize, and the mechanics of speed and rapid response make them a reasonable genre for engaging drill and practice work.

Simulations

Background

Although simulation games are not the oldest of the computer game genres, the simulation genre has had enduring popularity since the debut of the popular *Sim-City* in 1989. The term "simulation" has become a broad term in discussions of digital game genres, with games ranging from vehicle, flight, sports, medical and social simulations; however, among the most notable simulations are construction and management simulation games. Construction and management simulation (CMS) games are a genre of games that focus on construction and management of resources. Unlike other genres, CMSs do not focus on progressive gameplay or rely on combat or conflict of competition; the gameplay is about balance—balancing growth with resource management. Typically, there is no victory or loss conditions in CMS games, although some may end or wither due to poor management or resources or neglect of the setting.

Narrative and Environment

Unlike other genres of digital games, typically, the narration mainly serves as a background or as a framework for CMSs. What little narrative exists is often in the form of scenarios that serve primarily to frame the environment and provide a context. The scenarios may provide a frame of time and issues of conflict, such as the expansion of ancient Rome or the discovery of a new land. The scenarios also frame the types of resources afforded, the needs of society and the types of cultivation possible.

Character

The player does not play a character role per se in CMSs, but instead is an omnipresent force that oversees the growth and development of the environment. The player may be cast in the role of mayor, owner or manager, but that is mainly a function of the scenario. The player's role is to develop, construct and manage resources.

Gameplay and Mechanics

At the core of simulation games is the leveraging of resources against the economy of building. In *Fundamentals of Construction and Simulation Game Design*, Adams (2013) discusses some of the fundamental mechanics behind CMSs by outlining the various types of resources (e.g., money, people, food, materials, etc.) and the sources of those resources (e.g., taxation, immigration, farms, environment,

32 • Aesthetics and Game Genres

etc.) against the elements that drain or diminish the resources (purchases, death, consumption, depletion, natural disasters, etc.).

Perspective

Typically, the player is not represented in the environment as an avatar or character, but instead interacts outside the setting. In 2D simulations, the player may view the setting from a top-down perspective or orthographic 2½D viewpoint. Some immersive settings allow players to move through the simulation, while others offer provisions for players to shift perspective from a wide angle overview to zoom into specific areas of the setting.

Interfaces

Typically, the interface for CMSs tends to be clear and easy to read. The environments tend to be clear and unobstructed by weather or atmospheric elements that might impede viewing the setting.

Strategy Games

Background

Like many digital games, the roots of strategy games are in traditional board games (*Chess*) and tabletop strategy games (*Risk*). The focus of the strategy game genre is on a central conflict that presents strategic, tactical, economic, development, exploration and logistical challenges. Strategy games require thought and planning rather than relying on physical dexterity. Initially, strategy games were played turn-based; however, with the advent of real-time gameplay, speed is now part of the mechanics of play. Strategy games often center on warfare or on some type of political conflict. Although the goal of gameplay is often conquest, players must manage a limited (and possibly growing) amount of resources to achieve the goal.

Narrative and Environment

The role of narrative is fairly limited in strategy games and mainly serves as the framework or theme to structure the central conflict. The most common themes include historical settings, fantasy, science fiction and modern day, but often the narrative is subsumed by the mechanics of the game.

Character

The player is situated in an omnipotent role and must prioritize and determine how to allocate resources. The player often is not cast in a role as a protagonist in the narrative, but instead serves as an overall commander.

Gameplay and Mechanics

Gameplay primarily consists of balancing tactical maneuvers with resource management. The primary mechanics involve resource management for exploration, cultivation, construction, warfare, defense and development. Players must determine how to allocate resources and balance various needs to dominate. War-based strategy games require players to address logistics, such as the balance of troops and strategies for warfare, whereas world-building strategy games may also include allocating resources for cultivating arts, education and culture against the needs for consumption, defense, exploration, building, agriculture and manufacturing. Inventory in strategy games are assets rather than individual items collected by characters.

Perspective

Strategy games vary in player perspective. Initially, most games were presented as 2D environments, with the camera angle being an overhead view looking down on the scene, much like viewing a map. Subsequent games were developed in orthographic view (2½D). As graphics capabilities improved for computers, strategy games began emerging as 3D environments. However, because strategy games are not played from a single-character perspective, most games allow players to change the viewpoint to view the entire game space.

Simulations and Strategy Games, Aesthetics and Learning

Much of the research about simulations and the limited work about strategy games in education are related to the cognitive aspects of design (Leutner, 1993; Rieber, 1996; Squire & Barab, 2004; Vogel et al., 2006); de Fritas & Oliver (2006) devised a framework to help tutors evaluate the potential of simulation games that most effectively meet the needs of their learning context.

Of the limited research related to aesthetics and design, Amory, Naicker, Vincent and Adams (1996) found that the students in their study identified design aspects such as graphics, sound and storyline, along with cognitive aspects such as visualization, logic and memory, as important aspects of their gameplay experience. Quinn's (1996) reflections on the design of his educational simulation, *Quest for Independence*, provide great insight that is still relevant today for the design of educational simulation games. *Quest for Independence* was a computer-based simulation to help learners develop independent learning skills. It was created using HyperCard.[6] Quinn identified some of the challenges he encountered during the design process that provide insight into the design of contemporary simulations (and strategy) games for learning. Some of the issues Quinn encountered were methods of representing routine tasks (going to work) and navigating through an environment (taking a bus). He also devised prompts to encourage learners to explore new areas of the environment. Raybourn (2006) presents the *Simulation*

34 • Aesthetics and Game Genres

Experience Design Method, a framework for the design of educational simulations. Raybourn's framework outlines four key aspects of design: interaction, narrative, place and emergent culture. While interaction, narrative and place are key aspects of game design, Raybourn's category for emergent culture is unique to educational game design. According to Raybourn, emergent culture includes assessment and feedback.

Although there is relatively little research about aesthetics in the design of game-based simulations, the few related studies address many of the same key elements of the need for rich environments that afford balance.

Virtual Worlds

Background

Although virtual worlds are not games per se, they are often grouped with games in discussions about game-based learning because of the game-like qualities of the environments. Additionally, virtual worlds have been used for games and for game-based learning, and many include affordances for construction—different from simulation games, but construction nonetheless. Three-dimensional virtual worlds have a unique history and emerged alongside digital games, often drawing upon the same sources of inspiration.

The roots of virtual worlds can be found in a variety of sources. The earliest roots can be traced back to the Multi-user Dungeons (MUDs) and, later, the emergence of Multi-user Object-Oriented (MOOs) environments. Unlike the game aspects of MUDs, MOOs were created to be social environments. Like MUDs, MOOs are text-based environments in which users interact in spaces comprised of textual descriptions. Among the most popular MOOs was *LambdaMOO*, created by Pavel Curtis, a researcher at Xerox Palo Alto Research Center (PARC) who, with the help of a few other experienced "mudders," launched *LambdaMOO*. Many of the controversies and problems encountered with *LambdaMOO*[7] have impacted not only the design of subsequent MOOs but also the subsequent design of 3D virtual worlds.

In 1985, Lucasfilm launched the first networked multi-user virtual world, *Habitat. Habitat* was an experiment in virtual or computer-mediated communities that ran for six years in the United States and Japan. It was also one of the first graphical multi-user environments. Whereas MUDs, MOOs and chats were text-based environments, *Habitat* was a 2D world in which visuals were used to construct both the environment and the objects within it (Farmer & Morningstar, 1991). It was also the first to use avatars as a visual representation of users (Damer, 1998). The 2D scenes that composed the setting of *Habitat* consisted of real-time animated scenes of the world.

During the mid- to late 1990s, many online graphical chat worlds began to emerge. One of the most popular of the graphic chat worlds was *The Palace. The Palace* was a 2D virtual world in which users were represented by a 2D graphical avatar. Around the same time, Mark Pesce and Tony Parisi teamed up in an

Aesthetics and Game Genres • 35

attempt to create a virtual reality interface to the Internet (Pesce, 1998). As 2D Web browsers were moving into the mainstream, Pesce looked for a means that would allow users to explore the Web in three dimensions (Pesce, 1998). In 1994, Virtual Reality Markup Language (VRML) emerged.

VRML served as the basis for several 3D virtual worlds, such as *OnLive! Traveler*, *blaxxun* and *Sony's Community Player* (Damer, 1998; Dickey, 1999, 2005, 2007). In the spring of 1995, Worlds Inc. launched one of the first 3D virtual worlds, *Worlds Chat*, soon followed by *AlphaWorld* (the predecessor version of *Active Worlds*). After the initial burst of development, interest in virtual worlds began to diminish as online games and social networking began to spark public interest. *Active Worlds* remained one of the few surviving virtual worlds due in part to a faithful following, the relative ease of user extensible options for building and the forays into using *Active Worlds* as an authoring platform for game-based learning (Dede et al., 2004[8]; Barab, Gresalfi, Dodge & Ingram-Goble, 2010[9]; Dickey, 2011b, 2011c).

In 2003, *There* and *Second Life* each launched their respective virtual world platforms. With advances in graphical capacity, *Second Life* emerged as one of the most popular virtual world platforms for game-based learning.

Environment

There is no one single narrative for virtual worlds—beyond the narrative surrounding the marketing. Most virtual worlds include some type of immersive environment and user extendibility to allow developers, world or island owners, and property owners (or renters) the option of creating their own narrative and environmental design to support the narrative. Most virtual worlds have provisions for avatars that serve as the visual representations of users in the environments. Mechanics vary greatly from platform to platform but typically include some provisions for avatar movement and chat, and options for building.

Summary

This review is by no means comprehensive for either the genres presented or the research about integrating and developing different game-based learning environments based on individual game genres. The purpose of this chapter is to provide a sampling of work to illustrate the differing aesthetics for different game genres and some of the challenges and issues related to aesthetics detailed in research about the design of game-based learning.

Notes

1. Some "hidden object" adventure-style games may include time management, but those are not typical of the genre.
2. Granted, online guides known as "cheats" and "walkthroughs" are widely available for most games and are sometimes consulted when one is having difficulty with some aspect of the game. However,

36 • Aesthetics and Game Genres

clues for solving puzzles should be contained within the game so that the skillful player does not have to resort to finding outside assistance.

3. Growing dialogue is emerging about gender selection and sexual preference in RPGs.
4. Games do actually end—they end when a game is terminated and the server closed. However, some games have managed to exist in various forms beyond the official termination of the game.
5. A *checkpoint* is a location within the level that allows players to continue the game or resurrect without having to begin the entire level anew.
6. HyperCard is no longer available; however, it had some interesting and accessible features that might still prove helpful to aid non-programmers in developing prototypes for games.
7. An infamous incident in *LambdaMOO* is chronicled by Julian Dibbell in *My Tiny Life* (Dibbell, 1999).
8. This represents one journal article among a range of fine work about the River City Project. A longer list of publications can be found at http://muve.gse.harvard.edu/rivercityproject/research-publications.htm
9. This represents one journal article among a range of fine work about the Quest Atlantis Project. A longer list of publications can be found at http://sashabarab.com/rsrch_qa.html

References

Achtman, R. L., Green, C. S., & Bavelier, D. (2008). Video games as a tool to train visual skills. *Restorative Neurology and Neuroscience*, 26(2008), 435–446.

Adams, D. M., Mayer, R. E., MacNamara, A., Koenig, A., & Wainess, R. (2012). Narrative games for learning: Testing the discovery and narrative hypotheses. *Journal of Educational Psychology*, 104(1), 235–249.

Adams, E. (2013). *Fundamentals of construction and simulation game design*. Indianapolis, IN: New Riders.

Adams, E. (2014). *Fundamentals of game design* (3rd ed.). Indianapolis, IN: New Riders.

Amory, A. (2001). Building an educational adventure game: Theory, design and lessons. *Journal of Interactive Learning Research*, 12(2/3), 249–263.

Amory, A. (2007). Game object model version II: A theoretical framework for educational game development. *Educational Technology Research & Development*, 55(1), 51–77.

Amory, A., Naicker, K., Vincent, J., & Adams, C. (1999). The use of computer games as an educational tool: Identification of appropriate game types and game elements. *British Journal of Educational Technology*, 30(4), 311–321.

Ang, C. S., Zaphiris, P., & Mahmood, S. (2006). A model of cognitive loads in massively multiplayer online role playing games. *Interacting with Computers*, 19(2007), 167–179.

Baltra, A. (1990). Language learning through computer adventure games. *Simulations & Gaming*, 21(4), 445–452.

Barab, S. A., Gresalfi, M., Dodge, T., & Ingram-Goble, A. (2010). Narratizing disciplines and disciplinizing narratives: Games as 21st century curriculum. *International Journal of Gaming and Computer-Mediated Simulations*, 2(1), 17–30.

Bartle, R. A. (1990). Interactive multi-player computer games. Colchester/Essex, UK: MUSE Ltd. Retrieved November 3, 2013, from ftp://ftp.lambda.moo.mud.org/pub/MOO/papers/mudreport.txt

Barton, M. (2007). The history of computer role-playing games Part 1: The early years (1980–1983). In *Gamasutra: The Art & Business of Making Games*. Retrieved November 3, 2013, from http://www.gamasutra.com/features/20070223a/barton_pfv.htm

Boot, W. R., Blakely, D. P., & Simons, D. J. (2011). Do action video games improve perception and cognition? *Frontiers in Psychology*, 2(226), 1–6.

Carbonaro, M., Cutumisu, M., Duff, H., Gillis, S., Onuczko, C., Schaeffer, J., Schumacher, A., Sigel, J., Szafron, D., & Waugh, K. (2006). Adapting a commercial role-playing game for educational computer game production. In *GameOn North America 2006*. Retrieved March 3, 2014, from http://www.cs.cmu.edu/~waugh/publications/gameon06.pdf

Cavallari, B., Jedberg, J., & Harper, B. (1992). Adventure games in education: A review. *Australian Journal of Educational Technology*, 8(2), 172–184.

Chen, H. P., Lien, C. J., Annetta, L., & Lu, Y. L. (2010). The influence of an educational computer game on children's cultural identities. *Educational Technology & Society*, 13(1), 94–103.

Childress, M. D., & Braswell, R. (2006). Using massively multiplayer online role-playing games for online learning. *Distance Education*, 27(2), 187–196.

Curtis, D. D., & Lawson, M. J. (2002). Computer adventure games as problem-solving environments. *International Education Journal*, 3(4), 43–56.

Damer, B. (1998). *Avatars! Exploring and building virtual worlds on the Internet*. Berkley, CA: Peachpit Press.

Dede, C., Nelson, B., Ketelhut, D. J., Clarke, J., & Bowman, C. (2004). *Design-based research strategies for studying situated learning in a multi-user virtual environment*. Paper presented at the International Conference on Learning Sciences, Mahwah, NJ, June 22, 2004.

de Fritas, D., & Oliver, M. (2006). How can exploratory learning with games and simulation within the curriculum be most effectively evaluated? *Computers & Education*, 46(2006), 249–264.

Dibbell, J. (1999). *My Tiny Life: Crime and Passion in a Virtual World*. London: Fourth Estate Limited.

Dickey, M. D. (1999). *3D virtual worlds and learning: An analysis of the impact of design affordances and limitations in Active Worlds, blaxxun interactive, and OnLive! Traveler; and a study of the implementation of Active Worlds for formal and information education*. Published doctoral dissertation, The Ohio State University.

Dickey, M. D. (2005). Brave new (interactive) worlds: A review of the design affordances and constraints of two 3D virtual worlds as interactive learning environments. *Interactive Learning Environments*, 13(1–2), 121–137.

Dickey, M. D. (2007). Virtual worlds for educators—Virtual worlds: A three-part webinar. *TeachU: Online Seminar Series*. The Ohio Learning Network.

Dickey, M. D. (2011a). World of Warcraft and the impact of game culture and play in an undergraduate game design course. *Computers & Education*, 56(1), 200–209.

Dickey, M. D. (2011b). Murder on Grimm Isle: The design of a game-based learning environment. In S. De Freitas & P. Maharg (Eds.), *Digital games and learning* (pp. 129–152). London, UK: The Continuum International Publishing Group.

Dickey, M. D. (2011c). Murder on Grimm Isle: The impact of game narrative design in an educational game-based learning environment. *British Journal of Educational Technology*, 42(3), 456–469.

Dye, M.W.G., Green, C. S., & Bavelier, D. (2009). Increasing speed of processing with action video games. *Current Directions in Psychological Science*, 18(6), 321–326.

Farmer, C., & Morningstar, F. R. (1991). The lessons of Lucasfilm's Habitat. In M. Benedikt (Ed.), *Cyberspace: First steps* (pp. 273–302). Cambridge, MA: The MIT Press.

Franceschini, S., Gorl, S., Ruffino, M., Viola, S., Molteni, M., & Facoetti, A. (2013). Action video games make dyslexic children read better. *Current Biology*, 23, 462–466.

Graft, K. (2013). Adapting the adventure game genre for the modern day with Broken Age. *Gamasutra: The Art & Business of Making Games*. Retrieved February 12, 2013, from http://www.gamasutra. com/view/news/204322/Adapting_the_adventure_game_genre_for_the_modern_day_with_ Broken_Age.php

Green, C. S., & Bavelier, D. (2003). Action video game modifies visual selective attention. *Nature*, 423, 534–537.

Green, C. S., & Bavelier, D. (2006). Effect of action video games on the spatial distribution of visuospatial attention. *Journal of Experimental Psychology*, 32(2), 1465–1478.

Green, C. S., & Bavelier, D. (2012). Learning, attentional control, and action video games. *Current Biology*, 22, 197–206.

Hafner, K., & Lyon, M. (1996). *Where the wizards stay up late: The origins of the Internet*. New York, NY: Simon & Schuster.

Jang, Y., & Ryu, S. (2011). Exploring game experiences and game leadership in massively multiplayer online role-playing games. *British Journal of Educational Technology*, 42(4), 616–623.

Jenkins, H. (2002). Game design as narrative architecture. Retrieved May 3, 2014, from http://web.mit. edu/21fms/www/faculty/henry3/games&narrative.html#1

Ju, E., & Wagner, C. (1997). Personal computer adventure games: Their structure, principles, and applicability for training. *The DATA BASE for Advances in Information Systems*, 28(2), 78–92.

38 • Aesthetics and Game Genres

Laurel, B. (1993). *Computers as theatre*. New York, NY: Addison-Wesley Publishing Co.

Leutner, D. (1993). Guided discovery learning with computer-based simulation games: Effects of adaptive and non-adaptive instructional support. *Learning and Instruction*, 3, 113–132.

Levy, S. (1984). *Hackers: Heroes of the computer revolution*. New York, NY: Penguin Books.

Malone, T.W. (1981). Toward a theory of intrinsically motivating instruction. *Cognitive Science*, 4, 333–369.

Manero, B., Fernández-Vara, C., & Fernández-Manjón, B. (2013). Stanislavski's system as a game design method: A case study. *Proceedings of DiGRA 2013: DeFragging Game Studies*. Atlanta, GA, August 2013.

Mathevet, R., Le Page, C., Etienne, M., Lefebvre, G., Poulin, B., Gigot, G., Proréol, S., & Mauchamp, A. (2007). BUTORSTAR: A role-playing game for collective awareness of wise reedbed use. *Simulation & Gaming*, 38(2), 233–262.

Moreno-Ger, P., Burgos, D., Martínez-Ortiz, I., Sierra, J. L., & Fernández-Manjón, B. (2008). Educational game design for online education. *Computers in Human Behavior*, 24(2008), 2530–2540.

Moreno-Ger, P., Martínez-Ortiz, I., & Fernández-Manjón, B. (2005). The <E-GAME> Project: Facilitating the development of educational adventure games. *Cognition and Exploratory Learning in the Digital Age (CELDA 2005)*. Porto, Portugal: IADIS.

Oei, A.C., & Patternson, M.D. (2013). Enhancing cognition with video games: A multiple game training study. *PLoS ONE*, 8(3), e58546.

Papargyris, A., & Poulymenakou, A. (2005). Learning to fly in persistent digital worlds: The case of massively multiplayer online role playing games. *ACM SIGGROUP Bulletin: Special Issue on Online Learning Communities*, 25(1), 41–49.

Pesce, M. (1998). A brief history of cyberspace. Retrieved April 3, 2012, from http://www3.zdnet.com/products/vrmluser/perspectives/mp.history.html

Quinn, C.N. (1991). Computers for cognitive research: A HyperCard adventure game. *Behavioral Research Methods, Instruments and Computers*, 23(2), 237–246.

Quinn, C.N. (1996). Designing an instructional game: Reflections on Quest for Independence. *Education and Information Technologies*, 1(3–4), 251–269.

Rankin, Y., Gold, R., & Gooch, B. (2006). 3D role-playing games as language learning tools. *EUROGRAPHICS*, 25(3).

Raybourn, E.M. (2006). Applying simulation experience design methods to creating serious game-based adaptive training systems. *Interacting with Computers*, 19(2007), 206–214.

Rieber, L.P. (1996). Seriously considering play: Designing interactive learning environments based on blending of microworlds, simulations and games. *Educational Technology Research and Development*, 44(2), 43–58.

Rollings, A., & Adams, E. (2003). *Game design*. Indianapolis, IN: New Riders.

Sancho, P., Moreno-Ger, P., Fuentes-Fernández, R., & Fernández-Manjón, B. (2009). Adaptive role playing games: An immersive approach for problem based learning. *Educational Technology & Society*, 12(4), 110–124.

Schell, J. (2008). *The art of game design: A book of lenses*. Burlington, MA: Morgan Kaufmann Publishers.

Sedano, C.I., Leenderts, V., Vinni, M., Sutinen, E., & Ellis, S. (2013). Hypercontextualized learning games: Fantasy, motivation and engagement in reality. *Simulation & Gaming*, 44(6), 821–845.

Sherwood, C. (1991). Adventure games in the classroom: A far cry from A says Apple. *Computers & Education*, 17(4), 309–315.

Simpson, J.M., & Elias, V.L. (2011). Choices and chances: The sociology role-playing game—The sociological imagination in practice. *Teaching Sociology*, 39(1), 42–56.

Squire, K., & Barab, S. (2004). Replaying history: Engaging urban underserved students in learning work history through computer simulation games. ICLS '04 *Proceedings of the 6th International Conference on Learning Sciences* (pp. 505–512). Mahwah, NJ.

Steinkuehler, C. (2006). The mangle of play. *Games & Culture*, 1(3), 1–14.

Taylor, T.L. (2009). *Play between worlds: Exploring online game culture*. Cambridge, MA: The MIT Press.

Torrente, J., del Blanco, A., Marchiori, E.J., Moreno-Ger, P., & Fernández-Manjón, B. (2010). <e-Adventure>: Introducing educational games in the learning process. In *Education Engineering (EDUCON)* (pp. 1121–1126). Madrid, Spain: IEEE.

Torrente, J., Moreno-Ger, P., Fernández-Manjón, B., & Sierra, J. L. (2008). Instructor-oriented authoring tools for educational videogames. *Eighth IEEE International Conference on Advanced Learning Technologies*, pp. 516–518. Santander, Cantabria: IEEE.

Villalta, M., Gajardo, I., Nussbaum, M., Andreu, J. J., Echeverría, A., & Plass, J. L. (2011). Design guidelines for classroom multiplayer presential games (CMPG). *Computers & Education*, 57(2011), 2039–2053.

Vogel, J. J., Vogel, D. S., Cannon-Bowers, J., Bowers, C. A., Muse, K., & Wright, M. (2006). Computer gaming and interactive simulations for learning: A meta-analysis. *Journal of Educational Computing Research*, 34(3), 229–243.

Watcharasukarn, M., Krumdieck, S., Green, R., & Dantas, A. (2011). Researching travel behavior and adaptability: Using a virtual reality role-playing game. *Simulation & Gaming*, 42(1), 100–117.

Media

Active Worlds (1995)—ActiveWorlds, Inc.
Asteroids (1979)—Atari
EverQuest2 (2004)—Sony Online Entertainment
Myst (1993)—Cyan-Brøderbund
Nancy Drew Games—Her Interactive: http://www.herinteractive.com/
Neverwinter Nights (2002)—BioWare
Pac-Man (1983)—Atari
Risk (1959)—Parker Brothers
Second Life (2003)—Linden Lab
SimCity (1989)—Maxis Software Inc.
Space Invaders (1978)—Midway
Tetris (1984)—Spectrum HoloByte

3
Aesthetics and Player Perspective

The focus of this chapter is on the different elements that construct player positioning in games: mechanics (camera view and movement), narrative, embodiment and immersion. This chapter begins with a discussion of the classic modes of player positioning in different games, both graphical and text-based. This section is followed by a discussion of how narrative perspective and point of view (POV) contribute to player perspective. This discussion is followed by a short analysis of how character design affordances and constraints foster embodiment. Following this analysis is a discussion of immersion through the lenses of two differing dramatic aesthetics (Aristotelian and Brechtian) and the educational implications of player perspective for the design of game-based learning.

Player Positioning

Graphical Games

Much of the early design of digital games used conventions from traditional board games as a guide. In board games, all of the action takes place on a single two-dimensional space, and the player—who is external to the game—manipulates and moves pieces. For example, with the game Monopoly, the entire game space consists of the game board. Players move pieces around the board. The entire game environment is fully displayed. The player views the board from above. The environment changes somewhat during gameplay as players buy *property* and add *buildings*, but primarily the environment is static and revealed at the start of the game. Examples of how digital games adopted this convention can be seen in the early single-frame games such as *Pong* and *Pac-Man*. All action occurs within a two-dimensional frame space with the player positioning being a *god's-eye* or top-down view of the game space. This style allows players to see the entire play space and develop strategies based on a world view. Although this was popular in early games, it is still used in many contemporary arcade-style games and mobile games (*Angry Birds*). With this type of play space, the player is external to the gameplay experience. The advantages of this perspective are that it is relatively easy to design and the game designer has control over the player's viewpoint.

42 • Aesthetics and Player Perspective

More advanced graphics capabilities supported the integration of the isometric view. The isometric view, such as that found in games like *SimCity* and *Civilization*, can roughly be described as 2½D. What is notable about the shift to an isometric view is that while the player still has an overall view of the scene, there are areas of the environment obscured or blocked from the player's view. There is a sense that the player is not able to see the entire gameplay environment; some parts are hidden from view. The game space emerges and develops as the player manipulates the viewpoint and progresses in gameplay. The advantage of isometric view is that the player is closer to the action than the top-down perspective; however, the player is still primarily external to the gameplay. Yet, with this style of game space, the player has some control over the viewpoint (camera). Typically, there are many constraints on player control of the viewpoint or camera, but the player is able to manipulate the camera to some degree and target specific areas to view.

In an attempt to move beyond the single-frame design, video games such as *Super Mario Bros.* incorporated the 2D *side-scroller*, which allowed players to explore spaces initially hidden from the first view. This shift from a single screen to a scrolling environment incorporated both a sense of motion and discovery into gameplay. Part of the environment is hidden from the player, and it is by moving left to right (or sometimes up and down) through the environment that the player is able to encounter and explore new game space. Typically, in side-scrollers, the player's character is positioned within the game (at the center of the screen or sometimes slightly left of center). With this model, the player is still external to the game space but, by manipulating a character through the play space, is able to encounter and explore new environments.

Similar to top-down design of game space is still-frame or a type of cinematic *mise-en-scène* used in some casual hidden-object and adventure games (*Bioscopia*, *Azada* and *Mystery Case Files*). The entire game is constructed of a series of renderings of complex, object-filled environments (often a series of rooms). The player interacts with elements in the images (by clicking on objects). Often, the player moves from room to room to solve puzzles and challenges in the quest to uncover an overarching narrative.

With the advent of faster processors and greater graphics capabilities, game designers were able to create increasingly more sophisticated and immersive game environments. In turn, as games became more complex, the visual representation and third-person perspective emerged that allowed players to view their characters within a 3D environment or setting. Initially, game players were somewhat limited in the degree to which a player could control the camera viewpoint to see the setting, but as the technology developed, so did the affordances for camera control. Third-person perspective allows players to view their characters within the scene. In addition to third-person perspective, third-person-trailing perspective allows the player to view the scene from over the shoulder of their character. Games such as *Quake* and *Doom* marked a departure of external player positioning and moved the player into the environment through the use of first-person POV. The result of this design shift is that players became part of the environment; they no longer viewed the entire game space within one or several frames, but rather the environment, information, events, actions and activities are initially obscured from view and encountered as the player moves through the graphical environment (Riddle, 2002).

The advantages of first-person perspective are that the player is somewhat positioned within the environment and that the "camera" or viewpoint is controlled by the player rather than having a fixed or preset viewpoint. This allows the player to move into the game space and encounter objects and environments through the eyes of the character/avatar. There are also disadvantages to first-person perspective. Adams (2014) argues that first-person perspective also limits the player in different ways. The player is not able to view his/her character and associated gestures, animations and customization. Similarly, first-person perspective can make some moves more difficult (e.g., jumping). First-person can also cause motion sickness for some people. Finally, as Adams notes, first-person perspective can limit the game design because the designer is not able to leverage various camera angles for dramatic effect.

Text-based Games

Not all games began as graphical environments; some began as text-based environments. In text-based environments, player perspective was not a function of graphic display or camera views, but instead a function of the narrative description. For example, early adventure-style games along with *MUDs* and *MOOs* were text-based environments. *MUD* is an acronym for Multi-user Dungeons or, as they are often referred to, Multi-user Domains or Dimensions; by extension, *MOO* is the acronym for MUD Object-Oriented. Text-based adventure games are game environments in which players interact with the game via text commands. They are programs for synchronous, networked communication that accesses a shared database. This database consists of text descriptions of a physical environment that is typically divided into *spaces, rooms, exits* and *objects* with which users interact by way of a text-based interface and by typing text commands. When a player enters the game, the player is typically presented with a narrative description of the current space along with objects and potential doors and portals. The player types commands to explore the space, examine objects and access different rooms or spaces.

Typically, the player is able to interact with various objects in the environment and, by doing so, uncovers an overarching narrative storyline. The player also encounters various puzzles or obstacles that must be solved or overcome to progress through the narrative and access additional spaces. Adventure games are among the oldest of the computer gaming genres, with roots that can be traced to text-based interactive fiction (Hafner & Lyon, 1996; Levy, 1984). Among the first adventure games (sometimes referred to as interactive fiction) is Crowther and Wood's Tolkienesque fantasy game, *The Colossal Cave Adventure* (also referred to

44 • Aesthetics and Player Perspective

as ADVENT or *Adventure*). In this game, users assumed identities, fought enemies and overcame obstacles to discover a treasure (Reid, 1994).

Early text-based adventure games such as *The Colossal Cave Adventure* and *Zork* place the player in a first-person perspective where the player is positioned in the game. The player encounters objects and environments in first-person perspective. Through trial and error, the player progresses through the environment and uncovers the narrative storyline and solves puzzles and challenges.

Example 1. The opening of The Colossal Cave Adventure:

You are standing at the end of a road before a small brick building. Around you
   is a forest. A small stream flows out of the building and down a gully.
>walk in (*player input*)
You are inside a building, a well house for a large spring.
There are some keys on the ground here.
There is a shiny brass lamp nearby.
There is tasty food here.
There is a bottle of water here.

>
(Crowther & Woods, 1977)

Around the same time as the emergence of *The Colossal Cave Adventure*, Roy Trubshaw, a student at the University of Essex, teamed up with Richard Bartle and created a multi-user text-based game and named it *MUD* for "multi-user dungeon." This first MUD (now referred to as MUD1) was a fantasy-based game that allowed users to communicate, collaborate and fight one another as they attempted to win treasures. On attaining enough treasures, users were granted privileges. One of the earlier versions of the game included the extensibility so prevalent in MUDs today. Most MUDs are now user-extensible systems that allow users to add to the database by creating *objects* and *rooms* for other users to interact with and in.

Similarly, MOOs were also text-based environments. In 1989, Jim Apnes, a graduate student at Carnegie Mellon University, created *TinyMUD*. Unlike the predecessor gaming MUDs, TinyMUD was the first social MUD. Apnes had removed the combat-oriented commands and thereby created an environment that focused on social interactions (Bruckman, 1997). Although game-like in many ways, MOOs were designed primarily for social interaction rather than gameplay.

Within MUDs and MOOs, the player is typically situated in first-person perspective. Some MUDs require or at least encourage players to adopt personae and to play as that personae or role throughout the gameplay. This type of role-playing game heavily informed the modern design of the Massively Multiplayer Online Role-playing Game (MMORPG) genre popular today (Taylor, 2009). The player perspective is first-person from the perspective of the player's self-created character. Within the narrative form, the player is positioned "in" the game. Many

MUDs and MOOs are user-extensible, meaning players can create and build onto the environment, thereby immersing the player deeper into the play experience.

With the onset of more advanced graphic capabilities, the core of text-based games such as MUDs and adventure-style games were impacted by new graphic capabilities. Adventure games evolved into graphic environments in which the player explored images of rooms and spaces to solve challenges and puzzles and unlock the overarching narrative. In most adventure games, players were no longer limited to a series of static images, but games also developed into simulated 3D environments (*Syberia*). However, typically in the adventure genre, players are situated in first- or third-person perspective.

Narrative: Perspective and Point of View

The terms "perspective" and "point of view" are often used synonymously in game design and, to some degree, perhaps they are synonymous; however, in literature, the term "perspective" denotes the character's (or characters') perspective in which the story is being told. The term "point of view" (POV), however, designates the narrator's mode. In first-person POV, the story is told through the narrator's voice. The narrator may be the protagonist or another character, but the story is a first-person account from the POV of the narrator. First-person pronouns such as "I," "me" and "my" denote the narrator's voice. The benefit of this POV is the reader is privy to the internal thoughts and feelings of the narrator character. Conversely, there are limitations to this POV because the reader is limited to only the view of the narrator. The reader knows only what the character knows, and the feelings and motivations of other characters have to be conveyed through dialogue and observable actions (body language).

> If you really want to hear about it, the first thing you'll probably want to know is where I was born, and what my lousy childhood was like, and how my parents were occupied and all before they had me, and all that David Copperfield kind of crap, but I don't feel like going into it, if you want to know the truth.
>
> *The Catcher in the Rye* by J. D. Salinger (1951, p. 3)

Second-person is rarely used in literature, though sometimes it is used in action games to frame the game and construct the role for the player. In second-person POV, the narration is addressed to the reader, and the reader is the agent of action (e.g., you walk into the abandoned hospital and you see signs of a recent struggle). This mode tends to distance the reader from the character rather than drawing him/her into the story.

Third-person POV can take several forms: third-person objective, third-person limited and third-person omniscient. In third-person mode, the narrator tells the story by describing the main character's actions, behavior and dialogue. There is no insight into the personal feelings of the character. Characters' thoughts,

46 • Aesthetics and Player Perspective

motivations and feelings have to be conveyed through actions and dialogue. In third-person limited, the narrator's voice expresses the internal thoughts and feelings of the main character, but typically only the main character.[1] The reader knows only what the main character knows, and the thoughts and feelings of other characters have to be conveyed through dialogues and actions. In third-person omniscient, the story is told by an omnipotent narrator who reveals the thoughts and feelings of several characters. This mode allows the reader to have insight into several characters but tends to distance the reader from the characters.

Both perspective and POV impact how a player is positioned in the narrative of a game. First and foremost is the role the player assumes in the game. Whether it is an omnipotent force from beyond (*Tetris*) or a renowned character from fictions such as *Nancy Drew*, the player experiences the game from the perspective of the role. The POV also impacts the experience. In the previously discussed text-based games, the player plays the game somewhat as himself/herself, as delineated by the use of second-person, whereas when the player is cast in a specific role, the shift to first-person helps create a bond between the player and the character role being portrayed.

Embodiment: Roles and Controls

Roles

In addition to a game's visual perspective and narrative POV, players are in some way situated within the game space as an agent, or they may force action upon objects in the game, as a pre-scripted character or as player-created character. In games such as *Tetris* and *Pong*, the player is a force or agent of action manipulating puzzle pieces or paddles.

As game development progressed and narrative began playing a stronger role in some genres, players were cast in the role of pre-scripted characters in games, notably action and adventure games. Games such as the *Tomb Raider (Lara Croft)* series, *Max Payne* series and the *Syberia* trilogy cast players in the leading role of the protagonist of the game. The personality, history and physical attributes and constraints impact how the player is embodied in the gameplay environment. Often, adventure and action/adventure game players are cast as pre-scripted protagonist characters and play the game as that character. In role-playing games, players often have the option of creating a unique character from a selection of options, but players' characters begin the games as low-level rank-and-file characters within a larger narrative. Within RPGs and games in which the player creates or configures a character, player perspective is to some degree shaped by the role the player inhabits in the game. The identity, personality, goals, nationality, alliance and physical attributes impact what the player experiences. For example, in both RPGs and MMORPGs, players often create characters within a central conflict and must often choose an allegiance within the conflict as well as characteristics and attributes. This in turn impacts what the player can see and do in the game, thereby impacting the player perspective.

Aesthetics and Player Perspective • 47

Avatar and Controls

Games may narratively cast the player in a role within the game, but the use of the controls and affordances and constraints of the character/avatar determine what the player has the option of viewing and to some degree how the player is embodied in the game. The camera view, motion and angle used to convey a scene impact how a player is positioned in a game. The interface and mechanisms that the player uses to control the character also impact how the player is positioned in the game. The types of mechanics of control include game console controllers, joysticks, keyboards and a mouse. Beyond the physical controls, there are two main methods of moving characters within the game: *point-and-click* and *direct control*. With point-and-click control, the player clicks on a location and the character moves to that location. Typically, the camera viewpoint is third-person. For example, in the game *Syberia*, to make the character of Kate walk down the street, the player clicks on various locations of the setting, and Kate walks to those locations. However, there are point-and-click games in which the player is cast as the lead character and plays as the lead character, but the character does not appear in the game. For example, in adventure games such as the *Nancy Drew* series, the player plays the game as Nancy and interacts with non-player characters as Nancy, but the physical representation of Nancy never appears. In contrast to point-and-click, *direct control* allows the player to pilot the character through the environment. Side-scroller games, contemporary action games and MMORPGs typically rely on this type of control. With direct control, player skills in navigation and speed can impact the game, progress and immersion.

The character is typically represented by some type of avatar that serves as the visual representation of the player in the game space. The character/avatar typically includes basic movement such as walking (both point-and-click and direct control) but may include other types of motion that may be player-controlled, such as jumping, climbing and fighting (often with direct controls). The avatar may also include other types of movements that are not player–controlled, such as gestures when talking and standing.

Embodiment is a function of the affordances and constraints of both the role and the controls. The character role shapes the gameplay experience through the personality, personal history and attributes. This impacts what the character can do within a game, and the narrative consistency of a character role impacts embodiment. Similarly, the affordances and constraints of the type of controls impact how the player is embodied in the game space.

Immersion

Perspective is a function of not only graphics and viewpoint (camera) but also the narrative of the game. Where the player is situated and constructed in relation to the game can impact the player's feelings of distance and immersion in the game environment. Taylor (2002) distinguishes between types of immersive experiences

48 • Aesthetics and Player Perspective

in games as diegetic immersion and situated immersion. Taylor characterizes diegetic immersion as the experience of a player being immersed in the act of gameplay, whereas situated immersion is the experience of a player being immersed in the experience of the game space through the player's character in the narrative environment. The differences between diegetic and situated immersion are not polar, but instead fluid states. With diegetic immersion, the player acts upon the game, whereas in situated immersion, the player acts within the game space.

Similarly, Adams (2004) identifies three types of immersive experiences: tactical immersion, strategic immersion and narrative immersion. According to Adams, tactical immersion is somewhat analogous to Csikszentmihalyi's "flow state interaction," which involves "deep concentration, high and balanced challenges and skills, and a sense of control and satisfaction" (Csikszentmihalyi, 1990, p. 83). Strategic immersion is a (Adams, 2004) in which the player is absorbed in the process of finding the moves that will lead to victory. The player is involved in the process of observing, calculating and deducting. Finally, narrative immersion involves the players becoming immersed in the narrative, both in terms of feelings about the characters and wanting to uncover the storyline.

Immersion is sustained by both player positioning and how a player participates in the gameplay experience. Games are simulated environments and as such require that players to some degree willingly embrace a suspension of disbelief (Coleridge, 1817). The notion of *suspension of disbelief* is a term coined by poet and philosopher Samuel Taylor Coleridge (1817). During a time in which fantasy had fallen out of popular favor, Coleridge maintained that if a writer infusing fantasy in fictional work is able to imbue the work with "human interest and a semblance of truth," the reader would willingly suspend disbelief and judgment to embrace the work (Coleridge, 1817, p. 290). Coleridge's notion of the suspension of disbelief is often discussed in the goal of game design because games often deal with fantasy and exaggeration and require that players to some degree "buy into" the fantasy to support engagement and immersion.

In *Hamlet on the Holodeck*, Janet Murray (2001) contends that the surrender of imagination is not a passive act on the part of participants as is often assumed in discussions of Coleridge's suspension of disbelief, but rather participants (readers, viewers, gamers, etc.) actively "create belief." Murray makes reference to *reader-response theory*, a literary theory that maintains that readers are active agents and the act of reading is a "dynamic interaction between text and reader" (Iser, 1978, p. 107). According to Murray, "When we enter a fictional world, we do not merely 'suspend' a critical faculty; we also exercise a creative faculty. We do not suspend disbelief so much as we actively *create belief*" (Murray, 2001, p. 110).

Whether by passive or active construction, Coleridge's suspension of disbelief has been embraced not only in game design but also in the design of virtual and simulated environments, and while some argued it as a goal, others argued against it. In the early to mid-1990s, there was much innovation in virtual space, and various themes of dialogue emerged about embodiment, presence and immersion in virtual space. Two differing but insightful discussions of the aesthetics of immersion in virtual space that emerged were Brenda Laurel's Aristotelian model of dramatic engagement and Carol Gigliotti's Brechtian model of dramatic reflection.

In Brenda Laurel's seminal work, *Computers as Theater* (1993), Laurel argued for an Aristotelian model of dramatic engagement to inform the design of interfaces and simulations. Laurel argued that the Aristotelian model of narrative provided a means to immerse, engage and evoke emotion from the user. Although Aristotle's outlined dramatic structure is merely a beginning, middle and end (*diesis*, *peripetia* and *lusis*), narrative theorists continue to attribute his identification of elements as being the foundation of drama structure (Halliwell, 1987). More contemporary outlines build upon Aristotle's original elements and often include variations of the five-stage model proposed by Gustav Freytag (1863). Freytag's five stages include exposition, rising action, climax, falling action and dénouement (resolution, revelation or catastrophe) (see Figure 3.1). The exposition provides the setting for the story and background information and introduces the main characters. The rising action includes the events and activities that contribute to building the story. The climax is the turning point of the story and key insight into the protagonist. The falling action typically involves the key conflict between the protagonist and antagonist. The dénouement is the end of the conflict and the resolution of the drama.

Laurel maintains that this model is pleasurable because it provides participants with a cathartic experience as they travel through the various stages. It is designed to evoke emotion and engagement. Laurel argues in her preface that "the notion of direct engagement opens the door to artistic considerations that are broader than the aesthetics of the screen."

In contrast to the engaging and cathartic model of immersion advocated by Laurel, in an article entitled "Aesthetics of a Virtual World," Carol Gigliotti (1995) offers a differing view for the design of immersive environment. Gigliotti argues for a Brechtian aesthetic for the design of immersion to interrupt the immersive experience. Bertolt Brecht was a noted early to mid-century German poet,

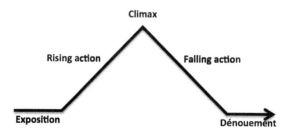

Figure 3.1 Freytag's pyramid of dramatic structure (Freytag, 1863, p. 115)
Adapted from Freytag, 1863, p. 115

50 • Aesthetics and Player Perspective

playwright and director who sought to use drama as a motivation for action. In the 1950s, Brecht criticized the Aristotelian model of dramatic structure for its goal of pleasure and engagement and instead argued that the role of drama should be to empower, teach and instruct audiences. According to Curran (2001, p. 167), "Brecht attacks Aristotelian catharsis as a kind of 'opium of the masses' arguing that empathizing with characters prevents viewers from reflecting critically on the social causes of human suffering." In Brecht's plays, the actors routinely address the audience out of character or "break the fourth wall" and interrupt the narrative to provide commentary on the action within the play. This interruption is designed to force the audience to reflect upon the choices made by the characters and reflect upon the impact of those choices. Gigliotti argues that the Brechtian aesthetic hinders participants from entering the pleasurable immersion of the Aristotelian model, and instead empowers participants to reflect and to consider the action to be taken. According to Gigliotti, the Brechtian aesthetics are "vehicles for imparting knowledge, a means of understanding the context in which that knowledge is developed and the encouragement to act on that knowledge" (Gigliotti, 1995, p. 297).

The notion of "breaking the fourth wall" and interrupting the fictive world of digital environments such as games and virtual worlds is not without controversy. "The fourth wall" is a term derived from the theater used to describe the imaginary wall or boundary between the front of the stage and the audience. The "fourth wall" is a perceived boundary and distance that preserves the illusion that the actors on stage cannot see or hear the audience, but that the audience is peering into the lives, actions and depictions on stage. Breaking the fourth wall typically involves an actor not delivering a monologue or soliloquy, but talking directly to the audience. This notion of the fourth wall extends into literature and film as well. Breaking the fourth wall can be a literary and cinematic device (also used in games). Examples of breaking the fourth wall can be seen in the film *Ferris Bueller's Day Off* and the television show *Malcolm in the Middle*, in which actors directly address the audience about events within the narrative. Both interactive design theorist Janet Murray (2001) and game designer Lee Sheldon (2014) address the impact of breaking the fourth wall. Murray argues that the fictive experiences provide a type of liminal trance in which the audience/viewer/reader can explore feelings and emotions outside of themselves from the safe distance of behind the fourth wall. Murray contends that immersive experiences are dependent on establishing distance and that we need to "define boundary conventions that will allow us to surrender to the enticements of the virtual environments" (p. 103). Similarly, Sheldon warns that creating an immersive experience can be challenging in games because, unlike film or literature, in games (and, by extension, virtual environments), players must interact with the environment through a console, mouse and/or keyboard. There are already a variety of mechanisms that may draw a participant out of the immersive experience without breaking the fourth wall. Sheldon cautions that designers should only break the fourth wall purposefully.

Educational Implications

A discussion of the aesthetics of player positioning holds much relevance for the design of game-based learning and indeed the integration of game-like elements for educational purposes. Player positioning, narrative, embodiment and immersion are all part of how a player is positioned in relationship to the game and impact the experience. For game-based learning, it is important to understand how these elements function and to make informed choices about how to position a learner in different types of learning experiences. Where and how the player/learner is positioned in relation to the game or learning environment will impact the experience. In graphical games, the shift from an outside, god's-eye perspective to a first-person perspective of playing a character embedded in the game space marked a shift in moving the player from outside of the game into becoming part of the gaming environment. The result of this shift creates more engaging experiences for the player (Riddle, 2002). Similarly, with text-based games and the integration of detailed narrative in graphical games, the perspective (role the player is playing) and the POV impact how the player is positioned as either internal or external to the game space. The use of first-person or even second-person POV includes the player in the game environment. Embodiment, as a function of the roles and the affordances as well as the constraints of the control mechanism, also impacts how a player is positioned. The consistency of the personality, history and attributes of the character role in which the player is cast or the creation of a unique character impacts how the player is constructed in the game. The type of controls (point-and-click vs. direct control) impacts player embodiment and immersion in the game space. Immersion, fostered by both player positioning and player participation, requires to some degree the willingness to embrace a suspension of disbelief (Coleridge, 1817). The aesthetics of the Aristotelian model of drama are a means of drawing players into an experience. In an article entitled "Engaging by Design," I argue that this shift of moving a player into a game has relevance for the design of educational material and game-based learning.

> These changes in design have growing relevance for the design of materials for both traditional classroom activities and digital interactive learning environments. A parallel between player positioning in game space and learner positioning within differing theoretical perspectives of learning can illuminate and inform instructional design about how to create engaging learning environments. For example, within a behaviorist perspective, the focus of the learning environment was to elicit the proper responses to stimuli. The positioning of the learner is external to the learning environment. Mastery of the desired material is the goal. However, the shift to a constructive epistemology marks a departure from an objectivist, systems approach to the design of instruction towards the development of engaging learning environments that support the construction of knowledge (Duffy & Cunningham, 1996; Jonassen, 1999). Problem-based learning

52 • Aesthetics and Player Perspective

and project-based learning are two examples of methods that reflect this epistemological shift in the design of instruction. In both of these methods, learners are taking a first-person perspective within the learning environment. No longer is the focus upon a "gods-eye view" and mastery of a specific set of exercises, but rather information, events, actions, and activities are obscured from view and encountered as the learner moves through the learning materials and environment.

(Dickey, 2005, p. 71)

While I still maintain this argument, I also believe it is important to recognize that the goal of most popular games is to entertain, whereas the goal of game-based learning is to educate. While popular games require players to synthesize, evaluate and strategize, the primary goal is entertainment, and player positioning and immersing the player in the gameplay are key parts in fostering an entertaining experience. However, immersive experiences may not be suitable for all educational experiences. Some of the goals of contemporary education are to foster learners who are reflective and can transfer knowledge from a synthetic experience to the real world. The immersive experience may not always provide the type of reflection or foster the type of third-person perspective that allows learners to become critical participants in the construction of knowledge. It is important to look at how and when breaking the fourth wall and interrupting the immersive experience may be more constructive toward meeting different learning goals. Differing aesthetics such as Gigliotti's Brechtian model can create rich environments for various learning goals.

Both Laurel (1993) and Gigliotti's (1995) differing views might seem to be better suited for a discussion of narrative, but they hold much relevance for the discussion of player perspective and the design of game-based learning. The Aristotelian model places the learner in the learning environment and as a participant in the space. The value in this model is that the learner is immersed and plays a part in the space. Certainly, there are benefits to this model in fostering learner engagement, but there are also limitations. With this model, does the learner have access to the entire environment or only a limited perspective? Is the learner able to "step back" from the experience and reflect and articulate learning? In opposition, the Brechtian aesthetic would interrupt the pleasure of narrative and immersion to challenge the learner. It is a model that may interrupt the pleasurable catharsis of the narrative immersive space, but it would challenge the participant to reflect. Laurel's Aristotelian aesthetic and Gigliotti's contrasting Brechtian aesthetic are important for the design of game-based learning because they represent two different but important perspectives of design for fostering learning. Laurel's Aristotelian model places the player/learner in a first-person perspective with the goal of immersing the player/learner in the environment, role and action—yet it is a seductive model and one in which the pleasurable, cathartic flow experience may impact the ability of the player/learner to reflect on knowledge and design

Aesthetics and Player Perspective • 53

a unique plan of action. In contrast, Gigliotti's Brechtian model is a more reflective aesthetic designed to cultivate knowledge and understanding. The immersive experience would be interrupted to prevent the player/learner from attaining the pleasurable, cathartic flow experience, but instead to contemplate and reflect on knowledge gained by the experience.

For the design of game-based learning, the aesthetics of player positioning play an important role in how the learner experiences the game-based environment. Both immersive and disruptive experiences have their place in the learning process. Understanding where to position a learner in terms of graphics, narrative, embodiment and immersion can provide educators and instructional designers with a better understanding of how to meet educational goals.

Guidelines for Learner Positioning in Game-based Learning

The following include questions to help guide educators and instructional designers in the development of game-based learning.

Perspective

1. Determine the relationship between the learner and the game space.
   - Is it important that the learner be in the environment?
   - How will the learner view the game-based environment (god's-eye or external force, first-person or third-person)?

Narrative

2. Determine the role of the learner.
   - Is the learner a pre-scripted character, or will learners create their own character and role?
   - How will this role be conveyed to the learner and reinforced?

Embodiment

3. Consider the types of controls and viewpoint and the learning goals.
   - What are the affordances of the avatar?
   - What are the affordances of the controls?
   - What do you want the learner to view and not view?

Immersion

4. Determine the type of immersive experience that best meets the needs of the learning goals.
   - Would the goals of learning best be supported by an environment that is emotionally immersive or reflective?

54 • Aesthetics and Player Perspective

Note

1. Occasionally, authors will deviate from and include short accounts of another character's thoughts and feelings (e.g., the Harry Potter series by J. K. Rowling).

References

Adams, E. (2004). Postmodernism and the three types of immersion. *Gamasutra*. Retrieved September 12, 2013, from http://designersnotebook.com/Columns/063_Postmodernism/063_postmodernism.htm

Adams, E. (2014). *Fundamentals of game design* (3rd ed.). Indianapolis, IN: New Riders.

Bruckman, A. (1997). *MOOSE Crossing: Construction, Community, and Learning in a networked virtual world for kids*. Doctoral dissertation, MIT.

Coleridge, S. (1817). *Biographia Literaria*, Chapter XIV. Retrieved September 14, 2013, from http://www.gutenberg.org/files/6081/6081-h/6081-h.htm

Crowther, W., & Woods, D. (1977). Adventure (aka ADVENT and The Colossal Cave Adventure) FORTRAN source code. Retrieved May 19, 2014, from http://mirror.ifarchive.org/if-archive/games/source/adv350-pdp10.tar.gz

Csikszentmihalyi, M. (1990). *Flow: The psychology of optimal experience*. New York, NY: Harper & Row.

Curran, A. (2001). Brecht's criticism of Aristotle's aesthetics of tragedy. *The Journal of Aesthetics and Art Criticism*, 59(2), 167–184.

Dickey, M. D. (2005). Engaging by design: How engagement strategies in popular computer and video games can inform instructional design. *Educational Technology Research and Development*, 53(2), 67–83.

Duffy, T. M., & Cunningham, D. J. (1996). Constructivism: Implications for the design and delivery of instruction. In D. H. Jonassen (Ed.), *Handbook of research for educational communications and technology* (pp. 170–178). New York, NY: Macmillan.

Freytag, G. (1863). *Die Technik des Dramas* (authorized translation from the 6th German ed. By Elias J. MacEwan, 1894). Retrieved May 19, 2014, from https://archive.org/details/freytagstechniqu00freyuoft

Gigliotti, C. (1995). Aesthetics of a virtual world. *Leonardo*, 28(4), 289–295.

Hafner, K., & Lyon, M. (1996). *Where the wizards stay up late: The origins of the Internet*. New York, NY: Simon & Schuster.

Halliwell, S. (1987). *The poetics of Aristotle*. Chapel Hill, NC: The University of North Carolina Press.

Iser, W. (1978). *The act of reading: A theory of aesthetic response*. Baltimore, MD: The Johns Hopkins University Press.

Jonassen, D. (1999). Designing constructivist learning environments. In C. M. Reigeluth (Ed.), *Instructional-design theories and models: A new paradigm of instructional theory* (Vol. II, pp. 215–240). Hillsdale, NJ: Lawrence Erlbaum Associates.

Laurel, B. (1993). *Computers as theatre*. New York, NY: Addison-Wesley Publishing Co.

Levy, S. (1984). *Hackers: Heroes of the computer revolution*. New York, NY: Penguin Books.

Murray, J. H. (2001). *Hamlet on the Holodeck: The future of narrative in cyberspace*. Cambridge, MA: The MIT Press.

Reid, E. (1994). *Cultural formations in text-based virtual realities*. Master's thesis, University of Melbourne.

Riddle, J. (2002). Cameras and point-of-view in the gamespace. In *SIGGRAPH2002 Proceedings* (p. 155). San Antonio, TX: ACM.

Salinger, J. D. (1951). *The catcher in the rye*. New York, NY: Little, Brown and Company.

Sheldon, L. (2014). *Character development and storytelling for games*. Crawfordsville, IN: Course Technology Cengage Learning.

Taylor, L. N. (2002). *Video games: Perspective, point-of-view, and immersion*. Master's thesis, University of Florida.

Taylor, T. L. (2009). *Play between worlds: Exploring online game culture*. Cambridge, MA: The MIT Press.

Media

Angry Birds (2009)—Rovio Entertainment
Azada (2007)—Big Fish Studios
Bioscopia (2003)—Viva Media
Civilization (1991)—MicroProse
Doom (1993)—id Software
Ferris Bueller's Day Off (1986)—Paramount Pictures
Tomb Raider (1996)—Eidos Interactive
Malcolm in the Middle (2000)—Fox
Max Payne (2002)—Remedy Entertainment
Mystery Case Files (2005)—Big Fish Studios
Nancy Drew (1998)—HER Interactive
Pac-Man (1980)—Namco
Pong (1972)—Atari
Quake (1996)—id Software
SimCity (1986)—Maxis
Syberia (2002)—Microids
Tetris (1984)—Sega

4
Aesthetics and Narrative Design

Introduction

The purpose of this chapter is to provide a discussion of the aesthetics of narrative design in games and to provide strategies for incorporating aesthetics of narrative design into game-based learning. This chapter begins with an overview of narrative in games, followed by three analyses of narrative structures found in games: the three-act story structure, the quest and long-form narrative. Within each analysis is a discussion of strategies used to integrate narrative within games, followed by a discussion of the educational implications related to each narrative structure. The chapter concludes with guidelines for developing and integrating narrative for game-based learning. Much of this chapter is based on my research in games and narrative. It includes updated and expanded work from several journal articles (Dickey, 2005, 2006, 2007, 2012).

Narrative in Game Design

Narrative is a ubiquitous structure that pervades our lives. Narrative is the manner by which humans both frame and recount their experiences (Polkinghorne, 1988). According to Bruner (1990), narrative is both a means of reasoning and a means of representation that is inherently sequential. It may be real or fantasy, based not on plausibility of facts, but rather on the integrity of structure internal to discourse (Bruner, 1990). Structural linguist Barthes (1975, p. 237)[1] contends that narrative is:

> present at all times, in all places, in all societies; indeed narrative starts with the very history of mankind; there is not, there has never been anywhere, any people without narrative; all classes, all human groups, have their stories, and very often those stories are enjoyed by men of different and even opposite cultural backgrounds: narrative remains largely unconcerned with good or bad literature. Like life itself, it is there, international, transhistorical, transcultural . . .

Within the field of game design, the role of narrative in games was at one time an issue of great debate (Aarseth, 2001; Frasca, 2001; Juul, 2001). Advocates

58 • Aesthetics and Narrative Design

of narrative in game design argued that a strong narrative line can create more immersive and engaging gameplay (Adams, 2001; Bringsjord, 2001), while opponents argued that central to gameplay is interaction, not storytelling (Juul, 1998; Laramée, 2002). One of the primary arguments against incorporating narrative into gameplay was that narrative is primarily linear in construct. According to both advocates and proponents of narrative in games, much of our concept and construction of narrative has been influenced by mediums such as books and films that are linear, and the typical narrative arc (i.e., exposition, rising action, climax, falling action and dénouement) works well for those mediums.[2] However, games, unlike books and movies, provide an interactive medium that is not necessarily linear in progression and, also unlike books and films, allows for input from the player. Although the degree of interactivity afforded players varies among game platforms, genres and mechanics, typically, most games allow players options that can interfere or alter the nature of linear narrative (Pedersen, 2003). The challenge of balancing interactivity with a cohesive narrative both impacts the design of games and is also a challenge for the design of game-based learning. Nevertheless, there are different aesthetics of narrative design that have emerged out of popular game design, along with conventions for integration that can help inform the design of game-based learning.

Narrative Structure: Three-act Story, Quest and Long-form Narrative

Despite the debates about the presence of narrative in games, narrative continues to play a significant role in many game genres. Stories are enjoyable and allow users to explore new places, situations and people. Stories draw upon our emotions yet provide a safe way to explore a myriad of feelings and experiences. According to Adams (2014), stories add entertainment to games by helping to immerse players and sustain interest in long games. It is for these reasons that narrative can also play a significant role in game-based learning.

Within various genres, there are style conventions for narrative. Among narrative style conventions are the three-act story structure based on the Aristotelian model of drama, the quest and, more recently, long-form narrative.

Three-act Story Structure

The three-act story structure is the time-honored structure used in books, films and television of beginning, middle and end (Onder, 2002; Novak, 2008). Within the three-act structure, the first act provides the foundations for the story (characters and setting), along with a presentation of the central problem or conflict. The middle act is typically the longest act and the act in which the main character(s) encounter the main obstacles for overcoming the problem, challenge or conflict presented in act 1. In the third act, the central problem, challenge or conflict is overcome or resolved and the act provides both a resolution and closure (see Figure 4.1).

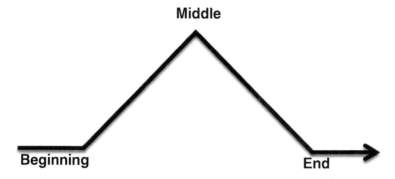

Figure 4.1 The three-act story structure

Variations of the three-act structure include both plot-based narrative and character-based narrative (Sikora, 2002). Plot-based narrative typically involves intricate scenarios in which the player's goal is to uncover a complex underlying storyline. Examples of plot-based narrative include *Myst* and *Riven*, in which the overriding focus is on the player performing actions that support and advance the plot and uncover the underlying story. In contrast to plot-based narrative is character-based narrative, which typically involves the player taking on the role of a pre-scripted character (Sikora, 2002). Examples of character-based narratives include the *Tomb Raider (Lara Croft)* and *Harry Potter* series, in which the action centers on a central character. In character-based narratives, the character often undergoes some type of transformation due to the trials and tribulations the character undergoes in the narrative of the game.

Genre Example: Adventure Games

There are many types of game genres, and each genre integrates a narrative storyline in varying degrees and ways (Sikora, 2002). It is difficult to characterize how narrative is handled in various game genres because game design is continually evolving and genres are not static categories but instead have elements and characteristics that overlap. For every sweeping statement of how narrative is used within a genre, counterexamples can nearly always be found. Given that fact, *typically*, narrative plays a more prominent role in adventure games, action/adventure and RPGs. Among the various gaming genres, the adventure game genre is one in which narrative typically plays a defining role in the design. The adventure game genre serves as a good model for the discussion of the three-act story structure because most adventure games includes many of the classical game devices used to convey narrative. For some of the most popular games of this genre, the storyline *is* the central focus of the game, and the gameplay is the means by which the story is revealed (e.g., *Myst*, *Syberia* and the *Drawn* series). Typically, in adventure games, the player is placed in first-person perspective in the role of the main character. It is through overcoming challenges that the player uncovers the story and advances the plot. Throughout various scenes in the game, players may collect objects, solve

60 • Aesthetics and Narrative Design

puzzles, gather information from a variety of sources and interact with non-player characters (NPCs). They then use these multiple modes of information to solve problems they encounter. The types of problems often require players to combine various objects and enact processes to form solutions.

Strategies: Plot Hooks, Characters, Backstory and Cutscenes

Plot Hooks. There are two main literary conventions that are found in many adventure games: plot hooks and characters. Plot hooks are literary conventions that typically are used at the beginning of the game to draw players into the game. Plot hooks may manifest in different forms (e.g., an urgent request for help, a central character who awakens in a strange location or a detective assigned to solve a crime). The purposes of plot hooks are to arouse curiosity and create intrigue, all of which leads the player to ask, "What is going to happen next?" Good plot hooks put players in the middle of the action without providing much exposition, which provides the impetus for the player to begin the game.

Characters. Another literary convention is the integration of compelling characters throughout the game. Often, in adventure games, the player is cast as the protagonist. Information about the personality, goals and motivation of the protagonist and characters can help establish a sense of emotional proximity between the player and the main character. Emotional proximity is characterized as the empathy and identification a player feels toward another character in a game. For example, in the beginning of the adventure game *Syberia*, the protagonist, Kate, is under pressure from her job, family and fiancé. She expresses feelings of stress and frustration as she attempts to appease each and still reconcile her own curiosity about the strange town she's entered. Feelings of stress and frustration are feelings with which most players can relate. Emotional proximity can be established through the use of multidimensional characters with both strengths and flaws (Freeman, 2003) and by having characters that change or grow through the duration of the game (Rollings & Adams, 2003).

Backstory and Cutscenes. The two main game devices used to both convey narrative and help players uncover the narrative storyline are backstory and cutscenes. A backstory is the background or history of the storyline. The purpose of a backstory is to provide a dramatic context for the action and interaction in the game (Crawford, 2003). A backstory may be as simple as a brief sketch of the main characters and key conflicts within the storyline (e.g., "A long time ago in a galaxy far, far away . . ."), or it may be as complex as a play guide with detailed histories of key characters and conflicts, along with maps that illustrate the game world.

Cutscenes are short sections of narrative interspersed and revealed during the course of gameplay. They may take many different forms, such as a radio broadcast, a journal entry, a story delivered by an NPC or even full motion video. The purpose of a cutscene is to further the storyline and reinforce the mood and tone of the game. Cutscenes are also used to provide players with key information. They often appear at the completion of puzzles or challenges (Hancock, 2002). Types of cutscenes include *flashbacks, parallel action, foreshadowing, cliffhangers* and *red herrings* meant to purposely trick the player (Hancock, 2002; Onder, 2002). Although narrative may also be supported through interactive elements such as the setting, interactions with NPCs and through player actions and feedback, cutscenes and backstory are often the primary devices for integrating narrative into gameplay. Narrative is most engaging when the narrative devices do more than just advance the story, but rather when the culmination of narrative support and player choices constructs the story.

Three-act Story Structure: Educational Implications (Motivation and Problem-solving)

Motivation

Motivation has long been a source of great interest in the design of educational materials, but among the most cited work in the field of game-based learning is Malone's (1981a, 1981b) seminal research about intrinsic motivation in games. In his work, Malone identified the elements of *challenge*, *fantasy* and *curiosity* as being main components in what makes games fun. Certainly narrative provides fantasy, but it also can be used to stimulate curiosity.

In adventure games, the goal of gameplay is to move through the game and successfully uncover a story. The story is typically one of mystery and intrigue with many twists and turns. Often, the plot is a three-act structure of beginning (exposition), middle (conflict) and end (resolution). The plot leads the player through different locations to explore, find clues and solve puzzles to uncover the story. The story serves as the motivation. Players are often cast as the lead character and situated in the environment and in the midst of the action. Elements of the story are interspersed in the form of cutscenes as a type of "reward" for solving puzzles and challenges.

Whether one subscribes to the notion of Aristotle's drama as a cathartic experience[3] or not, a good story is enjoyable. What is central to a good adventure game is the plot—the cause and effect of actions and events that lead the player through the narrative. Typically, most adventure games rely on plot conventions from different types of *genre fiction*: science fiction, fantasy and mystery. Although genre fiction is sometimes looked upon as a lower literary form, what it provides is a clear focus on story without requiring the reader to struggle with interpretation, as in some forms of literary fiction (Grossman, 2009). What is central to most genre fiction is the plot. The storylines are not complex literature, but they are good stories, and a good story is enjoyable and motivating.

The use of compelling characters can also serve as motivation. Typically, most adventure games center on the experiences of one central character. Characters that are relatable to players help establish a type of emotional proximity between the player and the character. Emotional proximity is the empathy and identification a player feels toward his/her character in a game. Similarities between player and character can help establish emotional proximity, but what is more important is creating characters with characteristics with which players can identify.

62 • Aesthetics and Narrative Design

Compelling and relatable characters are motivating because we become invested in the welfare of the characters and want to know the outcome of their fate within the story.

Problem-solving

The role of the basic three-act narrative may be most informative in how it serves as a cognitive framework for problem-solving. Polkinghorne (1988) contends that humans use narrative not only to frame thought but also to guide and inform actions. Robinson and Hawpe (1986) further assert that narrative is a type of causal thinking in which the narrative (cognitive) schema identifies categories (protagonist, situation, conflict, outcome, etc.) and relevant types of relationships (temporal, motivational and procedural) and integrates experiences (which do not necessarily occur in narrative form) into a plausible storyline. An example of how humans seek narrative structure can be found in a 1946 study by A. E. Michotte (1963) on the perception (attribution) of causality (as reported by Polkinghorne, 1988; Sarbin, 1986). Michotte's initial experiments consisted of showing observers two animated squares: one black square and one red square. Initially, the squares were separated. The black square moved rapidly toward the red square, and at the moment of contact, the black square stopped and the red square moved away from the black square. The majority of observers described the demonstration as the black square launching or pushing the red square (p. 20). Michotte deemed this description the *Launching Effect*. In a second example, Michotte showed the same two squares, but as the black square reached the red square, the black square continued at the same speed and the red square moved along with the black square at the same speed. Observers described this animation as the black square carrying the red square. Michotte described this as the *Entraining Effect*. What is most interesting about Michotte's studies is that the participants were merely observing colored squares moving in predefined patterns. There was no launching or entrainment, yet the observers imposed a simple narrative that implied causality of one square acting upon the other (Polkinghorne, 1988; Sarbin, 1986).

The three-act narrative structure as found in many adventure games provides an environment in which players can identify and construct causal patterns that integrate what is known (backstory, environment, rules, etc.) with that which is conjectural yet plausible within the context of the story. The setting and the backstory establish boundaries of what is plausible and possible. Within the game *Syberia*, for example, the main character, Kate, is a New York-based lawyer sent to the alpine village of Valadilene to conclude the acquisition of a famous mechanical toy factory. The setting is fairly realistic. Elements such as faxes and cell phones reinforce a sense of realism within the game. In Valadilene, she encounters several mechanical *automatons* that are somewhat fantastical, yet, because they are "mechanical," the fantasy still works within the realistic scope of the game. Given the setting and main character, it is more plausible for players to seek solutions to problems in more realistic forms—such as combining mechanical objects, reading diaries and initiating dialogue with NPCs—than to seek magical spells or potions for solutions to the obstacles Kate encounters. In this example, the narrative as established in the backstory and reinforced in the opening establishes the boundaries. Players make conjectures about overcoming obstacles and solving problems based upon what is plausible within these boundaries. Discovery and trial and error play a role in this process, but the narrative provides a cognitive framework for problem-solving by establishing what is plausible.

Problem-solving is also a function of the narrative framework through the use of characters. Typically, players take on the role of the lead character in adventure games, but they often encounter a series of NPCs who play specific roles in relation to the narrative line. For example, in *Syberia*, the player is cast as the protagonist, Kate. She encounters the character of Oscar (an automaton) who serves as a guide throughout different parts of the narrative. Although initially their relationship is a bit antagonistic, Oscar provides a type of metacognitive support by asking Kate discerning questions, offering opinions and allowing Kate to reflect and engage in dialogue for problem-solving. Plausibility is reinforced through the interplay between the characters and the environment. Narrative in adventure games provides a type of support for problem-solving by serving as a cognitive framework and by outlining the affordances and constraints with the environment and storyline.

Narrative Structure: The Quest

The quest is another common narrative structure found in literature ranging from the works of Homer, Chaucer, Cervantes and Joyce, and manifests in such popular films as *Star Wars*, *The Wizard of Oz* and, most recently, *Frozen*. Central to the quest is a journey and some type of final goal. The journey is typically a physical journey that requires the protagonist to explore new environments, but it may also be an emotional or metaphorical voyage. During the journey, the protagonist encounters various obstacles and must overcome challenges. The journey culminates in a final confrontation or challenge in which the protagonist must prevail to be victorious.

The Hero's Journey

One of the most frequently cited sources of guidance for the design of narrative in games is Joseph Campbell's outline of the quest structure, often referred to as the *hero's journey* (Crawford, 2003; Dunniway, 2000; Rollings & Adams, 2003). Vogler (1998) clearly outlines 12 stages of the hero's journey based upon Joseph Campbell's *The Hero with a Thousand Faces* (1973), in which Campbell identifies myths that seem to reoccur in different cultures throughout history. Although there are many variations (Vogler's included), Campbell's *hero's journey* contains the following stages:

1. Ordinary World
2. Call to Adventure

64 • Aesthetics and Narrative Design

3. Refusal of the Call
4. Meets a Mentor
5. The First Threshold
6. Threshold Test
7. Initiation
8. Allies and Enemies
9. The Innermost Cave
10. Culmination Ordeal
11. The Road Back
12. Return with Elixir

In the first stage, the hero is situated in the ordinary world (or whatever may be construed as ordinary). In some way, the hero is presented with a problem, challenge or event that necessitates that the hero leave the comfort and familiarity of the ordinary world (a tornado hits Kansas, Phileas Fogg attempts to circumnavigate the world in 80 days, a young boy discovers he is a powerful wizard[4]). At this point, the hero may refuse, have reservations or in some way be prevented from undertaking the adventure. Next, the hero encounters a mentor or someone who may offer advice or guidance (Glenda the Good Witch; Passepartout, the new valet; Hagrid, a half-giant groundskeeper). Once the hero commits to the journey, the adventures begin. During this process or journey, the hero encounters various obstacles and challenges that must be overcome in order to progress. The hero also forms allies and creates enemies that help and hinder in overcoming these obstacles and challenges. All of the obstacles, tests and challenges lead the protagonist to the *innermost cave*. The innermost cave is the site for the central challenge for the hero; it is the event all other challenges have been leading toward. Often, during the peak challenge, there is a moment when all seems lost (Dorothy is trapped by the Wicked Witch, the deadline is not met and the bet is lost, the hero "dies"); yet inevitably, the hero overcomes the challenge and survives (Dorothy throws water on the Scarecrow and inadvertently kills the Wicked Witch, the realization of a mistaken date due to changes in different time zones, good prevails and the hero lives). Now that the hero has survived, the next stage is the journey home, yet the journey back is often fraught with problems and challenges and potentially leads to one last conflict or challenge before the hero returns to the ordinary world (see Figure 4.2).

Genre Example

The quest is a common narrative structure found in varying degrees in many game genres; however, it is a particularly common narrative structure found in RPGs to provide a context for gameplay. For the purposes of this analysis, this discussion will focus on the integration of the quest in RPGs because it is a genre in which the quest plays a more prominent role and that exploits the full affordances of the quest. Typically, within RPGs, players select or create a character from a selection of characteristics and attributes. The character is faced with some type of

Aesthetics and Narrative Design • 65

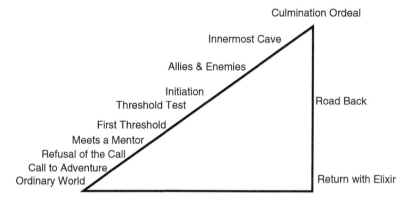

Figure 4.2 The hero's journey (Campbell, 1973)
Adapted from Campbell, 1973

quest that needs to be completed. This quest often requires the character to travel to a location. During the travels, the character gains new skills through successfully overcoming a series of obstacles and challenges (see Chapter 2). Examples of popular RPG games include the *Elder Scrolls*, *Diablo* and *Fable* series.

Strategies for Integrating Character Development and Small Quests

Characters. The use of compelling characters is another literary device integrated into game design, although there are some notable differences between different genres. In RPGs, typically the players create their own characters from a selection of characteristics and attributes. Unlike adventures games, in which the player takes on a pre-defined role, within RPGs, the player creates a low-level character that is part of the "rank and file" and, through the trials and tribulations of the journey, develops and enhances skills and attributes. What makes the player's character compelling is the personalization and unique qualities that the player creates.

Character design is another literary device present in games that is integrated through the use of the quest. Throughout the environment, players' characters interact with various NPCs. These characters serve different functions: guidance, inspiration, obstacles and assistance. NPCs serve as backdrop characters to fill out a city or town, but also serve as key components in extending the narrative. They may provide key information about situations or problems and provide insight that signals changes in the storyline. They provide a means for players to enhance their characters by requesting assistance or offering "work." They serve as nemesis, enemies and obstacles by confronting a character.

Small Quests. The core of RPG design and often central to gameplay is the narrative interactive environment. In various genres such as adventure games, the game centers on a single storyline, and the focus of gameplay is on uncovering the narrative storyline during gameplay. However, within RPGs, the narrative is not always as tightly controlled or revealed. The narrative is often embedded within

66 • Aesthetics and Narrative Design

the environment and is manifested in different ways, such as the player's character encountering an object (a "magic" book or a strange bottle of liquid) or reading a summons or a "call to action" notice posted in the environment. Often, these small quests are embedded in the form of an NPC posing a short narrative tale in which he or she requests the aid or assistance of the player's character. These requests for assistance are often framed as a small task or quest (e.g., deliver a package, find a lost book, escort an ally). Players may opt to select and complete or reject from several small quests within an area. Upon the successful completion of a small quest, a player's character is rewarded. The reward may come in the form of currency, goods or items to benefit the character. The character also typically earns points or "experience." These rewards allow players to continually enhance their character's attributes and skills.

Depending upon the extent of the narrative, these small quests may be a simple one-stage quest (defeat a specified enemy), or they may be more complex and require the player to complete several small quests to completely uncover a longer narrative (e.g., collect several herbs, grind the herbs to make ink, give the ink to a scribe to write a decree). Common types of small quests include *bounty quests, FedEx quests, collection quests, escort quests, goodwill quests* and *messenger quests.* Each quest type requires different actions from the player. Both the selection of the small quests and the successful completion advances gameplay and reinforces the player's role in the overarching narrative and narrative space. Some of the events and NPCs that appear in the main story small quests may reappear throughout the game.

Educational Implications: Motivation and Problem-solving

The narrative design of the quest provides much fodder for the design of game-based learning by supporting motivation and problem-solving, but in different ways than in the three-act structure. While both can provide insight into how to integrate narrative in game-based learning, the quest provides a framework for participation.

Motivation

The narrative design of the quest supports player motivation by providing opportunities for exploration, control and achievement. One of the key elements Malone (1981a, 1981b) identified as being intrinsically motivating in games is curiosity. The quest, in addition to providing a motivation through the (fantasy) narrative, also fosters curiosity through the narrative environment. The narrative is a progression and plays a key role. Players must travel through the environment and explore in order to find and complete small quests. As a narrative structure, the quest is a structure that fosters curiosity.

Typically, within RPGs environments, players are presented with a selection of small quests. The successful completion of smaller quests allows a player's character to gain points and attain advanced levels that, in turn, provide players with a choice of increasingly more difficult tasks. According to Malone and Lepper (1987) and Cordova and Lepper (1996), choice helps foster motivation by providing learners with some control. Most RPGs are structured as a series of levels. The use of levels limits the number of quests in which players can participate. Side quests offer additional options, but typically there are limited numbers of side quests as well. Research conducted by Iyengar and Lepper (1999, 2000) examined not only the motivating aspects of choice but also the demotivating aspects of choice when participants are presented with too wide of an array of choices. The use of levels and the limited numbers of small quests prevent players from becoming overwhelmed with choices.

Achievement

In addition to fostering curiosity and control, the quest narrative structure as realized in RPGs also fosters a sense of *achievement* during ongoing gameplay. Because the quest typically involves a long and arduous journey, players develop skills and enhancements throughout the narrative experience by successfully completing small quests. The development of skills and enhancements as well as moving through stages of the narrative environment help mark progress, which in turn fosters a sense of achievement when small quests are completed. Both Malone (1981a) and, later, Malone and Lepper (1987) note the importance of achievement in fostering motivation in gameplay.

Problem-solving

The quest narrative structure as realized in RPGs provides a model for a flexible design that fosters exploration, control and achievement. Yet, at the same time, there are elements within the design of a narrative environment that help scaffold players in the gameplay experience by providing a cognitive framework for problem-solving. The environment provides affordances or possibilities for action (Gibson, 1977). Players integrate information (setting, backstory, conflict, etc.) with the affordances of the environment to form conjectures about combinations and processes that will enable them to overcome obstacles and accomplish a task. Players are put in a position of having to make conjectures about causal relationships based on the type of information they have encountered while exploring. The various types of small quests expose players to the affordances of the environment. For example, during the process of completing a bounty quest, players are often required to travel into new areas of the gameplay environment. While traveling to their destination, players are exposed to new resources. These new resources may be necessary or helpful in completing subsequent small quests. Plausibility is established through the narrative and supported with the affordances of the environment. Research in situated learning reveals that cognition is more likely to be dependent upon context and affordances of a place and situation than by formal reasoning (Brown, Collins & Duguid, 1989; Lave & Wenger, 1991; Suchman, 1987). The actions required through participating in small quests may foster a type of metacognition or, perhaps more precisely, a type of meta-inferencing

68 • Aesthetics and Narrative Design

(Collins, 1978) by exposing players to resources and information that may aid them in completing future small quests.

Long-form Narrative

Narrative structures like the three-act story structure and the quest are two structures of narrative design in popular games; however, there is growing debate about the utility of the three-act story structure and whether this is necessarily the best model for game design. According to Abernathy and Rouse (2014), the three-act story structure is not an effective model for contemporary games—particularly in open-styled games (e.g., MMORPGs) in which players have choices and different options based upon those choices. The difficulty with open-style games is that the player may end up bypassing elements used to convey a central storyline. Abernathy and Rouse (2014) advocate looking toward long-form narratives such as that found in contemporary television shows such as *The Walking Dead*, *Game of Thrones* and *Breaking Bad*. This type of long-form narrative has become an increasingly popular form of storytelling found in popular fiction. In literature, long-form narratives may center on compelling characters (J. K. Rowling's Harry Potter series) or on a narrative environment (George R. R. Martin's A Song of Ice and Fire/Game of Thrones series). Where long-form narrative storytelling may provide the most insight is in the type of central focus: character or environment. In character-driven narrative, the focus is on a character or a small set of characters (the Harry Potter series, *Breaking Bad*, *Mad Men*), whereas when the focus is on the environment (*Game of Thrones, The Walking Dead*[5]), there is the potential for following generations of characters over spans of time. With this format, there is also more potential for user-extensibility.

Abernathy and Rouse (2014) cite Jeremy Bernstein's (2013) structural narrative as a guide for creating episodic narratives in which Bernstein outlines a storyline made up of a series of sequences, each with its own internal structure (setting, conflict, rising action and climax) that in turn contributes to the larger narrative. According to Abernathy and Rouse (2014), the long-form serialized storytelling consists of frequent small arcs that are embedded within larger and larger arcs. For example, Abernathy and Rouse look to the structure of long-form episodic television and the "substructures" that comprise individual episodes that form the larger arc, which in turn form the overarching narrative of the series. Similarly, Adams delineates different forms of long-form narratives as episodic, serial and limited series. As game design develops, so does game-based learning. The field of education has a long history of borrowing, appropriating and looting from popular media. The research of popular games can provide guidance and insight into both design and research of game-based learning.

Strategies

There are differing approaches to address how long-form narrative meets the changing needs of game design. Bernstein (2013) advocates the eight-sequence approach to filmmaking, devised by University of Southern California film professor Frank Daniels, in which the storyline is divided into eight sequences, each with its own three-act structure. Abernathy and Rouse (2014) argue that for open-styled games, there is no narrative structure, but instead, the narrative focus should be upon game characters and the gameplay objectives. They contend that storytelling should evolve around the game's structure.

Adams (2014) provides insight into different forms of long-form narrative by delineating the following types: episodic, serial or consistent worlds (Adams, 2014). The episodic structure proposed by Adams (2014) is similar in many ways to many television series in which there are consistent characters and settings, but each show is a self-contained story in which the plot is introduced, conflict arises and the conflict is resolved. This is somewhat similar to Bernstein's proposal (2013). For the most part, episodes can be watched in any order because they are self-contained stories that do not build upon or rely upon information from one show to the other (see Figure 4.3).

In contrast, serial structure provides a model in which there are several storylines that extend through the duration of several episodes, forming multi-episode arcs. In turn, these multi-episode arcs contribute to a larger storyline arc. These multi-episode arcs may vary across episodes at varying rates of progression. Episodes are not self-contained storylines, but instead, are parts of varying storylines. Soap operas are examples of serial storytelling that is situated in a fairly consistent environment, but with changing characters (see Figure 4.4).

The goals of game-based learning are different than those of games created for entertainment. Narrative in game design is a topic of much contention both in terms of the function and in terms of how to create cohesive stories that allow for player choice, input and interactivity. The very nature of interactivity and

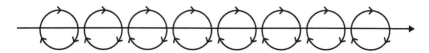

Figure 4.3 Episodic long-form narrative

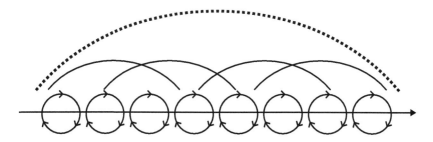

Figure 4.4 Serial long-form narrative

70 • Aesthetics and Narrative Design

choice seemingly prevents the type of cohesion necessary for the type of emotional investment that great stories elicit from readers. While this task is difficult for game design, it would seem to be impossible for game-based learning. Yet the goals of popular games and game-based learning are different, and the function of narrative in game-based learning is not for entertainment but rather as a tool of instruction. The episodic and serial narrative structure provides guidance in structuring narrative in ongoing environments and collaborative environments such as MMORPGs.

Genre Example

Similar to RPGs are MMORPGs, which are networked games that are essentially online collaborative RPGs. MMORPGs have become one of the most popular contemporary game genres, and among the most popular MMORPGs are *Ever-Quest*, *Guide Wars* and *World of Warcraft*. The roots of MMORPGs can be found in tabletop games such as *Dungeons and Dragons*, digital RPGs and text-based Multi-user Dungeons or Domains (MUDs) (see Chapter 2). Like tabletop games and single-player RPG digital games, the MMORPG genre is one in which players create a unique character that must overcome a series of trials and tribulations that enhances skills. Unlike RPGs, there is often no one final end to an MMORPG (beyond the game being terminated). Many popular MMORPGs continue to progress by developing new content.

Many games genres are single-player environments in which the storyline and gameplay stop when the player stops playing and resume when the player begins again. In contrast, MMORPGs are networked, persistent, communal environments and, as such, gameplay continues even when a player logs off. Within the MMORPG genre, there is no one single storyline for players to uncover, but rather the gameplay experience is an overarching narrative environment in which the player becomes enmeshed in an environment of narrative spaces (Jenkins, 2002) and interacts with other players. Communal play is central to MMORPGs.

Educational Implications

Collaboration

As learning environments become more collaborative, it is important to look at the range of how narrative is integrated into collaborative game spaces. In long-form narratives such as those found in MMORPGs and in addition to small quests that can be accomplished by individual players, there are also collaborative quests that require the organized efforts of several players. Typically, these collaborative quests are embedded in part of the narrative environment and are part of storylines that contribute to the wider narrative. Collaborative quests may be similar in form to single-player small quests but require the collaboration of several players to complete. A collaboration quest may require a variety of different types of player characters with differing skills, attributes and enhancements. Completion of the quests may involve an entire storyline arc.

The episodic and serial narrative design provides insight into how to design narrative environments for game-based learning. Examples of serial narratives such as those found in MMORPGs provide insight into how narrative can support collaboration among learners. Malone (1981a) noted the importance of collaboration in games and later noted that cooperation may foster interpersonal motivation (Malone & Lepper, 1987). Similarly, studies of environments such as educational MOOs and virtual worlds note the importance of collaboration in fostering motivation. Bruckman (1997), Dickey (2003, 2011a, 2011b) and Riner's (1996) respective research illustrates how collaboration in game-based environments allows for the emergence of peer role models and an appreciative audience.

Role-playing

Long-form narratives such as MMORPGs provide a structure in which players invest in long-term gameplay. Some games may not seemingly end, but continue to extend and build new content. As such, players spend a great deal of time developing a character within the narrative environment. Players may invest hundreds of hours developing and advancing their characters, resulting in a type of emotional proximity players may feel toward their characters. Much research has been conducted about the emotional proximity that players develop for their characters or avatars (Herz, 2001). Work by such diverse researchers as Stone (1995), Turkle (1995), Curtis (1992), Reid (1994), Jakobsson (2002) and Jakobsson and Taylor (2003) have investigated how role-playing in digital environments fosters personal and social reflexivity. Dibbell's (1995) landmark article "A Rape in Cyberspace" illustrates the depth of emotional proximity players have toward their characters.

Long-form narratives such as MMORPGs are essentially role-playing games and, as players develop their characters, they are in a sense taking on a role. Role-playing has long been an established technique used for educational activities. Fields such as medicine, social studies and language learning routinely use role-playing as a teaching and learning technique. Role-playing (fantasy) in games fosters intrinsic motivation (Malone, 1981b). Based on the integration of role-playing in science and math activities, Resnick and Wilensky (1997) argued that role-playing can help students understand complex systems and relationships. Riner's (1996) and Riner and Clodius' (1995) early research of educational MOOs revealed that role-playing fostered opportunities for collaboration both within and across classrooms. Similarly, Dede (1996) argued that role-playing within a digital environment may foster more risk-taking due to the level of anonymity of a character/avatar. One of the more compelling studies into how character/avatar creations can be motivational is Bruckman's (1997) ethnographic study of two girls' interactions in an online text-based environment, MOOSE Crossing, which

72 • Aesthetics and Narrative Design

provides unique insight into how character development within a narrative environment can be intrinsically motivating.

Informing Design for Game-based Learning

The three-act story structure, the quest and long-form narrative are different approaches for integrating narrative into games. Adventure games, RPGs and MMORPGs are just three different game genres in an array of genres; however, they are types of games that use these different forms of narrative in different ways, which in turn can be used to inform the narrative design of game-based learning. In adventure games, the narrative design (three-act story structure) plays a central role because the game is about uncovering a story. The use of the quest narrative design in traditional RPGs provides framework for exploration, control and achievement. The long-form narrative design emerging out of contemporary games and MMORPGs provides a framework for collaboration and emotional proximity for long-term engagement.

These three forms of narrative design provide models for the design of game-based learning. Although game-based learning may not be a game per se, it includes the use of game elements for teaching and learning. It is consistent with the current wave of instructional design that centers on the learning environment. This shift toward the development of learning environments has been in part fueled by the epistemological shift toward constructivism and a greater focus on problem-solving and problem-based learning. The use of narrative as a framework for an environment and interaction provides instructional/learning designers with diverse models to support different learning goals. The three-act storyline structure found in adventure games provides a model of how to design a learning environment in which a story, account or history is of central importance. The quest narrative structure found in RPGs provides a model of how to integrate narrative into a learning environment in which the focus of learning may be upon a transformation, process and/or discovery. The long-form narrative structure found in MMORPGs provides a model of how to create an ongoing narrative environment in which the focus of learning may be upon a history and/or an enculturation into a field of practice (Lave & Wenger, 1991).

Guideline for Integrating Narrative in Game-based Learning

The integration of narrative is far from unique in education. Goal-based Scenarios (Schank, Fano, Bell & Jona, 1993; Schank, Berman & Macpherson, 1999), Case-based Learning and even WebQuests are common models in which narrative is integrated in learning. However, although narrative may be a component in these models, there is relatively little guidance about how to develop narratives and how to integrate them for learning. This chapter is not meant to suggest that game design narrative replace any components of Goal-based Scenarios, Case-based Learning or even WebQuests, but rather to present strategies for creating compelling narratives for interactive learning environments and game-based learning environments.

1. *Function*

   When developing narrative for game-based learning, it is important to establish the role of narrative and the degree to which it plays a role. If the function of narrative is merely to frame a learning activity, then the role is to establish the setting and perhaps outline an initial conflict. According to Rieber (1996), fantasy (narrative) in games is either *exogenous* or *endogenous* to the context of a game. He characterizes *exogenous* fantasy as a type of "sugar coating" that is frivolous and having no impact on gameplay (p. 49). He argues that *endogenous* fantasy (narrative), on the other hand, is integral to the content of the game; there is no separation between content (fantasy) and gameplay. According to Rieber (1996), *endogenous* fantasy may be more suited to educational games because it may potentially motivate learners who might be interested in the fantasy.

2. *Type*

   If narrative is to play a greater role, then it is important to determine how it will be interspersed throughout the game-based learning activity by establishing whether the narrative will be linear or nonlinear. According to Adams (2014), linear stories limit the amount of freedom a player or (in the case of game-based learning) learner is afforded. The central point in a linear narrative is to uncover the story, so actions not related to that goal will not advance the gameplay. However, as Adams notes, linear stories can evoke more emotional power because the plot is a construct of the game and the integrity of the plot is not impacted by the player. Instead, the player's choices and conquests merely act to uncover more of the story. This is a good narrative structure when story and emotional investment are important for the overarching goal of game-based learning or the goal of learning is to present a story, account or history.

   The quest narrative structure found in RPGs provides a model of how to integrate narrative into a learning environment in which learners may self-define the roles they play and where to some degree they have the freedom to determine their transformation within the environment. The quest narrative structure is a good structure when transformation, process and/or discovery are the goals of learning.

   Long-form narratives are examples of narratives in which the player makes choices and those choices impact the narrative experience for the player. Adams (2014) argues that nonlinear narratives are not as emotionally immersive for players because there is less control over how the player encounters and uncovers the narrative. Player choices may impact when and if a player encounters key plot information. However, what may be lost in emotional investment in terms of storyline may end up being

74 • Aesthetics and Narrative Design

recouped in the type of emotional proximity players develop by investing in the development of their character. This form of narrative structure is good when a single storyline is not the focus in game-based learning but, instead, when the narrative environment frames the setting and supports activities within the setting.

3. *The Quest*

After determining the function of narrative for game-based learning and the type, the next step is to develop the plot by identifying the setting, characters and conflict. Although the quest provides a great framework for RPGs (and role-playing activities for game-based learning), it can also serve as a guide for developing a tight linear narrative such as that found in adventure games. Regardless of style, the underlying stage of Campbell's (1973) hero's journey provides guidance for how to shape a three-act storyline:

- Beginning: Stages 1–4
- Middle: Stages 5–9
- End: Stages 10–12

Below is an outline of the quest and how the various stages function in *The Wizard of Oz*.

1. *Ordinary world*: The hero is situated in the ordinary world (or whatever may be construed as ordinary). *Example*: Dorothy is living on her family farm in Kansas.

2. *Call to adventure*: Suddenly, the hero/protagonist is presented with a problem, challenge or event that necessitates that s/he leaves the comfort and familiarity of the ordinary world. *Example*: A tornado strikes Dorothy's house and she lands in Oz.

3. *Refusal of the call*: The hero initially may refuse, balk or have reservations about undertaking the adventure. *Example*: Dorothy is reluctant to wear the ruby slippers.

4. *Meets a mentor*: The hero meets a mentor or someone who may offer advice, guidance or insight into the call to adventure. *Example*: Glenda the Good Witch convinces Dorothy that the great and powerful Wizard can help her return home to Kansas.

5. *Encounters first threshold*: The hero commits to the adventure. During this process or journey, the hero encounters a challenge that must be overcome in order to progress. *Example*: Dorothy encounters the Wicked Witch of the West before embarking for Emerald City.

6. *Threshold test*: The hero passes the first test. *Example*: Dorothy accepts the ruby slippers.

7. *Initiation*: The hero is tested and through the various tests grows or is transformed. *Example*: Dorothy has several encounters with the Wicked Witch of the West on her way to Emerald City.

Aesthetics and Narrative Design • 75

8. *Allies and enemies*: The hero encounters allies and enemies. *Example*: Dorothy meets the Scarecrow, the Tin Man and the Cowardly Lion (brains, heart and courage). Together, they travel to Emerald City and overcome several assaults (angry trees and field of poppies).

9. *The innermost cave*: The hero arrives in the *innermost cave*, or the site of the central challenge. *Example*: Dorothy is captured by flying monkeys and is taken to the castle of the Wicked Witch. Her companions are also captured while attempting to rescue her.

10. *Culmination ordeal*: The *culmination ordeal* is the situation toward which all of the challenges have been leading. This is when the hero confronts the main antagonist or challenge. In most games, this is often termed the *Big Boss*. *Example*: Dorothy throws water on the Scarecrow and inadvertently kills the Wicked Witch.

11. *The road back*: Although the hero has defeated the main antagonist/challenge, s/he may encounter problems on the return to ordinary life. *Example*: Dorothy realizes the Wizard is a man in a control booth. The balloon in which she is to travel home leaves without her.

12. *Return with the elixir*: The hero returns to the ordinary world. *Example*: Dorothy awakens to find her adventures were a dream.

Design Heuristics for Integrating Linear Narrative in Game-based Learning[6]

1. *Setting*: The setting is a key aspect for integrating narrative in game-based learning. Determine the setting, including the physical, temporal, environmental and emotional, and ethical dimensions of the setting (Rollings & Adams, 2003). For more information about setting, see Chapter 6.

2. *Characters and roles*: Determine the characters to be included in the game-based learning environment. The first character is the learner. Who is the learner? What is the learner's role in the game-based learning environment? In the quest, the hero encounters many characters and situations that play certain roles in the journey. Identify the characters the learner will encounter. These roles should serve a particular function. For more information about character design, see Chapter 5.

3. *Conflict*: Identify the initial challenge, goal or task. At the core of the quest is a major challenge; it is the apex or climax of the narrative. In a game-based learning environment, the central challenge may be a problem or project that will serve as the catalyst of the storyline and the goal for learning. Identifying this component is vital to developing the storyline. It will likely be mentioned in the backstory and call to action.

4. *Obstacles*: Identify potential obstacles and develop puzzles, minor challenges and resources. Within the quest, before the protagonist encounters the key conflict, s/he must overcome smaller obstacles and challenges. In a game-based learning environment, these might include learning procedures, skills and content knowledge that will help learners complete the central challenge.

76 • Aesthetics and Narrative Design

Embedded in the environment (and throughout the journey) may be models, exemplars, resources and tools that learners may encounter (or have to search for) that might facilitate problem-solving and help learners complete challenges or overcome obstacles.

5. *Backstory*: In a learning environment, the backstory will likely outline the environment, ethical, physical, emotional and temporal dimensions of the narrative, as well as including a profile of the protagonist(s). The central challenge or initial "call to action" may be introduced at this time.

6. *Plot integration*: Develop cutscenes, characters or other elements to support the development of the narrative storyline. Cutscenes provide the ongoing narrative. They may be used to deliver key information or plot hooks. In an educational context, they might provide feedback on whether learners have successfully accomplished a task or aspect of instruction and set up the next stage of the narrative by presenting another problem, conflict or challenge.

Notes

1. At the time Barthes wrote *An Introduction to the Structural Analysis of Narrative* (1975), he was a structural linguist/theorist, but, with subsequent work, moved into post-structuralism.
2. It should be noted that artists have challenged and created nonlinear pieces within these mediums (*Citizen Kane, Pulp Fiction*).
3. For an in-depth discussion, see Chapter 3.
4. These are references to the following novels: *The Wizard of Oz, Around the World in 80 Days* and the Harry Potter series.
5. Although the current television version of *The Walking Dead* focuses on a small group of characters, characters come and go.
6. This is a revised and abbreviated version of a heuristic I presented in Dickey, 2006.

References

Aarseth, E. (2001). Computer game studies, year one. *Game Studies: The International Journal of Computer Game Research*, 1(1). Retrieved January 23, 2014, from http://www.gamestudies.org/0101/editorial.html

Abernathy, T., & Rouse, R. (2014). Death to the three-act structure: Toward a unique structure for game narratives. *Game Developers Conference*. Los Angeles, CA, March 17–21, 2014.

Adams, E. (2001). Replayability, Part one: Narrative. *Gamasutra*, 05.21.01. Retrieved December 14, 2013, from http://www.gamasutra.com/features/20010521/adams_01.htm

Adams, E. (2014). *Fundamentals of game design* (3rd ed.). Indianapolis, IN: New Riders.

Barthes, R. (1975). An introduction to the structural analysis of narrative. *New Literary History* 6(2), 237–272.

Bernstein, J. (2013). Reimagining story structure: Moving beyond 3-acts in narrative design. *Game Developers Conference: Next (GDC: Next)*. Los Angeles, CA, November 5–7, 2013.

Bringsjord, S. (2001). Is it possible to build dramatically compelling interactive digital entertainment (in the form, e.g., of computer games)? *The International Journal of Computer Game Research*, 1(1). Retrieved March 3, 2014, from http://www.gamestudies.org/0101/bringsjord/index.html

Brown, J., Collins, A., & Duguid, P. (1989). Situated cognition and the culture of learning. *Educational Researcher*, 18 (1), 32–42.

Bruckman, A. (1997). *MOOSE Crossing: Construction, community, and learning in a networked virtual world for kids*. Doctoral dissertation, MIT.

Bruner, J. (1990). *Acts of meaning*. Cambridge, MA: Harvard University Press.

Campbell, J. (1973). *The hero with a thousand faces*. Princeton, NJ: Princeton University Press.

Aesthetics and Narrative Design • 77

Collins, A. (1978). Fragments of a theory of human plausible reasoning. *Proceedings of the 39th Conference on Theoretical Issues in Natural Language Processing-2 (TINLAP-2)* (pp. 194–201). New York: ACM.

Cordova, D. I., & Lepper, M. R. (1996). Intrinsic motivation and the process of learning: Beneficial effects of contextualization, personalization, and choice. *Journal of Educational Psychology*, 88(4), 715–730.

Crawford, C. (2003). *Chris Crawford on game design.* Indianapolis, IN: New Riders.

Curtis, P. (1992). Mudding: Social phenomena in text-based virtual realities. Berkeley, CA. Retrieved January 5, 1999, from: ftp://parcftp.xerox.com in pub/MOO/papers/DIAC92

Dede, C. (1996). The evolution of constructivist learning environments: Immersion in distributed, virtual worlds. In B. G. Wilson (Ed.), *Constructivist learning environments: Case studies in instructional design* (pp. 165–175). Edgewood Cliffs, NJ: Educational Technology Publications.

Dibbell, J. (1995). A rape in cyberspace; or how an evil clown, a Haitian trickster spirit, two wizards, and a cast of dozens turned a database into a society. In M. Dery (Ed.), *Flame wars: Discourse of cyberculture.* Durham, NC: Duke University Press.

Dickey, M. D. (2003). Teaching in 3D: Pedagogical affordances and constraints of 3D virtual worlds for synchronous distance learning. *Distance Education*, 24(1), 105–121.

Dickey, M. D. (2005). Engaging by design: How engagement strategies in popular computer and video games can inform instructional design. *Educational Technology Research and Development*, 53(2), 67–83.

Dickey, M. D. (2006). Game design narrative for learning: Appropriating adventure game design narrative devices and techniques for the design of interactive learning environments. *Educational Technology Research and Development*, 54(3), 245–263.

Dickey, M. D. (2007). Game design and learning: A conjectural analysis of how Massively Multiple Online Role-Playing Games (MMORPGs) foster intrinsic motivation. *Educational Technology Research and Development*, 55(3), 253–272.

Dickey, M. D. (2011a). World of Warcraft and the impact of game culture and play in an undergraduate game design course. *Computers & Education*, 56(1), 200–209.

Dickey, M. D. (2011b). Murder on Grimm Isle: The design of a game-based learning environment. In S. De Freitas & P. Maharg (Eds.), *Digital games and learning* (pp. 129–152). London, UK: The Continuum International Publishing Group.

Dickey, M. D. (2012). Game design and the importance of narrative. In S. Garner (Ed.), *Design and designing: A critical introduction* (pp. 112–123). Oxford, UK: Berg Publishers.

Dunniway, T. (2000). Using the hero's journey in games. *Gamasutra*, 27.11.00. Retrieved September 21, 2013, from http://www.gamasutra.com/view/feature/3118/using_the_heros_journey_in_games. php

Frasca, G. (2001). Ludology meets narratology: Similitude and differences between (video) games and narrative. *Ludology.org Game Theory*. Retrieved December 13, 2013, from http://www.jacaranda. org/frasca/ludology.htm

Freeman, D. E. (2003). *Creating emotion in games: The craft and art of emotioneering.* Indianapolis, IN: New Riders.

Gibson, J. J. (1977). The theory of affordances. In R. Shaw & J. Bransford (Eds.), *Perceiving, acting, and knowing: Toward an ecological psychology* (pp. 67–82). Hillsdale, NJ: Lawrence Erlbaum Associates.

Grossman, L. (2009). Good books don't have to be hard: A novelist on the pleasure of reading stories that don't bore; rising up from the supermarket racks. *The Wall Street Journal*, August 29, 2009. Retrieved May 10, 2014, from http://online.wsj.com/news/articles/SB1000142405297020370660 4574377163804387216

Hancock, H. (2002). Better game design through cutscenes. *Gamasutra*, 04.02.02. Retrieved May 12, 2014, from http://www.gamasutra.com/features/20020401/hancock_01.htm

Herz, C. J. (2001). Gaming the system: What higher education can learn from multiplayer online worlds. The Internet and the university. *EDUCAUSE Forum on the Future of Higher Education.* Retrieved February 15, 2004, from http://www.educause.edu/ir/library/pdf/ffpiu019.pdf

Iyengar, S. S., & Lepper, M. R. (1999). Rethinking the value of choice: A cultural perspective on intrinsic motivation. *Journal of Personality and Social Psychology*, 76, 349–366.

78 • Aesthetics and Narrative Design

Iyengar, S. S., & Lepper, M. R. (2000). When choice is demotivating: Can one desire too much of a good thing? *Journal of Personality and Social Psychology*, 76, 995–1006.

Jakobsson, M. (2002). Rest in peace, Bill the bot. Death and life in virtual worlds. In R. Schroeder (Ed.), *The social life of avatars: Culture and communication in virtual environments* (pp. 63–76). London: Springer-Verlag.

Jakobsson, M., & Taylor, T. L. (2003). The Sopranos meets EverQuest: Social networking in massively multiuser networking games. *MelbourneDAC, the 5th International Digital Arts and Culture Conference*. Melbourne, Australia, November 2003.

Jenkins, H. (2002). Game design as narrative architecture. Retrieved September 10, 2004, from http://web.mit.edu/21fms/www/faculty/henry3/games&narrative.html#1

Juul, J. (1998). A clash between game and narrative. *Paper presented at the Digital Arts and Culture conference*. Bergen, Norway, November 1998.

Juul, J. (2001). Games telling stories? A brief note on games and narratives. *Game Studies: The International Journal of Computer Game Research*, 1(1). Retrieved April 3, 2014, from http://www.gamestudies.org/0101/juul-gts/

Laramée, F. D. (2002). *Game design perspectives*. Hingham, MA: Charles River Media.

Lave, J., & Wenger, E. (1991). *Situated learning: Legitimate peripheral participation*. Cambridge, UK: Cambridge University Press.

Malone, T. W. (1981a). Toward a theory of intrinsically motivating instruction. *Cognitive Science*, 4, 333–369.

Malone, T. W. (1981b). What makes computer games fun? *BYTE*, 6, 258–277.

Malone, T. W., & Lepper, M. R. (1987). Making learning fun: A taxonomy of intrinsic motivations for learning. In R. E. Snow & M. J. Farr (Eds.), *Aptitude, learning and instruction III: Conative and affective process analyses* (pp. 223–253). Hillsdale, NJ: Lawrence Erlbaum Associates.

Michotte, A. (1963). *The perception of causality*. New York, NY: Basic Books.

Novak, J. (2008). *Game development essentials*. Clifton Park, NY: Thomson Delmar Learning.

Onder, B. (2002). Storytelling in level-based game design. In F. D. Laramée (Ed.), *Game design perspectives* (pp. 291–298). Hingham, MA: Charles River Media.

Pedersen, R. E. (2003). *Game design foundations*. Plano, TX: Worldware Publishing Inc.

Polkinghorne, D. E. (1988). *Narrative knowing and the human sciences*. Albany, NY: State University of New York Press.

Reid, E. (1994). *Cultural formations in text-based virtual realities*. Master's thesis, University of Melbourne.

Resnick, M., & Wilensky, U. (1997). Diving into complexity: Developing probabilistic decentralized thinking through role-playing activities. *Journal of the Learning Sciences*, 7(2), 153–172.

Rieber, L. P. (1996). Seriously considering play: Designing interactive learning environments based on the blending of microworlds, simulations, and games. *Educational Technology Research & Development*, 44(2), 43–58.

Riner, R. D. (1996). Virtual ethics↔Virtual reality. *Futures Research Quarterly*, 12(1), 57–70.

Riner, R. D., & Clodius, J. A. (1995). Simulating future histories: The NAU solar system simulation & Mars settlement. *Anthropology & Education Quarterly*, 21(2), 121–127.

Robinson, J. A., & Hawpe, L. (1986). Narrative thinking as a heuristic process. In T. R. Sarbin (Ed.), *Narrative psychology: The storied nature of human conduct* (pp. 3–21). New York, NY: Praeger.

Rollings, A., & Adams, E. (2003). *Game design*. Indianapolis, IN: New Riders.

Sarbin, T. (Ed.) (1986). *Narrative psychology: The storied nature of human conduct*. New York, NY: Praeger.

Schank, R. C., Berman, T. R., & Macpherson, K. A. (1999). Learning by doing. In C. M. Reigeluth (Ed.), *Instructional-design theories and models: A new paradigm of instructional theory* (Vol. II, pp. 161–182). Hillsdale, NJ: Lawrence Erlbaum Associates.

Schank, R. C., Fano, A., Bell, B., & Jona, M. (1993). The design of goal-based scenarios. *The Journal of the Learning Sciences*, 3(4), 305–345.

Sikora, D. (2002). Storytelling in computer games. In F. D. Laramée (Ed.), *Game design perspectives* (pp. 273–277). Hingham, MA: Charles River Media.

Suchman, L. A. (1987). *Plans and situated actions: The problem of human-machine communications.* Cambridge, UK: Cambridge University Press.

Stone, A. R. (1995). *The war of desire and technology at the close of the mechanical age.* Cambridge, MA: The MIT Press.

Turkle, S. (1995). *Life on the screen: Identity in the age of the Internet.* New York, NY: Simon and Schuster.

Vogler, C. (1998). *The writer's journey: Mythic structures for writers* (3rd ed.). Studio City, CA: Michael Wiese Productions.

Media

Around the World in 80 Days (film) (1956)—United Artists
Breaking Bad (2008)—ACM
Diablo (1996)—Blizzard Entertainment
Drawn (2009)—Big Fish Studios
Dungeons and Dragons (1974)—Gary Gygax and Dave Arneson
Elder Scrolls (1994)—Bethesda Softworks
EverQuest (1999)—Sony Online Entertainment
Fable (2004)—Big Blue Box
Frozen (2013)—Walt Disney Animation Studios
Game of Thrones (television series) (2011)—HBO
Guide Wars (2005)—NCsoft
Harry Potter series (1998: Initial American release of Harry Potter and the Sorcerer's Stone)—J. K. Rowling
Tomb Raider (Lara Croft) (1996)—Eidos Interactive
Mad Men (2007)—AMC
Myst (1991)—Cyan
Riven (1997)—Cyan
Star Wars (1977)—20th Century Fox
Syberia (2002)—Microids
The Walking Dead (television series) (2010)—AMC
The Wizard of Oz (movie) (1939)—Metro-Goldwyn-Mayer
World of Warcraft (2004)—Blizzard

5
Aesthetics and Character Design

I don't care if it's realistic as long as it's believable.

Chuck Jones (1989)

Introduction

The purpose of this chapter is to provide a discussion about the role and design of characters in games and game-based learning. The chapter begins with an overview of the affective domain and emotional intelligence, followed by a review of research about the integration and design of characters (pedagogical agents) for learning. The next section focuses on methods for character design from such fields as literature, game design and theater. This section is followed by a review of methods and strategies for visual design. The final section includes guidance and strategies for developing compelling characters (pedagogical agents) for game-based learning.

Overview

The field of game design is a continually evolving field of study as game developers strive to find ways to design engaging experiences. Recent research from Microsoft's User Research Group provides some stimulating information about narrative and memory. In the research group, players were interviewed and asked to retell narratives from books, TV, movies and games. According to Hendersen (2014a), players provided longer and more detailed narratives for books, TV shows and movies than they were able to recount about games. Henderson observed that, in games, players tended to remember the beginning (backstory) and big moments, but were not always able to connect these to the narrative of a game. Although this research is focused on entertainment games, it is relevant to the integration of narrative into game-based learning. According to Hendersen (2014a), although players had some difficulty recounting narrative in games, one aspect in which recall was the same across different media (books, TV, movies and games) was in retelling of memorable characters. Hendersen notes that there was no discernible difference in players' recall of memorable characters, and players expressed a strong understanding and affection for memorable characters.

82 • Aesthetics and Character Design

This research is insightful for the design of game-based learning. Unarguably, more research needs to be conducted and in the context of game-based learning, but these findings hold much relevance for both narrative and character design in game-based learning. Most of the research about game-based learning has focused on motivational aspects and learning outcomes, but little work has been conducted about how different aspects of design, like narrative, character and environmental design, impact learners. Hendersen argues that "schemata are a more useful way to understand what is memorable and what is not, which is why ensuring a narrative makes sense to players is key to a strong experience" (Hendersen, 2014b).

Recent research on game design and narrative illuminates the importance and value of character design in games (Henderson, 2014a; Abernathy & Rouse, 2014). We remember memorable characters from games and other media because of the emotional impact or resonance of a character and how that character makes us feel. A well-designed character can resonate with our own experiences, take us on an unexpected journey and teach us about ourselves—they are what drive narrative and, most importantly, make us feel something by tapping into our emotions and creating bonds. The very fact that a well-designed character can engage our emotions is a primary reason why character design should play an important part in game-based learning design.

The Affective Domain

Emotions are important because they drive our attention—which in turn impacts memory and learning. In an era in which too often the expressive arts are being eclipsed by cognitive-focused curriculum, it is important that we remember the value of emotion and recognize the role it plays in constructing the whole individual (Dewey, 1902). The function of emotion in the learning environment is important because emotions "influence our ability to process information and accurately understand what we encounter" (Darling-Hammond et al., 2003, p. 90).

Bloom's Taxonomy: Affective Domain

In 1956, educational psychologist Benjamin Bloom categorized knowledge into three domains: cognitive, affective and psychomotor. The three domains are often loosely defined as knowing (cognitive), feeling (affective) and doing (psychomotor). Within the scope of the cognitive domain are knowledge, comprehension, application, analysis, synthesis and evaluation, which form the basis of learning objectives. The outline of this domain starts from the lower-order thinking and moves to more complex. The impact of Bloom's taxonomy is widespread in educational theory and instructional design and is often referenced in discussions of learning goals and objectives. Although Bloom's explication of the knowledge domain has had great impact on contemporary education and instructional design, the cognitive domain is only one of three domains of knowledge. Bloom

Aesthetics and Character Design • **83**

also delineated the affective domain and the psychomotor domain. Of the three categories, educational theory, instructional design and learning design have most often focused on the cognitive domain, followed by the psychomotor domain. Of the three, the affective domain seems to be discussed, integrated and perhaps understood the least. To some degree, this is understandable because much of the focus of contemporary education is situated within the cognitive domain and the science-based traditions influenced by the behaviorist perspective of learning and the shift toward cognitivist perspectives. The affective domain revolves around emotions, attitudes and feelings and how people react emotionally.

What makes the affective domain difficult is that it is concerned with feelings and emotions. In an era of standardized tests and the widespread devaluing of expressive curricula, the question is where do feelings and emotion belong in education? Feelings and emotions are messy and not easily measured. Similarly, values and beliefs are often culturally constructed, and learners from diverse populations may not share the same belief systems and values, so, in many regards, it is easier to ignore or sublimate the affective domain and privilege the cognitive domain. As Pierre and Oughton (2007) concede, the affective domain is not easily quantified, and "tests of cognitive knowledge can be marked right or wrong, but emotions exist on a continuum." After all, the goal of education has traditionally been placed on the acquisition of facts. But humans are complex, and while Bloom's categorization allows us to focus on specifics of cognition, Pierre and Oughton (2007) argue that while "attitudes are not directly observable . . . the actions and behaviors to which they contribute may be observed." In other words, the affective domain is important because it impacts the cognitive domain and the psychomotor domain, and vice versa. While it is unarguably helpful to view knowledge as separate domains, humans do not function as beings with separate domains, but rather our emotions are part of how we learn.

Bloom's classification of skills and objectives within the affective domain include receiving, responding, valuing, organizing and characterizing. Similar to the cognitive domain, the trajectories of these objectives begin with lower order (receiving) and move to higher order (organizing and characterizing). *Receiving* is the willingness to listen and be aware. *Responding* is the reaction or response to a phenomenon. *Valuing* centers on the recognition of worth or value attached to a person or phenomenon. *Organizing* centers on determining a hierarchy of importance in prioritizing values. *Characterizing* involves internalizing values and integrating them into behaviors (see Table 5.1).

Table 5.1 An outline of the affective domain and associated functions

Affective Domain	Functions
Receiving	Willingness to listen to become aware
Responding	Reaction or response to a particular phenomenon
Valuing	Recognition of worth or value attached to a person or phenomenon
Organizing	Prioritize hierarchy of values
Characterizing	Internalize values and manifest in behaviors

84 • Aesthetics and Character Design

Of the limited research into the affective domain, much has centered on student attitudes toward a particular subject (math) and feelings of anxiety about a subject (math), or in the area of character development. But within the scope of the affective domain is receiving, responding, valuing, organizing and characterization, and by following the trajectory of categories, one is able to follow the path of change. Central to Bloom's delineation of the affective domain is a willingness to be aware, respond and change. That is where the affective domain may offer the most relevance in a discussion of character design. In the discussion of narrative design (see Chapter 4), it was noted that characters can impact our emotions. A well-designed character can be memorable and resonate and impact our feelings. As noted in the discussion of narrative, main characters (protagonists) are often transformed or changed by the experiences they encounter throughout their heroic journey. In many game genres, the player takes on the role of the main character, so the player (to some degree) goes through the transformation as the character. As the character goes through some type of transformation, they, in effect, model the affective domain.

Emotional Intelligence and Emotional Design

In a book titled *Emotional Design* (2004), renowned design theorist Donald Norman confronts the role of emotion in design and the types of feelings humans have for designed objects. According to Norman, there are three levels of design that impact our emotional response and experience of use: visceral, behavioral and reflective. The visceral level is the biological level and is the response to "powerful emotional signals from the environment that get interpreted automatically at the visceral level" (Norman, 2004, p. 65). It includes such emotional responses as taste, touch and smell but also includes innate responses to attractiveness and sensuality. The behavioral level is about use, functionality and performance. According to Norman, good behavioral design consists of four components: function, understandability, usability and physical feel (Norman, 1988, 2004). The reflective level is about culture, interpretation, understanding and reasoning. Norman's discussion about emotional intelligence is important because emotions are part of the human experience, and we are continually impacted and informed by our emotions. This in turn translates into how we design products, artifacts and educational media, and can inform how we design and develop different elements for game-based learning. Henderson (2014a) and Abernathy and Rouse's (2014)[1] respective work outlines the need to create compelling characters, but part of what makes a character compelling is the way a character resonates emotionally. Emotional design is part of constructing compelling characters.

Pedagogical Agents

Recent developments in networking are allowing educators and instructional designers unprecedented opportunities for creating compelling interactive learning environments. Text-based virtual realities such as MUDs and MOOs have been used by educators for a variety of initiatives, but, more recently, interactive virtual worlds have been gaining notoriety in the research of instructional design along with the emergence of game-based learning environments and the rise of serious/educational games. Within each of these types of technologies, learners often encounter various types of pedagogical agents in the form of bots (MUDs, MOOs[2] and virtual worlds) and non-player characters (NPCs) in games. Regardless of the form, these pedagogical agents play a type of character in the learning environment. There is relatively little research about character design in game-based learning—likely this is due to the fact that research about game-based learning is just beginning to emerge. Nevertheless, significant research has been conducted about the design of pedagogical agents and their impact on learning. Pedagogical agents are another form of character found in learning environments.

Much of the research about pedagogical agents focuses on the need for creating emotive and embodied agents and models for design. Among some of the earliest research and development of pedagogical agents is Joseph Bates's article "The Roles of Emotion in Believable Agents" (1994), based on his work with the Oz project (Bates, 1992). In this often-referenced paper, Bates identified key elements and sources for guidance in creating *believable agents*. Bates references key work in animation (Disney) along with foundational cognitive-based research into emotions (Ortony, Clore & Collings, 1988). Bates argues that while both are informative about creating believable agents, artists "who have explored the idea of believable character" provide important insight for design (1994, p. 1).

Within the work on the need for creating embodied pedagogical agents, much research has been proposed about how to create embodied agents. Towns, Fitzgerald and Lester (1998) proposed an emotive-kinesthetic behavior sequence framework for creating lifelike pedagogical agents with emotive expression. Similarly, Cassell et al. (1999) proposed a model for embodied conversational characters complete with *conversational function* and behaviors (verbal and nonverbal). Doswell (2004) advocates for an embodied pedagogical agent that is conversational and responsive to learners while scaffolding their needs. McQuiggan and Lester (2007) argue that affective reasoning as part of human social interaction needs to be incorporated into the design of agents. They contend that there is a need to integrate empathy and empathetic responses into the design of agents. Similarly, Zakharov, Mitrovic and Johnston (2008) maintain that emotions play an important part in learning and that pedagogical agents need to be developed that are able to identify and respond to the "affective states" of learners.

What is notable about the research about pedagogical agents is this trajectory from basic embodiment through movement and dialogue to the present, in which the affective domain and emotion are playing a greater role in how pedagogical agents are conceived. As research into the design of pedagogical agents has progressed, so has the recognition about the important connection between emotion and learning. This is informative about the pedagogical needs of character design for game-based learning. Emotion plays a role in learning, and good characters

86 • Aesthetics and Character Design

and compelling narratives are ways to evoke emotion. Research from the design of pedagogical agents provides some compelling arguments for creating characters that are able to identify and respond to learners in game-based learning environments.

There is also considerable work about the impact of pedagogical agents that would inform the design of game-based characters. Some of Isbister's early work focused on the design of agents. According to Isbister and Nass (2000), users were less concerned or impacted by personalities of pedagogical agents as by consistency. Users preferred characters that were consistent and complementary to their own personality traits. Moreno, Klettke, Nibbaragandla and Graesser (2002) found that college students reported that likeability of pedagogical agents was not as important as efficacy. Their findings revealed that personality may not play as strong of a role in agent design as providing an agent perceived as being credible. Atkinson (2002) noted the importance of embedding the agent within the learning environment as opposed to being external. In the ongoing effort toward creating embodied agents, Baylor, Ryu and Shen (2003) found that participants learned more with an animated agent, although they reported that the agent was less helpful when it was animated. Ryu and Baylor's (2005) findings revealed that there were two key constructs students were most responsive toward in pedagogical agents: agents that (1) were informative and useful, and (2) had social presence and a "personality." Sahimi et al. (2010) found that neither agent realism nor gender had an impact on students, but that agents were more effective when embedded in the learning environment. Although this is merely a small foray into the research about the impact of pedagogical agents and there is not a clear trajectory of findings, what is revealed and informative for character design in game-based learning is the value of embedding agents in the learning environment and that the perception of a helpful personality may not be of as much importance as presence. This provides some interesting fodder for development of different character roles.

Finally, a growing but significant body of work is emerging about aesthetics and design for pedagogical agents. Gulz and Haake (2006) argue that the "visuo-aesthetic experience" of pedagogical agents is important for motivation and engagement and should not be treated as a secondary issue. Similarly, Veletsiano (2007) argues that although little research has been conducted about the impact of agents' aesthetic properties and how they impact learning, work in other fields of design has shown that aesthetics can impact metacognition and perceptions of ease of use. Veletsiano speculates about how aesthetics might influence learning. The work of Gulz and Haake (2006) and Veletsiano (2007) holds relevance for character design in game-based learning, not merely in terms of creating engaging characters, but in terms of harnessing aesthetics for learning.

Much of the research about pedagogical agents has focused on function and embodiment in creating human-like agents with presence and emotion that are responsive to the emotions of learners. However, research has also been conducted into the visual design of agents and characters. The function of a character is a key aspect for character design because it serves to define the role; however, the appearance, movement and dialogue of a character also are important for conveying these roles. There is a significant body of research from various fields of psychology that helps to inform the design of pedagogical characters based on public perceptions of attractiveness, agreeableness and dominance. Much of this work has been leveraged in the design of pedagogical agents and characters (Bates, 1994; Isbister, 2006b; Isbister & Nass, 2000; Johnson, Rickel & Lester, 2000; Nass, Isbister & Lee, 2000). According to Isbister (2006a), both agreeableness and dominance of a character can provide more depth in character development. Based on research about perceptions of personality, Isbister argues that agreeableness impacts how game players perceive their relationship to a character. People tend to have a positive association with characters deemed attractive (Zebrowitz, 1997).

Character Design

Although much of the educational focus of character design has been situated in the development and impact of pedagogical agents, the potential impact and importance of character design for game-based learning environments should not be understated. Great characters in games, movies and literature can motivate, inspire, teach and provide insight and opportunities for reflection. They evoke feelings to impact our emotions. A great character in a game can serve a variety of functions and reinforce a sense of immersion in the environment (Dickey, 2012).

Character design within games includes the role the character plays in the game, the function of the character and the visual design of the character. Fields such as literature and even behavioral psychology can help inform design aspects of role and function and provide guidance in how characters convey aspects of personality through dialogue, while visual fields such as comics and animation provide guidance in how to visually communicate those aspects.

The following sections outline strategies used in literature, theater, game design and animation for developing compelling characters. The focus on each section is to outline the trajectory of character development by drawing on strategies and research from such diverse areas as game design, animation, kinesthetic and behavioral studies and research to inform character design in game-based learning. The goal of this section is to provide guidance for the design and development of compelling characters for a variety of learning environments. This section begins with a discussion of character roles and function. This is followed by a discussion of visual design. Finally, aspects of dialogue are addressed. Following this section are guidelines for creating characters in the form of a heuristic for character design in game-based learning.

Literature: Character Roles and Functions

In addition to a storyline, many games include a variety of characters scattered throughout the gameplay environment. In some game genres (adventure and

88 • Aesthetics and Character Design

action), the player may take on the part of a pre-scripted character within the narrative and play the game as that character. Often, the player/character will encounter a variety of NPCs throughout the game, and those NPCs often serve a variety of functions within a game. They may play the role of enemies or allies, or serve as a means of conveying information. Compelling characters can motivate, challenge and even emotionally impact players. As in other forms of media, creating compelling characters can be very challenging, particularly for those without a background in creative writing. Nevertheless, there are strategies for character design in games that can provide guidance for the design of game-based learning. Prior to the visual design, a designer must first understand the role and function of a character in a game. Vogler's (1998) outline of Jung's archetypes offers guidance on the development of roles. The following seven character archetypes typically appear within the classic quest structure: Hero, Mentor, Threshold Guardian, Herald, Shapeshifter, Trickster, and Shadow. These archetypes are based upon Jung's archetypal patterns, which Jung argues are part of our collective unconscious (1953). Although Vogler (1998, p. 30) advocates Jung's notion of character archetypes, he stresses that archetypes should not be considered as fixed roles, but rather as a "function performed temporarily by characters to achieve certain effects in a story" and to consider the psychological function of the archetype and the dramatic function in the progression of the storyline. The following overview provides an outline of each character role and function. Below is a table that includes a short description of the role or purpose of each character type and how these roles manifest in game design.

The Hero

The hero's role functions as the main agent of action who undertakes the journey from a first-person perspective. The hero is someone whom the audience can identify with on some level and yet also admire. The purpose of the hero is to give the audience a "window" or point of view into the story within the quest and other types of narratives.[3] The hero should have multiple "universal" qualities with which audiences can relate. The hero should also have qualities the audience find admirable so the audience will embrace the hero and perhaps wish to live vicariously through him/her. The hero should also have some flaws to make him/her a character with dimension and relatable to audiences (e.g., Harry Potter is courageous but also very quick to anger). According to Vogler, the function of the hero is to serve as an agent of action and change. The hero is what drives the storyline, but at the same time is someone who is impacted by the events and thereby undergoes some type of transformation. What is most telling about the hero is how the hero responds to pressure and the qualities that emerge as a result of pressure.

The Mentor

The role of the mentor is to provide guidance. The mentor's function is to in some way educate the hero, whether it is through training or providing insight into a

Aesthetics and Character Design • **89**

problem or conflict. Within any story, there may be several characters who serve as mentors (e.g., in the Harry Potter series, *Hagrid, Dumbledore, Sirius, Arthur, Molly* and *Lupin* all serve as mentors at different times). According to Vogler, the mentor's function is also to motivate the hero. In addition to providing key information and guidance, the mentor provides reassurance, inspiration or even the necessary push to send the hero into action. In Vogler's view, the mentor typically appears near the beginning of the narrative.

Threshold Guardian

The threshold guardian functions as a character or even a situation that in some way tests the hero with some obstacle. Threshold guardians are not typically the main enemy or villain, but merely an obstacle the hero must overcome. A threshold guardian can be something as simple as the weather or as complex as a hero's personal insecurities. How the hero handles resistance and overcomes the obstacle is telling about the hero. In the example of *Harry Potter and the Sorcerer's Stone*, platform 9¾ at King's Cross tube station could be considered a threshold guardian.

The Herald

The herald functions to signal change and present new information, whether in the form of a person, some news or even an inner force that sparks the call to duty. The herald serves to motivate the hero to action. Typically, the herald enters near the beginning of the narrative to spur the hero into action (e.g., Hagrid visits Harry's home after the messages from Hogwarts have been ignored.)

The Shapeshifter

The shapeshifter functions as a character or situation in which doubt must be overcome. The shapeshifter might take the form of a person who in some way changes or has a hidden side or element, or it can take the form of a situation that causes instability. The function of the shapeshifter is to present some form of challenge and doubt that the hero must overcome. In the example of *Harry Potter and the Sorcerer's Stone*, Professor Quirrell appears to be a harmless ally, but instead is a host for the evil Lord Voldemort.

The Trickster

The trickster functions as another type of obstacle in the form of a character who causes problems either by design or by accident. A trickster can provide comic relief as well as serving to help keep the hero's ego under control. In the Harry Potter series, Fred and George Weasley serve as tricksters throughout the series.

The Shadow

Finally, the shadow functions as the main antagonist in the form of a character or situation. The function of the shadow is to provide a worthy opponent to the

90 • Aesthetics and Character Design

hero. The shadow may take the form of a person (Voldemort, Darth Vader, the Wicked Witch of the West), or may be an internal struggle the hero needs to overcome.

Table 5.2 below includes a table of character types and functions.

Game Design: Character Roles and Function

Most of the literature about the design of characters for games begins with the role and the function of a character. The character's role is both the role that the character plays in gameplay as well as the role in the narrative. Defining the role of the player in gameplay involves looking at the types of gameplay mechanics (see Chapter 7) and the genre (see Chapter 2). For some genres, such as adventure games, the player may be taking on the role (hero/protagonist) in the game, and the character's role is predefined. For example, in the game *Syberia*, players play the game as Kate. They interact in the environment through the character of Kate and the scripted dialogue between Kate and other characters. In other genres, the role of the player may be as an external force that is acting upon the gameplay environment (strategy games). Adams (2014) refers to these as specific and nonspecific avatars (representations of players in the game). Yet in other genres, such as MMORGPs, the player

Table 5.2 Character types and roles

Character—ROLE	Role—FUNCTION
Hero	The hero is the protagonist and typically the lead character in a game. Depending upon the genre, this is the role the player adopts when playing the game.
Mentor	The mentor provides both guidance and insight to aid the protagonist. Typically, the mentor is an ally of the protagonist. The mentor may appear throughout the game to offer the protagonist advice, information or insight, or even to supply tools to assist the protagonist.
Threshold Guardian	The threshold guardian is an obstacle or hurdle that the protagonist must overcome or move past. The challenge of overcoming the obstacle helps prepare the protagonist for future challenges.
Herald	The herald is a source of information for the protagonist. The herald may be a person or may take a different form, such as an announcement, a newspaper or a letter.
Shapeshifter	The shapeshifter may take different forms (an ally, companion or some other form), but the function of the shapeshifter is to provide an element of doubt.
Trickster	The trickster may also take different forms, but functions as some form of an obstacle that must be overcome.
Shadow	The shadow is the antagonist of the central conflict for the protagonist. It may be an enemy (Darth Vader, Voldemort, Wicked Witch of the West), or it might be an internal struggle the protagonist is attempting to overcome.

Adapted from Vogler, C. (1998). *The writer's journey: Mythic structures for writers* (2nd ed.). Studio City, CA: Michael Wiese Productions.

self-selects from an array of attributes to create a unique, low-ranking character. One of the first steps is to determine a character's game purpose by defining how the character interacts in the gameplay environment (Walsh, 2007).

The term "role" also refers to the role of a character in the narrative of a game. Laurel (1993) was among the first to provide guidance for the design of game characters. Laurel drew upon Aristotle's (1954) criterion for dramatic characters in her outline of character design. According to Laurel, characters should be (1) good—they should do what they intend (actions follow thought), (2) appropriate—they should be appropriate to the actions they perform (match between traits and action), (3) realistic—deeds match thoughts and actions (causal connection between thoughts, traits and actions), and (4) consistent—actions are consistent (traits should not change arbitrarily).

Much of the discussion about character roles and functions either references Vogler (Adams, 2014) or provides roles that correspond to Vogler's (1998) outline of Jung's (1953) archetypes. For example, Schell's (2008) list of character functions include:

1. Hero: the character who plays the game
2. Mentor: gives advice and useful items
3. Assistant: gives occasional tips
4. Tutor: explains how to play the game
5. Final boss: someone to have the last battle against
6. Minions: bad guys
7. Three bosses: tough guys to battle against
8. Hostages: someone to rescue

Similarly, Sheldon (2014) outlines the following roles:

1. Protagonist—Player
2. Villain—Antagonist
3. Mentors
4. Sidekicks
5. Merchants
6. Trainers
7. Quest givers

Regardless of the terms used, roles and functions generally include the hero, the villain (shadow), sidekicks (trickster) and mentors.

Personality and Traits

Adams (2014) stresses that the goal of character design is to create characters that are appealing, believable, identifiable and distinctive. Most discussions of character design stress the importance of developing multidimensional characters and

92 • Aesthetics and Character Design

not relying on one-dimensional stereotypes. Isbister (2006a) outlines the following *big five* personality traits as a guide for delineating personality types:

1. Agreeableness: friendly and compassionate vs. detached and suspicious
2. Dominance: prominent and outgoing vs. submissive and reserved
3. Openness: broad-minded and curious vs. closed and cautious
4. Conscientiousness: efficient and organized vs. careless and carefree
5. Neuroticism: sensitive and self-conscious vs. confident and secure

Both Walsh (2007) and Sheldon (2014) recommend elucidating character traits such as mobility, skills, profession, race, gender, ethnicity and status. Miller (2004) provides the following strategies to help scaffold the development of characters.

1. Probe: develop the character's backstory and psychological profile (family, schooling, history, hopes and fears)
2. Motivation: identify character's goal
3. Personality: highlight character traits and quickly convey them
4. Avoid stereotypes or play against them
5. Visual design: characters need a distinct look (body language and attire)
6. Make characters fun: not "funny" but distinctive
7. Names: provide distinctive names
8. Dialogue: use dialogue to convey personality

Most discussions about character design stress the importance of revealing characters through actions and interactions rather than through descriptions (Laurel, 1993; Adams, 2014; Schell, 2008; Isbister, 2006b; Walsh, 2007; Sheldon, 2014; Miller, 2004). There are several methods for revealing the personality of a character. The physical appearance provides a great deal of information about a character— provided the character appears in the game. In some games, the lead character—the role the player fills—is not seen in the game. For example, in the Nancy Drew series, players are cast in the role of Nancy, but she never appears in the series. Her personality is clearly conveyed, but the methods used to convey personality come from dialogue, her interaction with other characters and interactions with aspects of the game. These are all methods of conveying character. Miller (2004) outlines the following five methods in which a character's personality can be revealed:

1. Physical appearance
2. Dialogue
3. Interaction with other characters
4. Actions
5. Other characters reveal

Motivation

Personality is not merely revealed through a combination of traits and characteristics but is also conveyed through relationships between characters. Creating engaging characters involves looking beyond surface aspects. However, as the old theater adage states, "there are no small parts, only small actors." This statement, often attributed to Constantin Stanislavski, holds relevance for the design of compelling characters (Manero, Fernández-Vara & Fernández-Manjón, 2013). Central to Stanislavski's method of acting is that an actor must find (or invent) a character's motivation. Stanislavski's method entails actors identifying their characters' objectives and the types of conflict their characters encounter. Manero et al. (2013) outline the following different types of conflicts characters may encounter:

- Intersubjective: a conflict between characters with opposing objectives
- Environmental: a conflict in which the environment prevents the objective
- Intimate: a conflict in which the action carries inner consequences

This approach provides strategies that can be applied to the development of characters within a game or game-based environment by providing designers with methods for developing complexity for different characters.

Visual Representations

The function of a character is a key aspect for character design because it serves to define the role; however, the appearance, movement and dialogue of a character are important for conveying these roles. Once the role and function of a character has been determined, the next step is to outline visual aspects of a character design, including the face, body, and motion and movement. There is a significant body of research from various fields of psychology that helps to inform the design of pedagogical characters based on public perceptions of attractiveness, agreeableness and dominance. Much of this work has been leveraged in the design of pedagogical agents and characters (Bates, 1994; Isbister, 2006a, 2006b; Isbister & Nass, 2000; Nass, Isbister & Lee, 2000; Johnson, Rickel & Lester, 2000).

Face Design

We are attracted to beauty. One of the guiding principles of animation outlined by Disney animators Frank Thomas and Ollie Johnston (1981) is appeal. According to Thomas and Johnston, all characters should be pleasing to view because our attention is drawn to attractiveness (Thomas & Johnston, 1981; Norman, 2004). Isbister (2006a, 2006b) provides some key guidelines for the visual design of characters. First and foremost, she advocates making all characters attractive (symmetry, prominent cheekbones, defined chin, large eyes), regardless of role (hero, villain, sidekick). We tend to credit attractive people and things with being more capable and interesting, and we view them more positively (Norman, 2004; Langlois, Kalakanis, Rubenstein, Larson, Hallam & Smoot, 2000). According to Isbister (2006b), both agreeableness and dominance of a character can provide more depth to character development. Based on research about perceptions of personality, Isbister argues that agreeableness impacts how game players perceive

94 • Aesthetics and Character Design

their relationship to a character. People tend to have a positive association with characters deemed attractive (Zebrowitz, 1997). According to Isbister, people feel more positive toward attractive faces, and this is transferred to having a more positive impression of a game; however, Isbister also notes that attractiveness is culturally constructed (2006a, 2006b).

Other guidelines include perceptions about facial structure. People perceive baby faces (round face with soft features) as warm and open, but also immature and lacking competence (Zebrowitz & Montepare, 2008). Mature faces are perceived as competent and capable of commanding respect (Zebrowitz, 1997). Finally, the use of eyeglasses can also impact perception. The wearing of eyeglasses is associated with intelligence (Gulz & Haake, 2006).

Body

The visual representation of a character's body is also impacted by attitudes of attractiveness. Fat bodies are often viewed negatively, whereas muscular bodies are viewed more positively. Thin bodies are viewed somewhat in between (Gulz & Haake, 2006). Views of weight and physical appearance are culturally constructed and dependent upon cultural norms. In addition to body shape, clothing plays a role in how a character is constructed and perceived. While findings about visual design for faces and bodies are insightful, the power of education is that it challenges and transforms learners. Character design that breaks conventions and challenges perceptions provides opportunities for learners to reflect and explore their own biases about attractiveness and attributing positive attributes to people and items of beauty.

Motion and Movement

Both comic artists (McCloud, 1994) and animators (Thomas & Johnston, 1981) have a long history of subtly exploiting the use of attractive vs. unattractive character design in visual media. However, visual design is just one aspect of character physical design; motion is also fundamental in how a character is conveyed to an audience. Bates (1994) advocated the use of principles of animation to inform the design of pedagogical agents that are able to convey emotions. Characters designed and portrayed by animation pioneers such as Walt Disney, Tex Avery and Chuck Jones provide classic examples in how design, motion and action can convey and reinforce character design. Frank Thomas and Ollie Johnston (1981) of Disney's legendary "nine old men" outlined the following 12 principles of animation that still serve as the foundation for giving characters personality and the "illusion of life."

1. Squash and stretch
2. Anticipation

Aesthetics and Character Design • 95

3. Staging
4. Straight-ahead action and pose-to-pose action
5. Follow-through and overlapping action
6. Slow in and out
7. Arcs
8. Secondary action
9. Timing
10. Exaggeration
11. Solid drawing
12. Appeal

These principles still provide foundational guidelines for aspiring animators. In 1987, renowned 3D animation pioneer John Lasseter (1987) adapted the original principles for use in 3D computer animation. These principles continue to inform character-based animation and provide guidance for conveying personality and character through motion and movement.

Lasseter's principles of traditional animation applied to 3D computer animation include:

1. Squash and stretch
2. Timing and motion
3. Anticipation
4. Staging
5. Follow-through and overlapping action
6. Straight-ahead action and pose-to-pose action
7. Slow in and out
8. Arcs
9. Exaggeration
10. Secondary action
11. Appeal

Squash and Stretch

Squash and stretch is the foundational principle to nearly all forms of animation. Squash and stretch refers to the illusion of rigidity of an object and the progressive transformation of an object during an action. Thomas and Johnston (1981) use the example of a bent arm and the bulge of the bicep that appears with a bent arm but flattens as the arm is straightened. One of the first exercises many animation students encounter is a "squash and stretch" exercise in which they apply principles of squash and stretch to convey the rigidity of a bouncing ball (sphere)—a ball that squashes (flattens) upon impact with the ground and stretches as it is descending toward the ground and again as it is ascending. The degree of squash and stretch would vary according to the pliability of an object. For example, in an animation of a dropped bowling ball, the bowling ball would remain fairly

96 • Aesthetics and Character Design

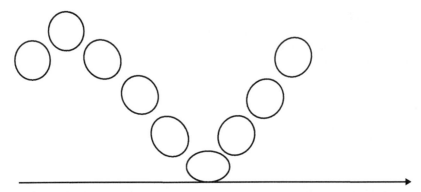

Figure 5.1 Squash and stretch

intact compared to an animation of a soft rubber ball, which would be animated with a greater degree of transformation upon impact and subsequent bounce (see Figure 5.1).

Timing

Timing refers to the speed of an action. The timing of an object reflects the weight and size of that object as well as conveying emotion. According to Lasseter (1987), the speed of movement of a character can convey whether a character is "lethargic, excited, nervous or relaxed."

Anticipation

Anticipation denotes the preparation for an action. Thomas and Johnston (1981) use the example of a man beginning to run—the man may start the action by slightly crouching, then spring into a run. That initial crouching signals or anticipates the start of a character running. According to Lasseter (1987), an action has three parts: the preparation for the action (anticipation), the action and the termination of the action. Anticipation helps convey what a character is doing by providing a "setup" to the action. The degree of the anticipation can convey the degree of effort required for an action.

Staging

Staging is derived from theater and the importance of conveying an action, personality, mood and emotion so that it can be seen by the audience. Staging works well in theater, films and animation where the viewpoint is controlled. Both Lasseter (1987) and Thomas and Johnston (1981) recommend framing a character and action in silhouette. A great example is Disney's iconic character Mickey Mouse. Mickey is always staged so that both ears are displayed in silhouette, regardless of the actual physical positioning; the ears always appear in all staging.

Staging of a character in games works better for some games in which the player has limited control over the camera view and the main character and NPCs can be "staged"; however, in immersive 3D environments, staging is more difficult because the player controls the camera. Character motions and movements have to be framed so that they convey emotion, action and personality from various angles.

Follow-through and Overlapping Action

Follow-through and overlapping action refers to the end stage of one action and its relationship to the next action. The follow-through action is the counterpart to anticipation. An action begins with the anticipation, the action and then the follow-through actions. For example, when walking, not all parts of the body stop when reaching a destination. Legs settle into a standing position as arms continue to swing slightly and clothing sways. Overlapping action denotes that actions are rarely isolated—as one action ends, another is beginning, and there are adjustments and accommodations based on the relationship between the two movements of the character. For example, in the action of a character walking across the room to pick up a book, the character would not come to a complete stop before picking up the book, but instead, as the character nears the book, the character would begin to raise an arm and open a hand to reach toward the book.

Straight-ahead Action and Pose-to-pose Action

Straight-ahead action and pose-to-pose action are in reference to two styles of hand-drawn animation. In straight-ahead action, the animator draws the action one frame after the other for a scene. In pose-to-pose, animators plan the action, draw key poses for the scene and fill in the in-between frames between the key poses. This is roughly the traditional animation version of keyframes and tweening.

Slow In and Out

Slow in and out refers to the spacing of *in-between* frames for subtlety and timing. The spacing of in-betweens impacts how velocity is conveyed. For example, a bouncing ball moves faster as it approaches the ground and leaves the ground than it does when it approaches the top of the bounce. Slow in and slow out can impact character timing and personality.

Arcs

Arcs are the visual path of action for movement. Movement is more interesting and less stiff when the path of action is an arc.

Exaggeration

The principle of exaggeration is to overemphasize the essence of the emotion and scene.

98 • Aesthetics and Character Design

Secondary Action

Secondary action refers to the action of an object fortified by a subsidiary action. Thomas and Johnston (1981) provide the example of a sad character wiping away a tear as he walks away. The wiping of the tear is a secondary action to sadly walking away. It reinforces the character's emotion. According to Thomas and Johnston, the secondary action must take place before or after the primary action or it will be lost in the movement.

Appeal

According to Thomas and Johnston, characters should have appeal. They argue that appeal is not the same as being cute or likeable, but rather all characters (including villains) should be pleasing to view. All characters should possess "a quality of charm, pleasing design, simplicity, communication and magnetism" (1981, p. 68) because attractive figures hold our gaze (and attention).

Both the list by Thomas and Johnston (1981) and Lasseter's (1987) subsequent list for 3D animation provide some guidance for how motion and movement convey and reinforce characters and emotion and the illusion of life. Much information about a character can be conveyed through visual design, motion and movement. Additionally, a great deal about the relationship between two characters can also be conveyed through motion and movement. Chuck Jones' infamous animation of simple characters—a line and a dot in the animation *The Dot and The Line: A Romance in Lower Mathematics*—is a great example of how motion and movement can convey personality and relationship.

Character Dialogue

In addition to visual design and motion and movement, much can be revealed and conveyed about a character through dialogue. Miller (2004) provides some guidance into the use of dialogue to reveal and support character design. Miller advocates using dialogue sparingly and only when there is no other means of conveying information. She stresses "showing" rather than "telling" about a character. She also provides the following guidelines for verbal communication for character design:

1. Keep communication short and to the point.
2. Use clear, simple words and informal language and grammar.
3. Character dialogue should reflect the character's personality.
4. Voiceover narration should be somewhat formal.
5. When using phone conversations, keep dialogue brief.
6. If using a news broadcast, follow typical style, pacing and format conventions.
7. After writing dialogue, read aloud to listen for awkward phrases, long lines and unnatural dialogue.

Freeman (2004) provides guidance in how to create emotion in games through applying "emotioneering" techniques. His guidelines for writing dialogue that convey personality of characters include:

Aesthetics and Character Design • **99**

1. Add color: Add "color" to the dialogue by conveying something of the personality of the speaker (gruff, sarcastic, pleasant) in the dialogue.
2. Prompt action: Dialogue should prompt the player into action but should also convey information about the speaker (personality, relationship) and the situation.
3. Splitting information: Often, the role of an NPC is to convey information; splitting information between two NPCs provides options of conveying different characters and relationships (and keeps dialogue short).

While good characters are memorable and impact emotions and add to the experience in games, good character design involves balancing needs, some game-based (mechanics), with a narrative storyline. However, strategies have been appropriated and developed that help inform the design of compelling and engaging characters.

Summary

Part of the emotional resonance we feel when playing games is a result of the types of characters that inhabit a game. Great characters in literature, movies and games have an emotional impact on us and resonate with our own feelings and experiences. Iconic characters such as Harry Potter, Scarlett O'Hara, Forrest Gump, Laura Ingalls Wilder and Tony Soprano resonate with us because they project our own fears, desires, strengths and failings, yet they may also motivate and teach while they entertain.

Heuristic for Character Design in Game-based Learning

This heuristic builds upon the guidance provided in Chapter 4 about narrative design. Central to narrative design for game-based learning is finding conflict—whether the conflict be problem-based learning; project-based learning; conflict in how the knowledge was uncovered (science), situated or evolved (history) or discovered (math); or conflicts in differences of what is actualized (language learning).

1. Identify any roles that characters need to fill (Schell, 2008). Define the role the character will play in relation to the learning environment.

   Vogler's list of archetypes provides guidance for different roles and functions in game-based learning, whether there is need for a linear narrative or characters within a narrative environment. The hero provides a way of thinking about how the learner will be situated in the game-based learning environment, whether cast in a particular role or "playing" themselves. The mentor can be conceived as a teacher, a guide or even types of resources to provide scaffolding. The herald can be an element that signals change—a character that presents a problem that needs to be solved or even a situation that presents a learning challenge that needs

100 • Aesthetics and Character Design

to be met. The threshold guardian can be some form of obstacle (time, constraints, need for additional knowledge or skills) that needs to be overcome. This might entail gathering data to proceed to inform a larger goal or learning a skill or tool before undertaking the main challenge. Shapeshifters and tricksters can also take different forms. They may be characters who place additional demands on the learner or interfere or create problems. They may also take the form of red herrings, dead ends and problems that arise during the learning process. Finally, the shadow is the final main obstacle. It may be in the form of a character (perhaps a "client" in case-based learning), or it might be the major challenge that the hero/learner must overcome. Outline the characters' personalities (strengths and weaknesses).

2. Identify the relationship the character has with the conflict, environment and other characters.

3. Create a backstory for each character. Identify the objective (goal/motivation) for the character. Determine the obstacles that are preventing the character from achieving the goal.

4. Outline the visual appearance of the character. Outline the motion and movement of the character. How do the character's appearance and movement convey information about the character?

5. Develop dialogue that fulfills the function of the role (guidance, challenge, information). How can the character's dialogue fulfill the needs, yet also convey emotional states and convey information about the relationship?

Notes

1. See the discussion of long-form narrative in Chapter 4 for an overview of Abernathy and Rouse's (2014) arguments about narrative for games.
2. See Chapter 2 for an in-depth explanation of MUDs and MOOs.
3. In serialized or long-form narratives, there may be several points of view or a change in point of view/protagonist over time (e.g., *Game of Thrones*, *Days of Our Lives*).

References

Abernathy, T., & Rouse, R. (2014). Death to the three-act structure: Toward a unique structure for game narratives. *Game Developers Conference*. Los Angeles, CA, March 17–21, 2014.

Adams, E. (2014). *Fundamentals of game design* (3rd ed.). Indianapolis, IN: New Riders.

Aristotle. (1954). *The poetics*. Translated by Ingram Bywater. In F. Solmsen (Ed.), *Rhetoric and poetics of Aristotle*. New York, NY: The Modern Library.

Atkinson, R. K. (2002). Optimizing learning from examples using animated pedagogical agents. *Journal of Educational Psychology*, 97(2), 416–427.

Bates, J. (1992). Virtual reality, art and entertainment. *PRESENCE: Teleoperators and Virtual Environments*, 1(1), 133–138.

Bates, J. (1994). The role of emotion in believable agents. *Communications of the ACM*, 37(7), 122–125.

Baylor, A. L., Ryu, J., & Shen, E. (2003). The effects of pedagogical agent voice and animation on learning, motivation and perceived persona. In D. Lassner & C. McNaught (Eds.), *Proceedings of World Conference on Educational Multimedia, Hypermedia and Telecommunications* (pp. 452–458). Chesapeake, VA: Association for the Advancement of Computing in Education (AACE).

Aesthetics and Character Design • 101

Bloom, B. (1956). *Taxonomy of educational objectives: The cognitive domain*. New York, NY: McKay.

Cassell, J., Bickmore, T., Billinghurst, M., Campbell, L., Chang, K., Vilhjalmsson, H., & Yan, H. (1999). Embodiment in conversational interfaces: Rea. *CHI Conference Proceedings* (pp. 520–527). Pittsburgh, PA: ACM.

Darling-Hammond, L., Orcutt, S., Stroble, K., Kirsh, E., Lit, I., Martin, D., & Comer, M. D. (2003). Feelings count: Emotions and learning (Session 5): The learning classroom: Theory into practice. *Annenberg Learner Course*. Retrieved October 18, 2013, from http://www.learner.org/workshops/workshop_list.html

Dewey, J. (1902). *The child and the curriculum*. Chicago, IL: University of Chicago Press.

Dickey, M. D. (2012). Game design and the importance of narrative. In S. Garner (Ed.), *Design and designing: A critical introduction* (pp. 112–123). Oxford, UK: Berg Publishers.

Doswell, J. T. (2004). Pedagogical embodied conversational agent. Proceedings of the *IEEE International Conference on Advanced Learning Technologies* (ICALT'04). Joensuu, Finland, August 2004.

Freeman, D. (2004, July). Creating emotion in games: The craft and art of Emotioneering™. *ACM Computers in Entertainment*, 2(3), Article 8a.

Gulz, A., & Haake, M. (2006). Design of animated pedagogical agents—A look at their look. *International Journal of Human-Computer Studies*, 64(2006), 322–339.

Hendersen, D. (2014a). Using user research to improve game narratives. *Game Developers Conference 2014*. Los Angeles, CA, March 17–21, 2014.

Hendersen, D. (2014b). Personal communication.

Isbister, K. (2006a). *Better game characters by design: A psychological approach*. New York, NY: Morgan Kaufmann.

Isbister, K. (2006b). Emotion and motion: Games as inspiration for shaping the future of interface. *Interactions*, Sept/Oct, 24–27.

Isbister, K., & Nass, C. (2000). Consistency of personality in interactive characters: Verbal cues, nonverbal cues, and user characteristics. *International Journal of Human-Computer Studies*, 53(2), 251–267.

Johnson, W. L., Rickel, J. W., & Lester, J. C. (2000). Animated pedagogical agents: Face-to-face interaction in interactive learning environments. *International Journal of Artificial Intelligence in Education*, 11(200), 47–78.

Jones, C. (1989). *Chuck amuck: The life and times of an animated cartoonist*. New York, NY: Farrar Straus Giroux.

Jung, C. G. (1953). *The collected works of C.G. Jung* (edited by H. Read, M. Fordham & G. Adler). New York, NY: Pantheon Books.

Langlois, J. H., Kalakanis, L., Rubenstein, A. J., Larson, A., Hallam, M., & Smoot, M. (2000). Maxims or myths of beauty? A meta-analytic and theoretical review. *Psychological Bulletin*, 126(3), 390–423.

Lasseter, J. (1987). Principles of traditional animation applied to 3D computer animation. *ACM Computer Graphics*, 21(4), 35–44.

Laurel, B. (1993). *Computers as theatre*. New York, NY: Addison-Wesley.

Manero, B., Fernández-Vara, C., & Fernández-Manjón, B. (2013). Stanislavki's system as a game design method: A case study. *Proceedings of DiGRA 2013: DeFragging Game Studies*. Atlanta, GA, August, 2013.

McCloud, S. (1994). *Understanding comics: The invisible art*. New York, NY: Harper Perennial.

McQuiggan, S. W., & Lester, J. C. (2007). Modeling and evaluating empathy in embodied companion agents. *International Journal of Human-Computer Studies*, 63(2007), 348–360.

Miller, C. H. (2004). *Digital storytelling: A creator's guide to interactive entertainment*. Burlington, MA: Focal Press Elsevier.

Moreno, K. N., Klettke, B., Nibbaragandla, K., & Graesser, A. C. (2002). Perceived characteristics and pedagogical efficacy of animated conversational agents. *Intelligent Tutoring Systems: Lecture Notes in Computer Science*, 2363(2002), 963–971.

Nass, C., Isbister, K., & Lee, E. J. (2000). Truth is beauty: Researching embodied conversational agents. In J. Cassell, S. Prevost, J. Sullivan, & E. Churchill (Eds.), *Embodied conversational agents* (pp. 374–402). Boston, MA: The MIT Press.

Norman, D. A. (1988). *The design of everyday things*. New York, NY: Doubleday.

102 • Aesthetics and Character Design

Norman, D. A. (2004). *Emotional design: Why we love (or hate) everyday things.* New York, NY: Basic Books.

Ortony, A., Clore, G., & Collings, A. (1988). The cognitive structure of emotions. *Applied Cognitive Psychology,* 6(2), 181–182.

Pierre, E., & Oughton, J. (2007). The affective domain: Undiscovered country. *College Quarterly,* 10(4), 1–7.

Ryu, J., & Baylor, A. L. (2005). The psychometric structure of pedagogical agent persona. *Technology, Instruction, Cognition and Learning,* 2, 291–314.

Sahimi, S. M., Zain, F. M., Kamar, N.A.N., Samar, N., Rahman, Z. A., Majid, O., Atan, H., & Fook, F. S. (2010). The pedagogical agent in online learning: Effects of the degree of realism on achievement in terms of gender. *Contemporary Educational Technology,* 3(2), 175–185.

Schell, J. (2008). *The art of game design: A book of lenses.* Burlington, MA: Morgan Kaufmann Publishers.

Sheldon, L. (2014). *Character development and storytelling for games* (2nd ed.). Boston, MA: Course Technology Cengage Learning.

Thomas, F., & Johnston, O. (1981, reprint 1997). *The illusion of life: Disney animation.* New York, NY: Hyperion.

Towns, S. G., Fitzgerald, P. T., & Lester, J. C. (1998). Visual emotive communication in lifelike pedagogical agents. In *Proceedings of Intelligent Tutoring Systems 98 Conference* (pp. 474–478). San Antonio, TX: Springer.

Veletsiano, G. (2007). Cognitive and affective benefits of an animated pedagogical agent: Considering contextual relevance and aesthetics. *Journal of Educational Computing Research,* 36(4), 373–377.

Vogler, C. (1998). *The writer's journey: Mythic structures for writers.* Studio City, CA: Michael Wiese Productions.

Walsh, A. S. (2007). Game characters. In C. Bateman (Ed.), *Game writing: Narrative skills for videogames* (pp. 103–126). Boston, MA: Charles River Media.

Zakharov, K., Mitrovic, A., & Johnston, L. (2008). Toward emotionally-intelligent pedagogical agents. *9th International Conference, Intelligent Tutoring Systems 2008* (ITS2008). Montreal, Canada, June 23–27, 2008.

Zebrowitz, L. A. (1997). *Reading faces: Window to the soul?* Boulder, CO: Westview Press.

Zebrowitz, L. A., & Montepare, J. M. (2008). Social psychology face perception: Why appearance matters. *Social and Personality Psychology Compass,* 2(3), 1497–1517.

Media

The Dot and the Line: A Romance in Lower Mathematics (1965)—Chuck Jones and Maurice Noble (directors); Warner Brothers

The Wizard of Oz (1939)—Metro-Goldwyn-Mayer

Harry Potter and the Sorcerer's Stone by J. K. Rowling (1998)—Scholastic

Nancy Drew Games—Her Interactive: http://www.herinteractive.com/

Syberia (2002)—Microids

6
Aesthetics and Environment Design

> ... a plot requires a stage, a space, wherein to develop and time in which to unfold.
> John Dewey, 1934

Within the framework of Dewey's aesthetic experiences, a story requires a setting in which the characters and actions develop and unfold. Game-based learning requires a setting of sorts to provide a context and to situate learning. The purpose of this chapter is to provide a discussion of different sources of environmental design that can provide guidance and insight into the design of environments for game-based learning. This chapter begins with the field of game design and a heuristic of game elements that shape the gameplay space. The focus of this section is on Adams' (2014) outline of game dimensions and includes a discussion of the relevance it provides for learning design and game-based learning. This section is followed by a discussion of experience design in storied spaces, evocative places and narrative environments. This discussion focuses on how differing aesthetics in physical spaces such as museums, cathedrals, casinos and amusement parks can educate, influence behavior and evoke emotions. Following this section is an overview of research about the educational use of virtual space (for game-like learning) and research about virtual world design. Included in this discussion is a heuristic for the integration of architectural elements to aid in navigation and wayfinding for game-based virtual environments.

Game Dimensions

Games are typically situated in some type of setting, whether it be a real-world setting (hide-and-seek), a playing field, a board (chess) or a computer-generated environment (2D, 3D, text descriptions in text-based games). In digital games, the game genre and design of the game setting greatly impact gameplay and the type of immersion experience afforded players (Laramée, 2002; Rollings & Adams, 2003). The environment is the space in which the gameplay occurs, and it forms a type of game world (Adams, 2014). Game environments can be realistic, fantasy, cartoon or some combination, yet the game space comprises more than just the artwork and imagery. The game environment is the culmination of the artwork,

104 • Aesthetics and Environment Design

along with the space design, narrative design and mechanics. While much of the literature about game design addresses game settings as a function of the game artwork or game mechanics, Adams' (2014) outline of the dimensions of game worlds provides a tangible and relevant heuristic for discussing the differing elements that comprise the game world. While Adams' (2014)[1] delineation of the dimensions of game worlds is primarily focused toward game design, his heuristic also provides thorough and accessible strategies for the design of educational games and game-based learning.

According to Adams (2014), a game setting can be defined by *physical, temporal, environmental, emotional* and *ethical* dimensions. The physical dimension defines the physical space in which the player's character/avatar or game pieces move around. This space is defined by the spatial dimension, scale and boundaries. The spatial dimension refers to the dimensions (2D, 2½D or 3D). In the past, 3D might have been thought only the domain of commercial game developers, but educational simulations and virtual worlds such as *Active Worlds, Second Life* and *Open Sims* have made 3D more accessible for different types of game-based learning. The physical dimension also outlines the scale and boundaries, which define the size and edges of the playing environment. For example, the physical dimensions of a digital chessboard for the setting for computer chess are likely to be significantly smaller in scale and have more distinctive boundaries than more elaborate settings such as one found in online games such as *World of Warcraft* or *EverQuest2*. The scale may refer to an absolute scale (e.g., the units of measure in a digital game) and the relative size of objects. For game environments in which the setting is attempting a type of realism, relative scale plays an important role in establishing credibility of the environment. The physical space is also defined by boundaries. For board games such as chess, the boundaries are typically the edge of the board; however, for larger game space settings, the boundaries may be architectural (such as rooms, walls and buildings) or environmental (such as water, land or even planets).

The temporal dimension defines the role of time in the game and how time is treated in the game world (Adams, 2014). It both describes temporal aspects, such as how much time a player has to complete an action, and defines the passage of time within the narrative of the game (nightfall, seasons and time passage). It also outlines the impact time passage will have on gameplay. For example, during several hours of playing the game *Diablo*, a player may cycle through day and night several times; however, the passage of time has little impact upon the game, whereas in a game such as *EverQuest2*, some objects and characters appear only during the day, while others appear at night. In the case of *EverQuest2*, day and night cycles are part of the gameplay experience. How time is implemented relative to the game environment may be represented as variable time or anomalous time. Variable time refers to how time in a game may be implemented at different speeds than real time. For example, in *EverQuest2*, 72 minutes of real time equals one day in *Norrath*, so day and night cycles are more frequent. The temporal dimension also addresses how the duration of time is handled in a game. Typically, in games,

Aesthetics and Environment Design • 105

actions occur much faster in relation to the same actions in the real world. Some games implement anomalous time (e.g., when the amount of time to accomplish two different tasks varies in real life, sometimes, those tasks are performed in the same duration of time in a game).

According to Adams (2014), the environmental dimension delimits both the game environment's appearance and atmosphere. The environmental dimension portrays the game setting as fantasy or realism. It also outlines the historical context, the geographical location and the overall mood and tone to be conveyed through the environment. Although the focus of the environmental dimension is visual, it also outlines the cultural context and supports the backstory of the game. The cultural context depicts how the characters in the game live. The environmental dimension is illustrated through the use of color, lighting and texture, along with the objects and even the sound design. It also extends to the supporting materials such as menus, interface and documentation. The environmental dimension is defined by the amount of detail and the style of the game (e.g., realism, realistic fantasy, futuristic, cartoon, manga, etc.). The environment as defined by the colors, textures, lighting and sound sets the stage and tone of the game. For example, American McGee's game *Alice*, a disturbed and distorted version of Alice from Alice in Wonderland, uses muted colors, distorted objects and dim lighting to induce the eerie and disturbing environment of a nightmare. In contrast, the drab colors and realistic shape and scale of objects in the *Medal of Honor* games convey a sense of realism more consistent with the subject of the game. According to Adams (2014), the degree of details supports greater immersion as long as the details do not impede gameplay. The environmental dimension also includes the background music, ambient sounds, and sounds made by characters and actions in the game.

The emotional dimension (Adams, 2014) describes the emotions of both the characters in the game and the types of emotions that the designer hopes to evoke within the game. The emotional dimension displays and reinforces both character development and the narrative framework of the game. Compelling multidimensional characters with which players can identify, placed in difficult situations that impact the characters emotionally, can help foster emotional proximity and investment for the player. Adams stresses the need to induce emotional resonance to focus games on the needs, goals and priorities of the characters rather than on the vague, overarching fate of "saving the world."

According to Adams (2014), the ethical dimension defines the moral aspects of the game. It is by defining this aspect that characters and roles logically follow rules that govern conventions within the context of the game. The ethical dimension is to some degree determined by the culture and history outlined in the emotional dimension, but there is more to this dimension than merely good vs. evil; it involves moral decision-making within the game and consequences of characters' actions. For example, in the game *America's Army*, shooting a fellow soldier will land a player in a virtual stockade. Where Adams' discussion of the emotional dimension is particularly noteworthy for game-based learning is his

106 • Aesthetics and Environment Design

examination of violence and how the ways in which it is portrayed impact how it is perceived in popular games. Adams notes that there is little consternation about violence when shooting aliens in games like *Space Invaders* or defeating opponents in chess (which is a war game, and when pieces are taken, they are in essence killed); yet in games like *Grand Theft Auto*, game violence often becomes the topic of great debate. According to Adams, the degree of realism is the defining factor in violence, not necessarily the ethics. This argument is particularly relevant for the design of game-based learning in which shooter-type games may be used as a type of "reward."

Relevance for Instructional/Learning Design

The use of settings aligns well with Dewey's notion of place for aesthetic experiences. As Dewey notes in his discussion of having an experience:

> The intimate nature of emotion is manifested in the experience of watching a play on a stage or reading a novel. It attends the development of a plot; and a plot requires a stage, a space, wherein to develop and time in which to unfold.
>
> (Dewey, 1934, p. 43)

Our experiences are grounded in space, some type of environment that provides context and content. Settings also play a role in Parrish's (2009) framework for integrating aesthetics into instructional design. According to Parrish, context plays a significant role in the learning experience:

> whether one accommodates or creates it, context must contribute to the cohesiveness of the learning experience by reinforcing all its components . . . insight can be gained from exploring ways to create context to enhance learning.
>
> (Parrish, 2009, p. 517)

In traditional instructional design models, context was often discussed in terms of Gagne's *conditions of learning* (Gagne, 1985; Gagne, Briggs & Wager, 1992). However, settings and scenarios are strategies that are employed in a variety of instructional methods and activities and in different degrees. Problem-based learning (Barrows, 1986; Duffy & Cunningham, 1996; Savery & Duffy, 1995), project-based learning (Blumenfeld et al., 1991; Thomas, 2000), anchored instruction (Bransford, Sherwood, Hasselbring, Kinzer & Williams, 1990; CTGV, 1990, 1993), scenario-based learning (Agostinho, Meek & Herrington, 2005), WebQuests (Dodge, 1995) and case studies (Ertmer & Quinn, 1999; Julian, Larsen & Kinzie, 1999) are methods that often employ the use of settings as a context to support learning. In many of these methods, the setting of the activity or scenario serves as a macro-context for embedding learning in complex and/or realistic environments (Duffy & Cunningham, 1996; Jonassen, 1999; Lave & Wenger, 1991; Perkins, 1992). Settings can play a significant role in cognitive apprenticeships and in framing situated learning. Situated learning is based on the model of situated cognition in which "knowledge is contextually situated and is fundamentally influenced by the activity, context, and culture in which it is used" (McLellan, 1996, p. 6). According to Brown, Collins and Duguid (1996), traditional schooling has made a practice of separating what students learn from how it's used. Situated learning takes context into account. Knowledge is both situated within a context and culture and developed through ongoing authentic activity.

Although settings to varying degrees play a role in various instructional models, rarely are settings as fully realized and supported as those found in gaming environments. Strategies for environment design such as Adams' (2014) game dimensions may be of great use in the design of game-based learning (digital and non-digital) environments, but could also provide insight into the design of traditional classroom-based learning environments by providing guides for delineating various dimensions to create a rich context for learning. Much of the research about the design of game-based learning has focused on learning design, with little discussion of aesthetics; however, much of the allure of popular games is due to the environment, both for gameplay and for supporting immersion. Educators and instructional designers are not game designers, but categorization of aesthetic elements such of those outlined by Adams (2014) provides a heuristic for creating a rich context for game-based learning.

Experience Design and Physical Spaces: Storied Spaces, Evocative Places and Narrative Environments

Game design provides great guides for how to fully realize a setting for game-based learning, but there are other sources of information as well. Whether it be a board, a screen, an immersive 3D environment or even a text-based description, these settings constitute "spaces"—spaces for experiences. As such, there are insightful resources for looking at how the design of space conveys knowledge, impacts behavior and provides a setting for experiences. Experience design provides insight into the types of components that contribute to creating "experiences" that are memorable and emotionally engaging. Various fields of interior and space design provide insight into how the design of environments such as museums, cathedrals, casinos, retail space and amusement parks educate, impact behavior, navigate and use design elements (light, color, sound) to provide settings for experiences.

Experience Design

"Experience design," a term often used in various fields of design, is defined as follows: a shift in the practice of design away from "increasing and improving functionality" toward focusing on the quality of the user experience

108 • Aesthetics and Environment Design

with the duration of engagement and design that is culturally relevant, functional and durable (Aarts & Marzano, 2003).

The term "experience design" is often used in relation to creating processes, products and environments that have an emotional impact on user experiences (Shedroff, 2001). Often used in marketing, the term is used to describe the focus on creating customer experiences that are memorable and that resonate. There are various physical environments that provide insight into how physical space design fosters experiences.

Storied Spaces: Museums and Cathedrals

Museums have a long history of being designed spaces that combine sensory experiences within a storied context (Falk, Dierking & Semmel, 2012; Wyman, Smith, Meyers & Godfrey, 2011). In addition to being places to store and display artifacts, museums also educate both conventionally and through the design and integration of information. Good museum exhibit design motivates and arouses curiosity through the placement of artifacts in a storied context that helps the visitor relate to the artifact and the culture. Information in various forms (text, audio, music) educate without overwhelming the visitor. Museum exhibit design integrates the physical space and the content through the use of hierarchal arrangements of artifacts and patterns of placement that help with navigating visitors, yet also providing space and time for contemplation. Museum exhibition design must also take into account various vantage points of viewers (standing, walking, and sitting) (Carliner, 2001). Both exhibition design and the museum space design provide guidance in how space can educate. Exhibition designers are well versed in immersing visitors in the content by engaging visitors in the story of the artifacts or topic. They do so by progressive layers, including the introduction to the gallery, theme labels and objects labels. Each successive layer draws the visitor into the "story" of the exhibit (Carliner, 2001; Wyman et al., 2011). Good exhibition design allows visitors to first skim information, and then move through progressive layers into more discrete object-based information. This both provides context and allows for choice. Storytelling techniques of beginning, middle and end provide a framework for guiding visitors to and through artifacts. Additionally, literary devices such as juxtaposition are used to maintain and reinforce the story. Juxtaposition is the act of placing two contrasting elements together or nearby to illustrate contrast, invite comparison or even display concurrent timelines. Exhibits also include types of compelling characters (in various forms) to make the story relatable (Carliner, 2001; Chittenden, 2011). Museum design provides insight into how physical space provides places for reflection, education and social functions. The lobby of many museums often sets the stage for the exhibition and provides the initial layer of theme. It also serves as a space for reflection as well as providing a social function (Mortensen, Rudloff & Vestergaard, 2014).

Aesthetics and Environment Design • **109**

Similarly, the design of gothic cathedrals provides an inspiring example of space designed to create experiences that are simultaneously sensorial, emotional and educational (Wilson, 1990). The very architecture of many classic cathedrals was designed to evoke emotions of awe, piety and holiness. Often referred to as "the poor man's bible," cathedrals were spaces designed not only as sacred experiences but also as environments to help educate a largely illiterate populace. Through the use of scale, shape, sculpture and pictures (stained glass), the interior of many cathedrals provide depictions of religious stories. Should a parishioner's attention stray from the liturgy of mass, his or her eyes would encounter various sculptures and stained glass images depicting religious stories. These depictions were purposefully designed to educate rather than distract. Often, elaborate stained glass windows contained an entire story composed of individual panels depicting parts of a story. While the windows, along with other artwork of many cathedrals, provided a means to educate illiterate parishioners through the use of imagery, the sheer scale of the architecture, of being a very small being in a very large space, fosters emotions of awe and reverence.

Evocative Places

While museums and gothic cathedrals are examples of environments that are designed for reflection, education and devotion, Las Vegas casinos and retail environments are also places in which the architecture and interior design is designed to evoke emotions and impact behavior, though perhaps in ways contrary to museums and cathedrals. The use of color, sound and navigation within casinos is legendary for creating sensorial experiences that are both evocative and seemingly timeless (Mayer & Johnson, 2003; Johnson, Mayer & Champaner, 2004; Lio & Rody, 2009). The use of color and faster music tempo can impact the pace at which players gamble, and the use of scents can impact the duration of gambling activity (Cornett, 2011). At one time, the prevailing model of casino design consisted of low ceilings, gaming consoles that blocked sightlines, complex mazes of machines and a notable lack of natural light and clocks. The prevailing design was to trap players. However, shifting notions of design have greatly impacted the art of casino design, and opulence and catering to players' experience is now reshaping casino design. Design in which players become part of, or characters in, the opulence is proving to greatly impact gambling behavior (Lehrer, 2012). More contemporary design has focused more on creating experiences that subtly impact behavior. Situating visitors in a lavish environment fosters feelings of opulence and entitlement. In a sense, visitors to such casinos become cast in the role of characters that belong in great wealth. Feelings of opulence and entitlement may perhaps translate into behavior of fiscal abandon.

The field of retail has also begun to leverage the notion of creating experiences that evoke emotion and impact behavior (Sherman, Mathur & Smith, 1997; Bitner, 1992). Research in the field of marketing contends that subtle environmental cues

110 • Aesthetics and Environment Design

or "atmospherics" such as lighting, color and design can impact consumer behavior (Dijksterhuis, Smith, van Baaren & Wigboldus, 2005; Turley & Milliman, 2000).

Narrative Environments: Disney

Environments that are well noted for experiential design are theme parks. Theme parks provide examples of how space can be designed to foster feelings of fun and fantasy. There are many legendary amusement parks (Coney Island, Busch Gardens, Dollywood), but none as legendary as Disney. Disneyland and Disney World are examples of how designed spaces foster experiences within a narrative environment (Jenkins, 2002; Weinstein, 1992). Disneyland[2] is comprised of a series of themed sectors that include *Main Street USA, Adventureland, New Orleans Square, Critter Country, Frontierland, Fantasyland, Mickey's Toontown* and *Tomorrowland.* Each of the themed areas is unique in appearance and character, yet, at the same time, they each blend into one another seamlessly.

Former Disney designer Don Carson (2000) provides much insight into the elements that foster unique "experiences" for visitors at Disneyland. In an article entitled "Environmental Storytelling: Creating Immersive 3D Worlds Using Lessons Learned from the Theme Park Industry," Carson outlines the key aspects of environmental storytelling that help immerse visitors in the Disney experience, and he discusses how they can be adapted for virtual environments and games. He offers three main rules that focus on place, role and actions. First and foremost, Carson stresses the importance of playing upon visitors' own experiences of the physical world and their knowledge of themes and settings. Carson uses the example of the ride *Pirates of the Caribbean* and how Disney incorporates all elements of our perceptions of pirates based primarily on depictions from movies and television. The theme of pirates is consistent and fully realized. Carson advocates leveraging the expectations initiated by a theme, emphasizing the theme and fulfilling expectations about that theme. All aspects of the environment should support the theme because elements that are not part of the theme will break the willing suspension of disbelief. Carson also advocates creating environments in which the audience/visitor always knows where they are—not always in terms of the overall world, but that they have a sense of the space/room that they occupy. Finally, Carson recommends providing clues for your audience to always understand who they are in the space and their role in that space.

Similarly, Scott Rogers (2009), game designer and now *Imagineer* for Disney, provides much insight into how design elements of Disneyland can inform the design of games and virtual environments. Rogers (2009) reinforces Carson's (2000) message of adopting a theme and remaining consistent with that theme. Rogers' (2009) outline provides an overall schematic for how to approach the design of environments based on the overall structure of Disneyland. Disneyland is a large environment that includes a variety of sectors or neighborhoods (e.g., *Fantasyland, Tomorrowland, Main Street USA*, etc.). There is a hierarchal arrangement in Disneyland that, starting from the top down, includes the world, land, attractions

Aesthetics and Environment Design • **111**

and experiences. In the example of Disneyland, Rogers characterizes Disneyland as the world. Lands within the world include *Fantasyland, New Orleans Square, Mickey's Toontown, Tomorrowland,* etc. Attractions are embedded in the "lands." For example, *Space Mountain* is a well-known attraction in *Tomorrowland,* and the *Haunted Mansion* is a popular attraction in *New Orleans Square.* Finally, Rogers advocates clearly defining the type of experience that visitors have moment to moment (e.g., feelings of nostalgia while strolling through *Main Street USA* and feelings of daring adventure while riding on the *Indiana Jones Adventure* ride). Like Carson (2000), Rogers (2009) advocates using the themes projected through the narrative to create an immersive experience.

Both Rogers (2009) and Carson (2000) note the importance of navigation in creating an experience. According to Rogers (2009), Walt Disney used *weenies* as a motivational aid for navigation. *Weenies*[3] are what Walt Disney called structures and attractions that serve as focal points of interest that beckon visitors to an area. Weenies placed in strategic locations serve to reinforce the narrative while also supporting visitor exploration. Attractions throughout the park serve as both weenies to draw visitors to locations as well as landmarks to help situate visitors in space. Both Carson (2000) and Rogers (2009) also stress the role of paths for navigation. Within the various sectors of Disneyland, there may be many paths for getting to the same location. As Carson (2000) notes, this allows each visitor to create his/her own unique experience and chart his/her own course through the park. It also allows visitors to select from direct paths or to explore through more circuitous routes. According to Rogers (2009), the variety of paths also serves to reinforce the theme and to provide hidden opportunities for the more adventurous explorers by providing hidden pockets of small interactive activities. According to both Carson (2000) and Rogers (2009), there are key elements built within and integrated into the environment that serve as subtle clues for navigation. For example, tree branches may be strategically designed to point in particular directions. Similarly, environmental elements such as rocks and boulders may be subtly shaped or arranged to guide directions in place of signs.

Both Carson (2000) and Rogers (2009) note the importance of how lighting is used in Disneyland. According to Rogers, light serves as a navigational aid by highlighting landmarks and key locations. For example, the infamous *Sleeping Beauty's Castle* serves as the main landmark throughout the entire park. It is well lighted during the evening, making it an accessible landmark. During the daytime, when lighting is not as effective, the effect of lighting is somewhat simulated by the use of the light colors of the castle that, in contrast to the rest of the environment, create a type of highlight. Lighting is also used to direct attention throughout the various attractions. Because our attention is drawn to light, key spotlights and subtle shifts of lighting guide our attention and reinforce the different themes. Lighting also serves as a navigational and behavioral aid. Because humans are drawn toward lighted areas, Disneyland uses light to subtly signal attendees' attention and to subliminally guide attendees toward the exit as the park closing time nears.

112 • Aesthetics and Environment Design

Although this review merely touches upon the vast knowledge of design that an in-depth study of museums, cathedrals, casinos and, most certainly, Disneyland might reveal, what is relevant to this review is the types of elements that foster emotion and contribute to experiences. Museum exhibition design provides insight into how an exhibit tells a story and the layers that reveal that story. Cathedrals illustrate how an environment can educate but also evoke emotional responses by being situated in a space. Similarly, the design of contemporary casinos can also evoke emotional response that impact behavior. Certainly, there are a great many untapped aspects of design to be found in an in-depth study of Disneyland that would yield much insight about education and emotional design, and this review merely touches the surface; however, what is common in the aesthetic design of these environments is that they all evoke emotion, they all educate on some level and, most importantly, story plays a defining role in creating an experience.

Design of Virtual Environments

Museums, cathedrals, casinos and amusement parks provide guidance about the aesthetics of physical space design that foster emotions, but there is much research about the design of virtual space that provides insight for the design of game-based learning. There are several areas of research of virtual environments that can inform design. Research into educational virtual reality and virtual worlds provides insight into interaction and engagement. The application of architectural and environmental design provides great insight into wayfinding and navigation strategies for virtual space design, and graphic design and game art provide insight into how color, shape and texture impact participants.

Virtual Reality and Virtual Worlds

Learning

Although real-world settings provide much valuable guidance for environmental and space design and how it impacts behavior, virtual worlds and virtual reality (VR) provide insight into the potential that virtual environments offer for learning (Dickey, 2003). The educational advantages of using VR-type settings are that 3D environments allow learners to view objects and environments from multiple perspectives, to experiment without real-world repercussions and to participate in active learning (Bricken, 1990; Dede, Salzman, Loftin & Sprague, 1999; Dede, 1995). The fact that learners are able to interact with virtual objects may lead to a better conceptual understanding of learning content and context (Bricken & Byrne, 1994).

A variety of educational initiatives has incorporated virtual environments both as a supplement to traditional classroom and extracurricular activities and as a primary medium for distance education (Barab, Hay, Barnett & Squire, 2001; Corbit & DeVarco, 2000; Dickey, 2003). Bers (1999) and Bers and Cassell (1999, 2000) used virtual environments to study how children construct identity

Aesthetics and Environment Design • 113

and how the use of storytelling aided in their constructed identities. Barab et al. (2001) used virtual worlds as a support in fostering undergraduate students' understanding of astronomy within a constructivist-based participatory learning environment. They found that virtual worlds can be used effectively as a tool to foster rich understandings. Bers and Cassell (1999) created a virtual world setting within a constructivist paradigm to study how children construct identity and the role of storytelling in identity construction. Bailey and Moar (2001, 2002) used the Vertex project to explore the use of virtual worlds within a constructivist paradigm and found that virtual worlds fostered collaboration, communication and storytelling with students 9–11 years old. Dickey's (2003, 2005, 2011) research into educational initiatives developed within communities of virtual worlds revealed that virtual world applications support a constructivist perspective by affording real-time communication along with a visual environment and resources to support collaboration. Despite the notoriety of *Second Life* in popular media, research is just beginning to emerge about the use of *Second Life* for education (Baker, Wentz & Woods, 2009; De Lucia, Francese, Passero & Tortora, 2009; Franklin, Mayles, Liu & Chelburg, 2008; Gillen, 2009; Good, Howland & Thackray, 2008; Jarmon, Traphagan & Mayrath, 2008; Yee, Bailenson, Urbanek, Chang & Merget, 2007). Of the emerging research, Franklin, Mayles, Liu and Chelburg (2008) found that the use of a virtual world as an authoring platform for student-created educational games was motivational for the students. Gillen (2009) used *Second Life* with students of similar ages to show how students make meaning and construct knowledge in multi-modal environments.

Design

Research of VR reveals some problems associated with the design of 3D environments that may potentially impact learning. Researchers have noted that users sometimes experience a type of disorientation in 3D environments and have difficulty navigating the environment (Darken & Siebert, 1996; Jackson & Winn, 1999; Salzman, Dede, Loftin & Chen, 1999; Dede et al., 1999; Marsh & Wright, 2000; Dede, 2003; Dickey, 2004, 2011). Problems associated with disorientation and wayfinding include identifying a specific place, relocating previously visited places and opportunities for fostering users' construction of cognitive maps of the environment. This concern is compounded when a virtual environment is being used for education and even more so when used as a medium for distance learning.

Various strategies have been explored for navigation in VR. Darken and Sibert (1996) propose the use of environmental cues to support wayfinding and navigation in large-scale virtual environments. They explored the use of overlaying semitransparent virtual maps and grids across the environment to aid users in searching large virtual environments. Those authors alternately proposed using cinematography conventions to aid users in wayfinding and navigation in virtual environments. Marsh and Wright (2000) argue that a real-world setting is

114 • Aesthetics and Environment Design

full of visual cues in the forms of shapes, objects, textures, patterns and details that aid in wayfinding. This level of visual information is difficult to achieve in a virtual environment because a high level of graphic detail imposes a great strain on processing and refresh rates. Marsh and Wright (2000) propose the use of cinematography conventions such as exit and entry points (doors, halls, paths), points of view (user's avatar looking off-screen) and the use of partial framing (placing objects/avatars partially off-screen to indicate that space exists beyond the screen). While both Darken and Sibert (1996) and Marsh and White (2000) offer intriguing design modifications, these modifications require a degree of control over the programming of a virtual environment. This level of control may not be available for educators and instructional designers wishing to implement virtual environments while restricted to using commercial applications.

Although work by VR theorists and researchers is insightful for the design of game-based environments, most of this work is based on models of information processing. This work does not purport to be more, and I by no means wish to indicate that it is in any way lacking. However, there are other lenses through which to view design and to provide insight into how aesthetics can be used to inform the design of virtual space for game-based learning. Heim (2001) proposed the Chinese art of environmental arrangement, feng shui, as a model for the design of flow (navigation) of a virtual environment. According to Heim (2001), feng shui addresses the weaknesses of cognitive systems theory by providing a model that supports qualitative associations in spatial awareness and incorporates the essence of flow or movement through space and time. While Heim's (2001) proposition of designing virtual environments that accommodate flow is compelling, guidelines and models from the field of architectural design provide insight about the use of architectural and environmental design aesthetics that can inform the design of game-based learning.

Navigation and Wayfinding: Virtual Space

Charitos' (1997) work on the design of virtual environments to support wayfinding and navigation offers insight and guidance for the design of game-based learning environments. Charitos advocates integrating architectural and environmental design strategies for supporting wayfinding and navigation within virtual environments. According to Charitos (1997), objects and elements we use in navigating our way through the physical world can also be effective devices for virtual environments. Objects such as *landmarks, signs, boundaries* and *thresholds,* and elements such as *paths* and *intersections,* which are commonly used physical environments, can serve as wayfinding guides and aids to help reduce disorientation and establish a sense of place in virtual environments. To some degree, Charitos' (1997) proposition addresses issues raised by both Darken and Sibert (1996) and Marsh and White (2000) by outlining different types of environmental cues. Charitos' (1997) recommendations are relevant to the design of game-based learning environments because he provides pragmatic criteria for

Aesthetics and Environment Design • **115**

objects and elements that can be easily implemented by educators and instructional designers.

Landmarks

A landmark is a prominent object in the environment that serves as a type of navigational guide by marking fixed points in space (Passini, 1984). According to Lynch (1960), a landmark is a point of reference, external from a viewer, and marked by physical characteristics that distinguish it from the surrounding environment. Characteristics that help distinguish a landmark include size, scale, spatial prominence, color and foreground/background contrast. Examples of landmarks include the Empire State Building in New York, the Tower Bridge in London and even Sleeping Beauty's Castle in Disneyland. Lynch's (1960) and Appleyard's (1969) respective work outlines criteria for distinguishing landmarks in an urban setting. These criteria include highly visible objects with prominent physical features that contrast with the surrounding area in form and style.

Signs

Signs play a primary role in aiding wayfinding in the environment by providing key information necessary for decision-making. According to Passini (1984), the classification of signs includes *directional signs, identification signs* and *reassurance signs*. Signs may convey information verbally through the use of text or nonverbally through the use of images (Arthur & Passini, 1992). *Directional* signs specify the direction toward a location, object or event by using either verbal information (text), nonverbal information (symbols) or a combination of both. *Identification* signs identify a place, object or even a person. Unlike directional signs, identification signs mark destinations rather than directions. *Reassurance* signs function as checkpoints during the wayfinding process. They provide reassurance to users that the chosen path will lead to the desired destination. Examples of directional signs can be found on highways reminding drivers of both direction and upcoming locales. Reassurance signs are often found in locations such as college campuses and in hospitals to reassure travelers of their progress toward their destination. Signs often appear at intersections to aid in decision-making about direction and route.

Boundaries

In a real-world setting, boundaries construct and define a space. Boundaries may take the form of something solid, such as a wall, or they may be constructed of something formless, such as light or regions of contrast (Lynch, 1960). Lynch refers to boundaries as "edges," but Charitos' (1997) nomenclature provides a more descriptive term for elements that demarcate one area from another. Examples of boundaries include walls that define a room or a building, hedges, curbs and partitions. The scale of a boundary can subtly communicate the purpose for designated places within an environment. Edges that are the most visually prominent are those that are "continuous in form and impenetrable to cross,"

116 • Aesthetics and Environment Design

such as lakes or rivers (Lynch, 1960, p. 62). Charitos (1997) advocates the use of collision detection in virtual environments to help establish solidarity and reinforce a boundary.

Thresholds

According to Charitos (1997), thresholds are some type of object that "signifies the transition between spaces." Examples of thresholds include openings such as doors and windows. Charitos argues that thresholds may visually appear as boundaries, but they lack the solidity of a boundary. Charitos recommends that thresholds be used to signify the transition from one space to another or the beginning and end of space. In virtual environments, devices such as teleporters or transporters can serve as thresholds because they shift the user from one setting or location to another in the virtual environment.

Paths

We encounter paths of many kinds as we navigate through environments in our daily lives. Paths take the form of sidewalks, streets, roads, railways, canals and even worn areas or paths in the landscape. According to Charitos (1997), paths are spaces that imply movement. The implication of movement is made evident through both formal qualities (texture, materials, lighting and structural elements) and spatial arrangement (length and breadth as distinguished by formal qualities). Paths function as navigation devices linking various places. Lynch (1960) notes that environmental elements (e.g., houses) are built along paths (e.g., roads) and arranged in relation to paths.

Intersections

According to Charitos (1997), intersections are points along paths where decisions must be made. For example, a crossroads in which two roads intersect is an intersection and requires travelers to make a choice. Charitos (1997) maintains that because interactions are decision points, it is imperative that they be considered a discrete spatial element. He suggests placing landmarks at major intersections because it is likely that the presence of a landmark will add to the individual qualities of the intersection and foster users' conceptual mapping of the environment.

Visual Design

Game design provides much insight into shaping the dimensions for game-based learning. Real-world environments provide insight into the design of space to evoke emotions, educate and impact behavior. Research in VR and virtual environments outlines the benefits and affordances of virtual environments for teaching and learning and provides insight into designing environments that accommodate the unique affordances of virtual environments. This research provides great insight about how to shape an environment, setting or context for learning.

However, the environment is more than mere space and pathways; situated in an environment, setting or context are elements, both environmental and visual, that visually construct a place. 3D, 2D and text-based games are filled with objects with which players interact. Depending upon the platform, style and medium, game art and visual design may include full scale cinemagraphics, 3D animation and a soundtrack. Rarely do educators have access to the types of resources and talent of game companies, architects and interior designers, and theme park designers, but tools such as virtual worlds, Web editors and even game design platforms provide accessible means for creating visual game-based environments. Additionally, there are elements that transcend mediums of physical space and virtual space (3D and 2D) that can also be integrated into text-based environments to aid in the design of game-based learning. Color, texture and light are important aspects of visual design that not only impact the aesthetics of space but also communicate and influence behavior by guiding focus.

The selection of colors can create a tone and mood for an environment. Bright colors convey a sense of playfulness, whereas muted colors might convey a more serious environment. Color can be used to reinforce the theme/narrative and can also provide elements of contrast to focus attention on some object or aspect in the environment. Contrasting warm colors (red, yellow, and orange) against cool colors (blue and violet) can focus attention and highlight objects and locations. Although the perception of colors is shaped by culture and it is difficult to make sweeping claims about what a color conveys, it is generally acknowledged that cool colors tend to recede and warm colors seem to move toward the viewer. *Sleeping Beauty's Castle* is well known in Disneyland and certainly meets all of Lynch's (1960) and Charitos' (1997) criteria for a landmark. As Rogers (2009) notes, the colors play an important role in the visual display. In the evenings, the castle is lighted and plays a prominent role in the landscape; however, lighting does not have the same impact during the daytime. Instead, the fact that the castle is lighter in color than most of the surrounding area provides a type of highlighting that allows the castle to be a prominent landmark during the day.

Lighting can also play an instrumental role in reinforcing themes and guiding attention. Our visual attention is drawn to light, and this is often used in games, theater and film to focus our attention on what the designer or director wants us to view. It is also used (particularly in magic) to divert our attention. Using variations of lighting can help spotlight and guide attention. The type and level of lighting helps establish the mood and tone. The careful use of spotlights and shadows can elicit feelings of trepidation, whereas brightly lighted environments can be inviting, though perhaps with less interest. Similarly, the use of textures can also reinforce themes and guide attention. According to Carson (2000, p. 3), color, lighting and texture can "fill an audience with excitement or dread." Carson advocates using textures and details to guide attention and to draw audiences into a scene. Textures also play a significant role in the visual design of an environment. Both Carson (2000) and Rogers (2009) note the importance

118 • Aesthetics and Environment Design

of textures for reinforcing theme and creating mood and tone for the theme. Textures provide details that inform visitors about the environment. Textures can convey the age and provide subtle information about whom or what may inhabit an environment.

Summary

The purpose of this chapter is to provide a discussion of aesthetic elements of environment from different perspectives with the goal of informing the design of game-based learning. This chapter is divided into three main sections: game dimension, physical space and virtual environments. The intent is to present the information from a very loose top-down perspective. The chapter began with an outline of game dimensions typically found in computer and video games (Rollings & Adams, 2003; Adams, 2014) and the relevance of outlining dimensions for game-based learning. The purpose of using this as a point of departure in a discussion about environments is that choices about dimensions will impact the shape and design of the game environment and setting. Following the discussion of dimensions is a discussion of the role of aesthetics in the design of space to suggest how aesthetic choice impacts experience in space. The discussion of space is divided into two parts: physical space (storied, evocative and narrative) and virtual space (VR and virtual environments). Within each section is a discussion of experience in both types of space. It should be noted that much of the research conducted about virtual world design has been from a cognitive perspective of information processing, and while this research is certainly informative, it does not address the impact of aesthetics in the design, but it does provide insight into the design of space. Following the review of VR and virtual worlds is a section about the use of real-world architectural elements to shape virtual space. This chapter concludes with one last section entitled Guidance for Game-based Learning Design, which provides an outline of game dimensions, a summary of findings from physical space design and an outline of architectural elements. This final section is not intended to be a blueprint for the design of environments for game-based learning, but instead to provide support and guidance.

Guidance for Game-based Learning Design

Although there are many great guides for game design, Adams' (2014) outline of game world dimensions provides a helpful way to frame the design of space for game-based learning. Most game worlds comprise five dimensions—physical, temporal, environmental, emotional and ethical—that support and impact gameplay. The careful blending of all five of these dimensions helps foster a sense of suspended disbelief and provides players with a sense of immersive engagement in the gameplay environment. The following section provides an overview of each of Adams' dimensions and how they relate to game design and game-based learning.

Aesthetics and Environment Design • **119**

Environment Dimensions

1. **Physical Dimension:** The physical dimension defines the physical space in which the player's character/avatar or game pieces move around. This dimension is comprised of scale and boundaries, which define the size and edges of the playing environment. The physical dimensions are determined by both the narrative and the scale and scope of the game and are part of the physical game space.
2. **Temporal Dimension:** The temporal dimension defines the role of time in the game. It not only describes temporal aspects, such as how much time a player has to complete an action, but also defines whether the game will include nightfall, seasons or time passage, as well as delineates the impact that time passage will have on gameplay. The temporal dimensions are defined by the narrative.
3. **Environmental Dimensions:** The environmental dimension defines both the game setting appearance and atmosphere. It characterizes the game setting as fantasy or realism, the historical context, the geographical location, and the overall mood and tone. The environmental dimension is manifested in the use of color and lighting; the shape, size and placement of objects within the environment; and the supporting materials, such as menus and documentation. The environmental dimensions are defined by the narrative and help reinforce the narrative.
4. **Emotional Dimensions:** The emotional dimension describes the emotions of both the characters in the game and the types of emotions that the design hopes to invoke within the player. The emotional dimensions are conveyed through the narrative, characters and physical design.
5. **Ethical Dimensions:** The ethical dimension defines the moral aspects of the game. It is by defining this aspect that characters and roles logically follow rules that govern conventions within the context of the game. The ethical dimensions are conveyed through the narrative and characters and help reinforce the narrative.

Physical Space Design

After determining the dimensions, it may be helpful to consider the type of emotional, educational and behavioral aspects that may be manifested or elicited through the design of the environment. The following is an overview of the findings about aesthetics design of physical space.

Physical Spaces: Education and Emotion

1. *Museums*
    *   Storied space: beginning, middle and end
    *   Layers of information, beginning with general theme and progressing into greater depth throughout the exhibition
    *   Juxtaposition
    *   Choice

120 • Aesthetics and Environment Design

- Spaces for reflection and social functions
2. *Cathedrals*
   - Storied space: narrative conveyed through the use of images and sculptures
   - Scale: evocative, inducing feelings of awe and reverence
3. *Casinos*
   - Storied space: story of opulence
   - Role: visitor is cast in the role of someone who fits comfortably within opulence
4. *Amusement parks (Disneyland)*
   - Storied space: overarching "Disney" narrative
   - Themed space: consistent
   - Activities support theme
   - Navigation and wayfinding: individualized, but guided
   - Weenies to focus attention

Architectural Design and Wayfinding

After determining the function of the space, the following provides guidance for navigation and wayfinding in virtual environments.

1. *Landmarks*
   - Prominent objects that serve as navigational aids
   - Unique characteristics
   - Contrast against background environment
   - Distinguish in features (size, scale, spatial prominence, color)
2. *Signs*
   - *Directional* signs specify the direction toward a location or object.
   - *Identification* signs identify a place, object or even a person.
   - *Reassurance* signs function as checkpoints.
3. *Boundaries*
   - Define a space (wall, hedge, curbs)
   - Demark one area from another
4. *Thresholds*
   - Transitions between spaces
   - Openings such as doors, windows
5. *Paths*
   - Spaces that imply movement
   - Link various areas
     o Sidewalks
     o Streets
     o Roads
     o Railways
     o Canals, etc.

6. *Intersections*
   - Crossroads: points where decisions must be made
   - Directional signs provide guidance

Notes

1. Much of this information also appears in Rollings and Adams' (2003) *Andrew Rollings and Ernest Adams on Game Design* and in *Fundamentals of Game Design* (Rollings & Adams, 2006). However, for the purposes of brevity, I will be referring to the most recent version of *Fundamentals of Game Design* (Adams, 2014).
2. Although the content of this discussion extends to Disney World as well as Disneyland, for the purposes of brevity and my own experiences, I center this discussion on the original Disneyland.
3. According to Disney lore, Walt Disney used the example of how his dog would follow wherever Walt Disney led when tempted with a hotdog wiener (weenie).

References

Aarts, E. H. L., & Marzano, S. (2003). *The new everyday: Views on ambient intelligence.* Rotterdam, The Netherlands: 010 Publishers.

Adams, E. (2014*). Fundamentals of game design* (3rd ed.). Indianapolis, IN: New Riders.

Agostinho, S., Meek, J., & Herrington, J. (2005). Design methodology for the implementation and evaluation of a scenario-based online learning environment. *Journal of Interactive Learning Research,* 16(3), 229–242.

Appleyard, D. (1969). Why are buildings known? *Environment and Behavior,* 1, 131–159.

Arthur, P., & Passini, R. (1992). *Wayfinding: People, signs and architecture.* New York, NY: McGraw Hill.

Bailey, F. & Moar, M. (2001). Walking with avatars. *Paper presented at CADE 2001 (Computers in Art and Design Education).* Glasgow School of Art, April 9 – 11.

Bailey, F., & Moar, M. (2002). The Vortex Project: Exploring the creative use of shared 3D virtual worlds in the primary (K-12) classroom. Paper presented at SIGGRAPH 2002, San Antonio. Published in *ACM SIGGRAPH 2002 Conference Abstracts and Applications,* pp. 52–54.

Baker, S. C., Wentz, R. K., & Woods, M. M. (2009). Using virtual worlds in education: Second Life' as an educational tool. *Teaching of Psychology,* 36(1), 59–64.

Barab, S. A., Hay, K. E., Barnett, M. G., & Squire, K. (2001). Constructing virtual worlds: Tracing the historical development of learner practices/understandings. *Cognition and Instruction,* 19(1), 47–94.

Barrows, H. S. (1986). A taxonomy of problem-based learning methods. *Medical Education,* 20, 481–486.

Bers, M. (1999). Zora: A graphical multi-user environment to share stories about the self. *Proceedings of the International Conference on Computer-Supported Collaborative Learning (CSCL'99).* Stanford, CA, December 1999.

Bers, M., & Cassell, J. (1999). Interactive storytelling systems for children: Using technology to explore language and identity. *Journal of Interactive Learning Research,* 9(2), 603–609.

Bers, M., & Cassell, J. (2000). Children as designers of interactive storytellers: "Let Me Tell You a Story about Myself . . . " In K. Dautenhahn (Ed.), *Human cognition and social agent technology* (pp. 61–83). Philadelphia, PA: John Benjamins Publishing Company.

Bitner, M. J. (1992). Servicescapes: The impact of physical surroundings on customers and employees. *Journal of Marketing,* 56(2), 57–71.

Blumenfeld, P. C., Soloway, E., Marx, R. W., Krajcik, J. S., Guzdial, M., & Palinscar, A. (1991). Motivating project-based learning: Sustaining the doing, supporting the learning. *Educational Psychologist,* 26, 369–398.

Bransford, J. D., Sherwood, R. D., Hasselbring, T. S., Kinzer, C. K., & Williams, S. M. (1990). Anchored instruction: Why we need it and how technology can help. In D. Nix & R. Sprio (Eds.), *Cognition, education and multimedia* (pp. 115–141). Hillsdale, NJ: Lawrence Erlbaum Associates.

122 • Aesthetics and Environment Design

Bricken, W. (1990). *Learning in virtual reality* (Memorandum M-90–5). Seattle, WA: Human Interface Technology Laboratory.

Bricken, M., & Byrne, C. M. (1994). Summer students in virtual reality: A pilot study on educational applications of virtual reality technology. In A. Wexelblat (Ed.), *Virtual reality: Applications and explorations* (pp. 199–218). Boston, MA: Academic Press.

Brown, J. S., Collins, A., & Duguid, P. (1996). Situated cognition and culture of learning. In H. McLellan (Ed.), *Situated learning perspectives* (pp. 19–44). Englewood Cliffs, NJ: Educational Technology Publications.

Carliner, S. (2001). Modeling information for three-dimensional space: Lessons learned from museum exhibit design. *Technical Communication*, 48(1), 66–81.

Carson, D. (2000). Environmental storytelling: Creating immersive 3D worlds using lessons learned from the theme park industry. *Gamasutra*. Retrieved November 15, 2013, from http://www.gamasutra.com/features/20000301/carson_pfv.htm

Charitos, D. (1997). Designing space in virtual environments for aiding wayfinding behavior. *The Fourth UK VR-SIG Conference*, Brunel University, November 1, 1997.

Chittenden, T. (2011). The cook, the marquis, his wife, and her maids: The use of dramatic characters in Peter Greenaway's *Peopling the Palaces* as a way of interpreting historic buildings. *Curator: The Museum Journal*, 54(3), 261–278.

Cognition and Technology Group at Vanderbilt (CTGV). (1990). Anchored instruction and its relationship to situated cognition. *Educational Researcher*, 19(6), 2–10.

Cognition and Technology Group at Vanderbilt (CTGV). (1993). Anchored instruction and situated cognition revisited. *Educational Technology*, 33(3), 52–70.

Corbit, M., & DeVarco, B. (2000). SciCentr and BioLearn: Two 3-D implementations of CVE science museums. In E. Churchill and M. Reddy (Eds.), *Proceedings of the Third International Conference on Collaborative Virtual Environments* (pp. 65–71). New York, NY: Association for Computing Machinery.

Cornett, K. (2011). The psychology behind casino design. *Timeout Chicago*, August 24, 2011. Retrieved from http://www.timeout.com/chicago/things-to-do/the-psychology-behind-casino-design

Darken, R. P., & Siebert, J. L. (1996). Wayfinding strategies and behaviors in large virtual worlds. *Conference on Human Factors in Computing Systems*. Vancouver, British Columbia, Canada, April 13–18, 1996.

Dede, C. (1995). The evolution of constructivist learning environments: Immersion in distributed virtual worlds. *Educational Technology*, 35(5), 46–52.

Dede, C. (2003). No cliché left behind: Why education policy is not like the movies. *Educational Technology*, 43(2), 5–10.

Dede, C., Salzman, M., Loftin, B., & Sprague, D. (1999). Multisensory immersion as a modeling environment for learning complex scientific concepts. In W. Feurzeig & N. Roberts (Eds.), *Modeling and simulation in precollege science and mathematics* (pp. 282–318). New York, NY: Springer-Verlag.

De Lucia, A., Francese, R., Passero, I., & Tortora, G. (2009). Development and evaluation of a virtual campus on Second Life: The case of SecondDMI. *Computers & Education*, 52(1), 220–233.

Dewey, J. (1934). *Art as experience*. New York, NY: Perigee.

Dickey, M. D. (2003). Teaching in 3D: Pedagogical affordances and constraints of 3D virtual worlds for synchronous distance learning. *Distance Education*, 24(1), 105–121.

Dickey, M. D. (2004). An architectural perspective for the design of educational virtual environments. *Journal of Visual Literacy*, 24(1), 49–66.

Dickey, M. D. (2005). Engaging by design: How engagement strategies in popular computer and video games can inform instructional design. *Educational Technology Research and Development*, 53(2), 67–83.

Dickey, M. D. (2011). The pragmatics of virtual worlds for K-12 educators: Investigating the affordances and constraints of Active Worlds and Second Life with K-12 in-service teachers. *Educational Technology Research and Development*, 59(1), 1–20.

Dijksterhuis, A., Smith, P. K., van Baaren, R. B., & Wigboldus, D. H. J. (2005). The unconscious consumer: Effects of environment on consumer behavior. *Journal of Consumer Psychology*, 15(3), 193–202.

Aesthetics and Environment Design • **123**

Dodge, B. (1995). WebQuests: A technique for internet-based learning. *Distance Educator*, 1(2), 10–13.

Duffy, T. M., & Cunningham, D. J. (1996). Constructivism: Implications for the design and delivery of instruction. In D. H. Jonassen (Ed.), *Handbook of research for educational communications and technology* (pp. 170–198). New York, NY: Macmillan.

Ertmer, P. A., & Quinn, J. (1999). *The ID casebook: Case studies in instructional design*. Columbus, OH: Merrill.

Falk, J. H., Dierking, L. D., & Semmel, M. (2012). *Museum experience revisited* (2nd ed.). Walnut Creek, CA: Left Coast Press.

Franklin, T., Mayles, J., Liu, C., & Chelburg, D. (2008). Games and engineers in the middle school science classroom: A case study. In C. Crawford et al. (Eds.), *Proceedings of Society for Information Technology and Teacher Education International Conference 2007* (pp. 1207–1212). Chesapeake, VA: AACE.

Gagne, R. (1985). *The conditions of learning* (4th ed.). New York, NY: Holt, Rinehart & Winston.

Gagne, R., Briggs, L., & Wager, W. (1992). *Principles of instructional design* (4th ed.). Fort Worth, TX: HBJ College Publishers.

Gillen, J. (2009). Literacy practices in Schome Park: A virtual literacy ethnography. *Journal of Research in Reading*, 32(1), 57–74.

Good, J., Howland, K., & Thackray, L. (2008). Problem-based learning spanning real and virtual worlds: A case study in Second Life. *ALT-J, Research in Learning Technology*, 16(3), 163–172.

Heim, M. (2001). The feng shui of virtual environments. *Crossings: eJournal of Art and Technology*, 1(1). Retrieved May 3, 2014, from: http://crossings.tcd.ie/issues/1.1/Heim/

Jackson, R. L., & Winn, W. (1999). Collaboration and learning in immersive virtual environments. In C. Hoadley & J. Roschelle (Eds.), *Proceedings of the Computer Support for Collaborative Learning (CSCL) 1999 Conference* (pp. 83–92). Mahwah, NJ: Lawrence Erlbaum Associates.

Jarmon, L., Traphagan, T., & Mayrath, M. (2008). Understanding project-based learning in Second Life with a pedagogy, training, and assessment trio. *Educational Media International*, 45(3), 157–176.

Jenkins, H. (2002). Game design as narrative architecture. Retrieved November 20, 2013, from http://web.mit.edu/21fms/www/faculty/henry3/games&narrative.html#1

Jonassen, D. H. (1999). Designing constructivist learning environments. In C. M. Reigeluth (Ed.), *Instructional design theories and models* (Vol. 2, pp. 215–240). Mahwah, NJ: Lawrence Erlbaum Associates.

Julian, M. F., Larsen, V. A., & Kinzie, M. B. (1999). Compelling case experiences: Challenges for emerging instructional designers. Paper presented at the annual meeting of the *Association for Educational Communications & Technology (AECT)*, Houston, TX, February 10–14, 1999.

Johnson, L., Mayer, K. J., & Champaner, E. (2004). Casino atmospherics from a customer's perspective: A re-examination. *UNLV Gaming Research & Review Journal*, 8(2), 1–10.

Laramée, F. D. (2002). *Game design perspectives*. Hingham, MA: Charles River Media.

Lave, J., & Wenger, E. (1991). *Situated learning: Legitimate peripheral participation*. Cambridge, UK: Cambridge University Press.

Lehrer, J. (2012). Royal flush: How Roger Thomas redesigned Vegas. *The New Yorker*, March 26, 2012. Retrieved from http://www.newyorker.com/magazine/2012/03/26/royal-flush-2

Lio, H., & Rody, R. (2009). The emotional impact of casino servicescape. *UNLV Gaming Research & Review Journal*, 13(2). Retrieved January 5, 2014, from http://digitalscholarship.unlv.edu/grrj/vol13/iss2/2

Lynch, K. (1960). *The image of the city*. Cambridge, MA: The MIT Press.

Marsh, T., & Wright, P. (2000). Using cinematography conventions to inform the design and evaluation of virtual off-screen space. *AAAI 2000 Spring Symposium Smart Graphics* (pp. 123–127). Stanford, CA: AAAI Press.

Mayer, K. J., & Johnson, L. (2003). A customer-based assessment of casino atmospherics. *UNLV Gaming Research & Review Journal*, 7(1), 21–31.

McLellan, H. (1996). Situated learning: Multiple perspectives. In H. McLellan (Ed.), *Situated learning perspectives* (pp. 5–17). Englewood Cliffs, NJ: Educational Technology Publications.

Mortensen, C. H., Rudloff, M., & Vestergaard, V. (2014). Communicative functions of the museum lobby. *Curator: The Museum Journal*, 57(3), 329–346.

Parrish, P. E. (2009). Aesthetic principles for instructional design. *Educational Technology Research and Development*, 57(4), 511–528.

124 • Aesthetics and Environment Design

Passini, R. (1984). *Wayfinding in architecture*. New York, NY: Van Nostrand Reinfold Company.
Perkins, D.N. (1992). Technology meets constructivism: Do they make a marriage? In T.M. Duffy & D.H. Jonassen (Eds.), *Constructivism and the technology of instruction: A conversation* (pp. 45–54). Hillsdale, NJ: Lawrence Erlbaum Associates.
Rogers, S. (2009). Everything I learned about level design I learned from Disneyland. GDC Vault. Retrieved November 2, 2013, from http://www.gdcvault.com/play/1305/Everything-I-Learned-About-Level
Rollings, A., & Adams, E. (2003). *On game design*. Indianapolis, IN: New Riders.
Rollings, A. & Adams, E. (2006). *Fundamentals of game design*. Indianapolis, IN: New Riders.
Salzman, M.C., Dede, C., Loftin, B., & Chen, J. (1999). A model for understanding how virtual reality aids complex conceptual learning. *Presence*, 8(3), 293–316.
Savery, J.R., & Duffy, T.M. (1995). Problem based learning: An instructional model and its constructivist framework. *Educational Technology*, 35(5), 31–38.
Shedroff, N. (2001). *Experience design*. Indianapolis, IN: New Riders.
Sherman, E., Mathur, A., & Smith, R.B. (1997). Store environment and consumer purchase behavior: Mediating role of consumer emotions. *Psychology & Marketing*, 14(4), 361–378.
Thomas, J.W. (2000). A review of research on project-based learning. Retrieved November 25, 2013, from http://www.bobpearlman.org/BestPractices/PBL_Research.pdf
Turley, L.W., & Milliman, R.E. (2000). Atmospheric effects on shopping behavior: A review of the experimental evidence. *Journal of Business Research*, 49, 193–211.
Weinstein, R.M. (1992). Disneyland and Coney Island: Reflections on the evolution of the modern amusement park. *The Journal of Popular Culture*, 26(1), 131–164.
Wilson, C. (1990). *The gothic cathedral. The architecture of the great church*. London, UK: Thames and Hudson.
Wyman, B., Smith, S., Meyers, D., & Godfrey, M. (2011). Digital storytelling in museums: Observations and best practices. *Curator: The Museum Journal*, 54(4), 461–468.
Yee, N., Bailenson, J. N., Urbanek, B.S., Chang, F., & Merget, D. (2007). The unbearable likeness of being digital: The persistence of nonverbal social norms in online virtual environments. *Cyber-Psychology & Behavior*, 10(1), 115–121.

Media

Active Worlds (1995)—ActiveWorlds, Inc.
Alice (2000)—Rogue Entertainment. Electronic Arts.
America's Army (2002)—The United States Army
Busch Gardens (1959)—Tampa, FL
Coney Island (1829)—New York, NY
Diablo (1996)—Blizzard. Electronic Arts.
Disneyland (1955)—Anaheim, CA
Disney World (1971)—Orlando, FL
Dollywood (1961/1986)—Pigeon Forge, TN
EverQuest2 (2004)—Sony Online Entertainment
Grand Theft Auto (1997)—Rockstar
Medal of Honor (1999)—Dreamworks Interactive
Open Sims (OpenSimulator) (2014)—Open source
Second Life (2003)—Linden Labs
Space Invaders (1978)—Midway
Syberia (2002)—Microids
World of Warcraft (2004)—Blizzard Entertainment

7
Aesthetics and Game Mechanics

Introduction

This chapter begins with an overview of game mechanics, followed by a discussion of core mechanics and mapping them with elements of constructivist learning environments. This section is followed by an outline of common secondary mechanics and a discussion of the types of cognition, based on Bloom's taxonomy, they foster. Following is a discussion of game mechanics in different genres (adventure games, puzzles, RPGs, small quests, arcade/shooter-style mechanics and construction mechanics) and how they foster cognition.

Aesthetics and Games

A discussion of game mechanics may seem somewhat incongruent in a book about aesthetics for game-based learning. After all, game mechanics may be better suited to a discussion of programming or systems design; nonetheless, they are also very relevant to the discussion of aesthetics both in terms of how they interact with elements such as narrative and environment, and because there is beauty and drama in the act of interaction. In an article titled "Chess as an Art Form," Humble (1993) provides a compelling argument about the aesthetics of playing chess. Humble contends that there is artistry and creativity in the act of playing chess. Chess serves as an "individual form of creativity" (p. 59) as players maneuver their game pieces within the constraints of rules and game space to create combinations and traps. Chess allows players to express their artistry through creative combinations of moves with economics of moves and patterns. It is the skillful combinations, economy of the moves and originality of the matched skills of the two players that make chess an art form. Humble contends that "chess offers a medium in which players strive to produce intellectual objects of beauty and imaginative power" (p. 60). Humble's (1993) arguments can easily be applied to digital games. Beyond the narrative, character and environment design, there are moves, combinations and strategies in the very act of gameplay that are both intellectual and beautiful in the creative combinations and economy within the affordances and constraints of the game space. The types of mechanics for an individual game are what allow for artistry in the act of interaction.

126 • Aesthetics and Game Mechanics

Beyond the artistry of interactivity, games are also a type of drama, not just in terms of narrative or storyline, but also through the act of competition. Humble (1993) maintains that there is a level of drama implicit in competition, and while his example is applied to chess, it can easily be extended to games. Games are competitive, whether it is against other players, against the computer or even beating one's previous performance (score); there is drama in the act of interaction in gameplay. Finally, there is relevance in discussing the aesthetics of game mechanics because mechanics and aesthetics are not separate components in a game, but rather part of the design continuum and are tightly related. By extension, the aesthetics of game mechanics help inform the design of game-based learning by looking at the types of mechanics (core and secondary) and how they may foster different types of artistry of intellectual engagement.

Core Mechanics

Overview

As the chapter on game genre reveals, there are many different types of game genres, yet characterization of genres is difficult because there are games that cross genres and there are elements within games that overlap but may be manifested differently in different genres. There have been several initiatives to map learning design to different game genres. Prensky (2001) offered a taxonomy in which he mapped types of learning to different styles of games. Similarly, Sherry and Pacheco (2006) advocate aligning learning outcomes to game genres that align to types of learning based on Bloom's taxonomy (1956). However, game genres are fluid characterizations and may not provide a thorough model for integrating game elements into game-based learning. Games are goal-oriented and rule-bound, and the game mechanics are the means by which those rules are manifest. Rather than mapping game genres to learning outcomes, looking at how different game mechanics operate and function may provide more insight into the design of interactivity in game-based learning.

Game mechanics are mechanisms for how rules are expressed in gameplay. As with definitions of game genres, there are differing views on the definition of what constitutes game mechanics (Dunniway & Novak, 2008; Sicart, 2008; Rouse, 2001; Jarvinen, 2008; Salen & Zimmerman, 2003; Adams & Dormans, 2012). However, central to nearly all discussions of game mechanics is the understanding that most games are goal-oriented and rule-bound. Rules determine what a player can and cannot do in a game, and they also define victory and loss conditions. Game mechanics are the mechanisms for how rules are manifested in a game. They form the core of the interaction. The setting and storyline serve as the framework for interaction, but the mechanics define the processes for the rules. Because games often blur and blend genres, it is difficult to concretely align game mechanics with various genres. Various game mechanics provide different types of rule-based interaction. However, it should be noted that the definition of game

Aesthetics and Game Mechanics • **127**

mechanics is a topic of much variation and debate. Because the purpose of this chapter is focused on elements of aesthetics for the design of game-based learning, the focus will be on generalities about game mechanics and how they relate to the design of game-based learning.

Core Mechanics

Although there is much discussion and variation about what constitutes game mechanics and how they are manifested in games, Adams and Dormans (2012) provide a succinct list of five types of game mechanics: *physics, internal economies, progressive mechanisms, tactical maneuvering* and *social interaction.* The physics of a game are the mechanics (rules) of how objects move and interact in the game space. A game adhering to Newtonian physics would likely include some sense of gravity and collision. In turn, a character in that game would likely adhere to some sense of gravity when running and jumping in the game. The internal economies are the rules that govern the "creation, consumption and exchange of quantifiable resources" (Adams, 2014b, p. 352). These may be resources as tangible as game money (e.g., money, gold coins) or as intangible as health, reputation and magic. One might also argue that social capital might also be a form of intangible internal economy in a game. Progressive mechanics dictate player progression in a game. Progressive mechanics are the mechanisms that block or unlock access and may take many forms, such as spatial barriers and enablers (walls, doors, locks), temporal barriers and enablers (time-locked activities, speed, pause features) and plot progression barriers and enablers, in which aspects of the narrative must be completed before the player can advance in gameplay (triggers and dialogue trees). Tactical maneuvering mechanics involve movement and control of a space or region. Tactical maneuvering mechanics include elimination mechanics (destroying enemies), capture mechanics (capture or control of a region), survival mechanics (eluding enemies) and race mechanics. Social interaction mechanics are mechanics that support social interaction and collaboration. Examples of social interaction mechanics include chat tools, group mechanics and rules governing role-playing in role-playing games (RPGs).

The core mechanics identified by Adams and Dormans (2012) of *physics, internal economies, progressive mechanisms, tactical maneuvering* and *social interaction* are also manifested and mutually informed by and help shape game aesthetics. Mechanics of physics inform and are informed by player perspective of motion and movement. The physics inform and are informed by the character design and certainly impact the narrative and environment design. Similarly, progressive mechanics inform and are informed by the narrative in terms of access to and through an area, the environment in shaping the space and objects in the environment, and the narrative (what is and is not plausible). In most aspects of game design, there is a reciprocal relationship between interactivity and aesthetics.

Adams and Dormans' (2012) list of core mechanics provides a good point of departure for addressing mechanics and game-based learning. While the goals

128 • Aesthetics and Game Mechanics

for popular entertainment games are very different than those of game-based learning, and the types of resources allocated to the design of commercial games is likely substantially different than that of most instructional designers, educators and learning design practitioners, Adams and Dormans' outline of core game mechanics provides a way to look at how to design interaction for game-based learning.

Educational Implications

The core mechanics outlined by Adams and Dormans (2012), viewed through the lens of learning design, can also provide a type of heuristic for educational interactive design and game-based learning. From a constructivist perspective, these core mechanics can roughly be aligned to the affordances of constructivist learning environments. Granted, this argument may initially seem somewhat speculative, but the movement toward constructivism and, by extension, constructivist learning environments represents an interruption of the systems-based approach toward instructional design. Games are environments that, while essentially a system of algorithms, manifest to players as rich environments filled with competition, drama and pathos. The core mechanics can provide new models and ways of thinking about constructivist learning environments.

The current focus in the field of instructional design is the cultivation of interactive learning environments (Hannafin, Land & Oliver, 1999; Jonassen, 1999; Winn, 2002). Essential to a constructivist theoretical perspective is the conviction that knowledge is constructed, not transmitted, and that learners are not passive recipients of knowledge but instead play an active role in the learning process (Duffy & Cunningham, 1996; Johnson & Johnson, 1996; Jonassen, 1999). Often, some form of problem-based or project-based learning is the focus. Jonassen (1992) outlined several key elements to foster the construction of knowledge. According to Jonassen, learners should have opportunities for exploration, manipulation and inscription systems, which allow learners to "externalize understanding" (Winn, 2002). Constructivist learning environments should also provide access to resources (models, exemplars and information gathering tools) (Jonassen, 1999; Jonassen, Peck & Wilson, 1999). Finally, environments should also include discourse opportunities between learners. Conversation and discourse foster collaboration and support social negotiation in learning (Jonassen, 1999; Lave & Wenger, 1991; Vygotsky, 1978). This in turn allows learners to share information, test understandings and reflect on learning (Duffy & Cunningham, 1996; Jonassen, 1999). It could be argued that the epistemological orientation of constructivist learning environments is somewhat congruent with core mechanics in games. The physics mechanics support experiential affordances for learners by providing the environment and exploration. The internal economies mechanics afford resources in varied forms. The progressive mechanics provide a type of scaffolding through the means of progression. The tactical mechanics provide resources, inscription and exploration, and, finally, the social mechanics support

Aesthetics and Game Mechanics • 129

Table 7.1 Core game mechanics (Adams & Dormans, 2012) and constructive learning

Core Mechanic	Constructivist Learning
Physics mechanics	Experiential
Internal economies mechanics	Resources
Progression mechanics	Scaffolding
Tactical mechanics	Inscription
Social mechanics	Discourse tools

Adapted from Adams and Dormans, 2012

discourse. Granted, this argument is somewhat tenuous, and the purpose is not to outline yet another model or system for instructional design but rather to look at how these different components relate and at model environments that can be harnessed for learning (see Table 7.1).

Secondary Mechanics

Core mechanics are the broad mechanics, and there is benefit in looking at distinctions between different types of secondary mechanics. Because games often blur and blend genres, it is difficult to concretely align game mechanics with various genres. However, at the risk of over-generalizing, some common tactical mechanics that can be found within action, simulation, role-playing and strategy games and MMO varieties include the following: *collection, elimination, avoidance, resource management, races* and *construction*. In a good game, mechanics are interwoven with the narrative, the environment and the affordances of the character design and player perspective.

Collection mechanics require players to collect a specific number of objects. This may include attaining certain scores or points; it may include defeating a specific number of enemies or attaining control over territories. Collection mechanics can be found in RPGs in which players may have to collect a number of objects (typically found only in dangerous terrain) and in strategy games or simulations in which players may need to collect objects to help build and reinforce defenses or support needs for future development. Elimination mechanics require players to defeat a number of enemies, agents or objects. Elimination mechanics may be in a wide variety of genres such as action, first-person shooters, RPGs, strategy games and simulations. They may be as seemingly simple as Pac-Man eating dots or as complex as finding strategies for defeating level or game bosses. Similarly, avoidance strategies require players to avoid losing objects, territories or even character lives. Resource management mechanics require players to balance and negotiate resources (tokens, money, health, character attributes and traits) to achieve a goal(s). Race mechanics require players to beat an opponent(s) in some type of race negotiating space, time or both. Construction mechanics require players to build, construct and/or alter an environment. It is important to note that several of these mechanics may be manifested in various ways in different genres.

130 • Aesthetics and Game Mechanics

Where a study of game mechanics may prove most insightful for the study of game-based learning is in looking at the types of knowledge they elicit. Bloom's taxonomy (Bloom, 1956) is a renowned classification of functions of the cognitive domain. The cognitive domains address the following cognitive forms, moving from lowest to highest: knowledge, comprehension, application, analysis, synthesis and evaluation. Anderson and Krathwohl (2001) provided a revised version of Bloom's taxonomy to include the following cognitive forms: remembering, understanding, applying, analyzing, evaluating and creating.

The following table presents a summary of these game mechanics, along with examples of their application in game genres and the types of cognitive forms they stimulate during gameplay. The purpose of this summary is not to provide a comprehensive analysis of game mechanics and cognitive forms, nor to be prescriptive in nature, but instead to initiate dialogue about how mapping mechanics to cognitive forms might inform the design of game-based learning (see Table 7.2).

Table 7.2 Game mechanics and cognition

Mechanics	Summary and Genre	Objectives	
		Bloom's Taxonomy (1956)	
Collection mechanics	This mechanic concerns the gathering or collecting of a specified number of objects (points, bounty, territory, etc.).	Knowledge Comprehension	Remembering Understanding
	Game genres: action, role-playing, simulation and strategy games		
Elimination mechanics	This mechanic requires players to defeat specified enemies, agents or objects.	Knowledge Comprehension	Remembering Understanding
	Game genres: action, role-playing, simulation and strategy games		
Avoidance mechanics	This mechanic requires players to avoid losing objects or territories.	Knowledge Comprehension	Remembering Understanding
	Game genres: action, role-playing, simulation and strategy games		
Race mechanics	This mechanic requires players to beat an opponent(s) in some type of race negotiating space, time or both.	Knowledge Comprehension	Remembering Understanding
Resource management mechanics	This mechanic requires players to balance and negotiate resources (e.g., tokens, money, health, character attributes and traits) to achieve one or more goals.	Knowledge Comprehension Application Analysis Synthesis Evaluation	Remembering Understanding Applying Analyzing Evaluating Creating
	Game genres: role-playing, simulation and strategy games		
Construction mechanics	This mechanic requires players to build, construct and/or alter an environment.	Knowledge Comprehension Application Analysis Synthesis Evaluation	Remembering Understanding Applying Analyzing Evaluating Creating
	Game genres: role-playing, simulation and strategy games		

Aesthetics and Game Mechanics • **131**

It should be noted that many types of secondary mechanics may be expressed in different ways in different game genres. For example, in RPGs, resource management is a pervasive and complex mechanic that may overlap economic, tactical and social interaction. Within RPGs, resource management is used to help the player's characters, yet resource management within a strategy game may involve land cultivation or the acquisition of territory to enhance holdings. Having knowledge of both the type and variety of game mechanics can inform the design of game-based learning because mechanics define the interaction in gameplay. Much of the success of the user experience of a game can derive from the successful application of game mechanics.

Game Mechanics: Adventure Games, MMORPGs and Action and Casual Games

Adventure Games: Puzzle Mechanics

The list of secondary mechanics provides an outline of different types of mechanics and how they may support different learning objectives; more specific mechanics can provide insight into how specific types of mechanics foster different types of learning. Examples of subsets of game mechanics are those found in adventure games and small quests in MMORPGs.

Adventure games include several common game mechanics, most notably collection and resource management, but they also typically include an assortment of puzzles. There are a variety of puzzle types, including some of the following common puzzles:

- Inventory manipulation
- Dialogue-based puzzles
- Mazes
- Environment puzzles
- Locks
- Jigsaw puzzles
- Slider puzzles
- Audio puzzles
- Combination puzzles

Inventory manipulations require players to gather items found in the environment and often combine them (e.g., find batteries and bulb to activate a flashlight). Once items have been combined, players must activate the object or use it within the environment. This requires the players to *analyze* and *apply*. Dialogue-based puzzles often require players to interact with non-player characters (NPCs) and often correctly select from pre-scripted dialogue. This requires players to *analyze, synthesize* and *evaluate*. Mazes require players to navigate through a complex labyrinth of interconnected paths or passages. There

132 • Aesthetics and Game Mechanics

are strategies that many games employ with mazes, but even without much strategy, players can triumph through trial and error. Environmental puzzles require players to manipulate or alter their surroundings within the game environment. This requires players to *analyze, evaluate* and *apply*. Jigsaw puzzles require players to correctly rotate and align corresponding puzzles pieces, which can typically be accomplished through trial and error, but visual or image recognition can play a role in the speed and ease with which players solve jigsaw puzzles. Similarly, slider puzzles require players to unscramble an image by sliding adjoining tiles. Audio puzzles require players to reproduce the correct combination of tones or a series of sounds. This requires players to *remember* or, in some cases, to *analyze*. Finally, combination puzzles require players to activate the correct sequence of numbers or other objects. This may require players to *remember, analyze* and *apply*.

RPG/MMORPGs: Small Quest and Character Mechanics

As previously addressed in discussions of narrative (see Chapter 4) and genres (see Chapter 3), there are a variety of small quests in MMORPGs that provide insight into secondary game mechanics and how they can foster different types of learning. What is particularly insightful about MMORPGs is that they are collaborative interactive environments and provide a good model of how mechanics function in a multiplayer environment. In an article titled "Game Design and Learning: A Conjectural Analysis of How Massively Multiple Online Role-playing Games (MMORPGs) Foster Intrinsic Motivation" (Dickey, 2007), I categorized a number of common small quests and described the types of actions players must perform in completing the quests. Although the context for this description was in a discussion of narrative design, this same list of small quests is also helpful for illustrating how different game mechanics are manifest and for exploring the types of knowledge they require or elicit. The list of small quests includes:

- Bounty quests
- FedEx quests
- Collection quests
- Escort quests
- Goodwill quests
- Messenger quests

The *bounty quest* typically requires players to defeat an enemy or number of enemies (NPCs or other players). This may require players to *remember, analyze* and *evaluate* the environment and the affordances and constraints of their skills and those of the enemies to be defeated. Additionally, in the course of finding the "bounty," players are exposed to new regions, which in turn may require players to *remember* the new locations. Bounty quests sometimes require players to defeat high-level NPCs, forcing players to collaborate with other players to complete the quest. The social mechanics help foster community as players collaborate and *strategize*. A *FedEx quest* requires players to take a package or object from one player or location and deliver it to another. While this sometimes tedious small quest can be overused, the benefit of this is that it often exposes players to new regions of a game and new resources that may be relevant for problem-solving in later stages of the game. The *collection quest* requires players to collect a variety of objects. The purpose and benefit of the collection quest is to help players progress in the game by requiring them to gain higher levels of skills by "leveling up." In turn, this scaffolds players in advancing to more difficult levels and performing more difficult tasks. The *escort quest* requires a player to escort an NPC from one area to another. This often involves strategic planning by coordinating timing, navigation and even collaboration with other players. Typically, the player must protect the character. This type of quest is a good device for conveying plot information, as the NPC being escorted conveys a story, intrigue or twist during the travels. *Goodwill quests* require a higher-level player to assist a lower-level player. This provides scaffolding to beginning players and helps initiate them into the gameplay environment. Finally, the *messenger quest* is a quest in which a player must find an NPC and talk with them. The benefit of the messenger quest is that the NPC may be offering some key advice, information or directions that will help guide and mentor the player in problem-solving.

Researchers from such diverse fields as cognitive psychology, knowledge management, learning theory and instructional design have characterized four types of knowledge: (a) declarative knowledge, (b) procedural knowledge, (c) strategic knowledge and (d) metacognitive knowledge (Ackerman, 1986; Anderson, 1983; Bloom, 1956; Bransford, Brown & Cocking, 2000; Brown, 1978; Gagne, 1985; Jonassen, 1996; Kraiger, Ford & Salas, 1993; Smith & Ragan, 1993; Wagner, 1987). Declarative knowledge entails facts, data, concepts and principles. Procedural knowledge consists of knowledge of how to perform a task, action or process. Strategic knowledge, the foundation of problem-solving, is an understanding of how to apply knowledge, principles and experiences to various and new situations. Metacognitive knowledge consists of reflection and regulation of one's thinking during an activity (Brown, 1978). I first presented the following table in 2007 in an article titled "Game Design and Learning: A Conjectural Analysis of How Massively Multiple Online Role-playing Games (MMORPGs) Foster Intrinsic Motivation" (Dickey, 2007). This table is an attempt to characterize how various quests might foster learning in various knowledge types (see Table 7.3).

The following is an excerpt from "Game Design and Learning: A Conjectural Analysis of How Massively Multiple Online Role-playing Games (MMORPGs) Foster Intrinsic Motivation" (Dickey, 2007), in which I outline how different types of small quests can be used to foster various types of knowledge.

134 • Aesthetics and Game Mechanics

Table 7.3 Categorizing small quests by knowledge domains (Dickey, 2007)

Knowledge Domain	Small Quest
Declarative Knowledge	Collection quests
	Goodwill quests
Procedural Knowledge	FedEx quests
	Messenger quests
Strategic Knowledge	Collection quests
	Bounty quests
	Escort quests
Metacognitive Knowledge	Bounty quests
	Escort quests
	Goodwill quests

With kind permission from Springer Science+Business Media: *Educational Technology Research and Development*, 55, 2007, 268, Michele D. Dickey, Table 2

With kind permission from Springer Science+Business Media: *Educational Technology Research and Development*, 55, 2007, 268–269, Michele D. Dickey

Declarative Knowledge

A collection quest is a quest in which players must collect a variety of objects or perform an activity a certain number of times. The purpose and benefit of the collection quest is to help the player progress in the game by accumulating points. This type of quest might be useful for fostering and reinforcing declarative knowledge because declarative knowledge indicates knowledge of facts and data. For example, students might be required to complete a quest in which they must label, identify, or define something. They may have to complete the act several times in different combinations or ways to complete the task. Similarly, goodwill quests are quests which require a player to help another lower-level player. Teaching or assisting a peer is a way to reinforce knowledge. This type of quest may be useful in fostering declarative knowledge by having one student peer mentor or assist another learner.

Procedural Knowledge

The Fed Ex quests and messenger quests are quests which move players through the environment and expose them to new areas and resources. They are also procedural in nature. The Fed Ex quest is procedural in that it may involve going to various places to collect items and manipulate items and then finally deliver them. Procedural knowledge focuses on knowledge about how to perform a task. In a learning environment, this type of task might be useful in fostering procedural knowledge by simulating how

Aesthetics and Game Mechanics • **135**

something is done. The learner might be required to find various objects or to complete actions in a particular order with the goal of demonstrating a process. Similarly, the messenger quest is also often procedural in nature in which players often are required to pass information along from one source to another. In turn, this might be used by a learner to first simulate or learn a process then to recount that process to another learner or to a narrative character.

Strategic Knowledge

The bounty quest requires players to defeat a character or number of characters, while the escort quest requires players to escort a NPC from one location to another. Both quests-types are often challenging and require players to plan and strategize. Strategic knowledge refers to knowledge of how to apply knowledge, principles, and experiences to various and new situations. Both bounty quests and escort quests require players to analyze their character's strengths and weaknesses and to balance those against the environmental factors they may encounter and the type of challenge. These types of small quests might be useful for assisting learners in integrating and fostering knowledge gained from exploration, interaction, and various procedures and applying that knowledge in a new or unique situation.

Metacognitive Knowledge

Both bounty quests and escort quests also require players to explore, observe, speculate, and make conjectures. Players make conjectures by gauging the demands of the quests while reflecting on their past experiences. In goodwill quests, players may articulate their experiences while assisting lower-level players. In turn, players may model, scaffold, and coach lower-level players. These types of quests might be helpful in helping learners foster and apply "adaptive expertise" in problem-solving (Bransford, Brown & Cocking, 2000; Hatano & Inagaki, 1986) by exposing learners to resources and processes and then providing a challenge in which they must make conjectures about combining resources, processes, and skills.

Character Design Mechanics

In RPGs and MMORPGs, character design is a defining mechanic. Players begin the game by first creating a character they will play. Adams (2014b, 2014c) identifies key aspects of character design mechanics as *functional* and *cosmetic* attributes. Functional attributes include characterization attributes such as race, gender and character class, physical attributes, mental attributes, moral attributes and social attributes. Players must select from various attributes to form their characters. Race typically includes variations of human-like and non-human races (elves, gnomes, orcs, dwarves, humans, etc.). Gender is typically male or female, although some games have provisions for non-gendered or undefined. Depending upon the storyline, the character classes may be fantasy-based (shamans, mages, wizards) or futuristic (Jedi). Physical, moral and social attributes define the physique, codes of morality and social attitudes. Cosmetic attributes include hair, skin, facial features and adornments. Players customize their characters by attributes. The individual combination of attributes and adornments makes each character unique. Throughout gameplay, players continually enhance their character's skills and attributes.

Character design is a key mechanic in RPGs and MMORPGs. In both genres, character development, to varying degrees, dictates the gameplay experience. Where a character begins and behaves is typically determined by the attributes selected by a player at the beginning of the game and enhanced during gameplay. In MMORPGs, character design also becomes a form of social mechanics. Jakobsson (2002) argues that, in MMORPGs, players' investment in their characters results in a form of social capital. Social capital is the belief that social networks have value and that trust is gained by participating in community spaces (Putnam, 1995, 2000). Social capital in MMORPGs is the result of a player's character's assets, and the network of affiliations accrued with the playing of one or more characters (Herz, 2001). The attributes, adornments, skills and traits of a character, along with the player's actions, enhance the player's individual status among other players. Social capital that results from a player-created character can be very instrumental in an MMORPG environment because it may assist or hinder players in advancing in gameplay (Jakobsson & Taylor, 2003).

Action and Casual Game Mechanics

Adventure game puzzles and RPG/MMORPGs have a variety of mechanics that are insightful for the design of game-based learning because the variety of mechanics requires more complex cognitive strategies. However, there are other genres with mechanics that may be simpler but still hold relevance for the design of game-based learning. Action games as discussed in Chapter 3 are games with underlying mechanics that require quick response. However, there are also mechanics within action games that provide options. Adams (2014a) maintains that the mechanics of action games should be "simple and obvious." Typical mechanics include lives, energy, power-ups, collectables, time limits and score (Adams, 2014a; Novak, 2008). Typically, in action games, players are given a number of lives, which are reprieves from defeats (deaths). Pending the game, players may earn or be granted additional lives when they attain a certain level. Energy is often a form of health for the player's character. As a character engages in gameplay, often, interaction (battles, fights, engagements) impacts the player's character by depleting energy or health. Often, in action games, players may have the opportunity to rejuvenate energy or health through a power-up or some resource (potion). Typically, players' energy is replenished when they attain a new level. Power-ups are rewards that players earn or that may sometimes randomly occur within the environment. Power-ups might include rejuvenation of health, new tools or weapons, or some new skill. Collectables are bonus objects that may appear but are not essential to gameplay. Time and score are two common mechanics that enhance gameplay by imposing constraints. Some games use time as a mechanic by requiring players to complete a certain action or number of actions within an allotted time frame. Most action games use some form of score or scoring system to define performance.

In general, arcade and casual games are less complex genres of games that typically require less investment of time than genres such as RPGs and adventure games; however, the underlying mechanics provide interaction that fosters different types of cognition (Trefry, 2010). Common casual game mechanics include matching, sorting and seeking. Matching and sorting mechanics are essentially pattern recognition. Games such as *Bejeweled* or *Bubble Witch Saga* require players to match a series of objects. Sorting mechanics such as word puzzles and solitaire require players to sort items into a pattern or find hidden patterns in an assortment. Seeking mechanics require players to find objects from an array of objects. Hidden object puzzles are common games that use seeking mechanics. Often, within these mechanics are mechanics of time, speed, score and level, which add to the engagement. The mechanic of time often imposes a time limit in order to complete a number of matches, sorts or even seeking. Score mechanics can impose limits on scores that must be achieved (possibly within a designated amount of time). Level mechanics are the progression from easier to more difficult versions of the game.

Action and casual game mechanics provide a model of mechanics that would be suited to practice and review. They often require players to recognize, identify and manipulate. Mechanics of time, speed, score and level enhance what might be a rote activity by adding layers of challenge and even competition. The mechanics evident in casual games would most likely fall within the scope of declarative knowledge, but could be used as a means to provide engaging practice.

Conclusion

Ultimately, the design of a great game is a unique combination of game mechanics and interaction along with narrative, character design and the interests of the player; however, an understanding of game mechanics and interactive elements can inform designers and educators about the array of interactive mechanics. One of the concerns about using educational games and game-based learning environments is that, in order for game-based learning environments to be most effective, the mechanics must be contextually intertwined with the learning goal. The mechanics must be intrinsic to the learning task or there is the risk that the learner will focus on winning the game or, more precisely, beating an algorithm rather than engaging with the learning task and content (Scoresby & Shelton, 2007; Streibel, 1986; Turkle, 1995).

138 • Aesthetics and Game Mechanics

References

Ackerman, P. L. (1986). Individual differences in information processing: An investigation of intellectual abilities and task performance during practice. *Intelligence*, 10, 109–139.

Adams, E. (2014a). *Fundamentals of action and arcade game design*. Indianapolis, IN: New Riders.

Adams, E. (2014b). *Fundamentals of game design* (3rd ed.). Indianapolis, IN: New Riders.

Adams, E. (2014c). *Fundamentals of role-playing game design*. Indianapolis, IN: New Riders.

Adams, E., & Dormans, J. (2012). *Game mechanics: Advanced game design*. Indianapolis, IN: New Riders.

Anderson, J. R. (1983). *The architecture of cognition*. Cambridge, MA: Harvard University Press.

Anderson, L. W., & Krathwohl, D. R. (2001). *A taxonomy for learning, teaching and assessing: A review of Bloom's taxonomy of educational objectives*. New York, NY: Addison Wesley Longman.

Bloom, B. (1956). *Taxonomy of educational objectives: The cognitive domain*. New York, NY: McKay.

Bransford, J. D., Brown, A. L., & Cocking, R. L. (2000). *How people learn: Brain, mind, experience, and school committee on developments in the science of learning*. Washington, DC: National Academy Press.

Brown, A. L. (1978). Knowing when, where, and how to remember: A problem of metacognition. In R. Glaser (Ed.), *Advances in instructional psychology* (pp. 77–165). Hillsdale, NJ: Lawrence Erlbaum Associates.

Dickey, M. D. (2007). Game design and learning: A conjectural analysis of how Massively Multiple Online Role-Playing Games (MMORPGs) foster intrinsic motivation. *Educational Technology Research and Development*, 55(3), 253–273.

Duffy, T. M., & Cunningham, D. J. (1996). Constructivism: Implications for the design and delivery of instruction. In D. Jonassen (Ed.), *Handbook of research for educational communications and technology* (pp. 170–198). New York, NY: Macmillan.

Dunniway, T., & Novak, J. (2008). *Game development essentials: Gameplay mechanics*. Clifton Park, NY: Thomson Delmar Learning.

Gagné, R. M. (1985). *The conditions of learning and theory of instruction* (4th ed.). New York, NY: Holt, Rinehart and Winston.

Hannafin, M. J., Land, S., & Oliver, K. (1999). Open learning environments: Foundations, methods, and models. In C. M. Reigeluth (Ed.), *Instructional-design theories and models: A new paradigm of instructional theory* (Vol. II, pp. 115–140). Hillsdale, NJ: Lawrence Erlbaum Associates.

Hatano, G., & Inagaki, K. (1986). Two courses of expertise. In H. Stevenson, H. Azuma & K. Hakuta (Eds.), *Child development and education in Japan* (pp. 262–272). San Francisco, CA: Freeman.

Herz, C. J. (2001). Gaming the system: What higher education can learn from multiplayer online worlds. *The Internet and the University, EDUCAUSE Forum on the Future of Higher Education*. Retrieved February 15, 2004, from http://www.educause.edu/ir/library/pdf/ffpiu019.pdf

Humble, P. N. (1993). Chess as an art form. *The British Journal of Aesthetics*, 33(1), 59–63.

Jakobsson, M. (2002). Rest in peace, Bill the bot. Death and life in virtual worlds. In R. Schroeder (Ed.), *The social life of avatars: Culture and communication in virtual environments* (pp. 63–76). London, UK: Springer-Verlag.

Jakobsson, M., & Taylor, T. L. (2003). The Sopranos meets EverQuest: Social networking in massively multiuser networking games. *MelbourneDAC, the 5th International Digital Arts and Culture Conference*. Melbourne, Australia, May 19–23, 2003.

Järvinen, A. (2008). *Games without frontiers: Theories and methods for game studies and design*. Doctoral dissertation, University of Tampere, Finland.

Johnson, D. W., & Johnson, R. T. (1996). Cooperation and the use of technology. In D. Jonassen (Ed), *Handbook of research for educational communications and technology* (pp. 1017–1044). New York, NY: Macmillan.

Jonassen, D. H. (1992). Evaluating constructivist learning. In T. M. Duffy & D. H. Jonassen (Eds.), *Constructivism and the technology of instruction* (pp. 137–148). Hillsdale, NJ: Lawrence Erlbaum Associates.

Jonassen, D. H. (1996). *Computers in the classroom: Mindtools for critical thinking*. Englewood Cliffs, NJ: Prentice-Hall.

Jonassen, D. H. (1999). Designing constructivist learning environments. In C. M. Reigeluth (Ed.), *Instructional-design theories and models: A new paradigm of instructional theory* (Vol. II, pp. 215–240). Hillsdale, NJ: Lawrence Erlbaum Associates.

Jonassen, D. H., Peck, K., & Wilson, B. G. (1999). *Learning WITH technology: A constructivist perspective*. Columbus, OH: Merrill/Prentice Hall.

Kraiger, K., Ford, J., & Salas, E. (1993). Application of cognitive, skill-based, and affective theories of learning outcomes to new methods of training evaluation. *Journal of Applied Psychology*, 78(2), 311–328.

Lave, J., & Wenger, E. (1991). *Situated learning*. New York, UK: Cambridge University Press.

Novak, J. (2008). *Game development essentials* (2nd ed.). Clifton Park, NY: Thomson Delmar Learning.

Prensky, M. (2001). *Digital game-based learning*. New York, NY: McGraw-Hill.

Putnam, R. D. (1995). Bowling alone: America's declining social capital. *Journal of Democracy*, 6(1), 65–78.

Putnam, R. D. (2000). *Bowling alone: The collapse and revival of American community*. New York, NY: Simon & Schuster.

Rouse, R. (2001). *Game design: Theory and practice*. Plano, TX: Worldware Publishing.

Salen, K., & Zimmerman, E. (2003). *Rules of play: Game design fundamentals*. Cambridge, MA: The MIT Press.

Scoresby, J. & Shelton, B. E. (2007). Linking game play activity and learning objectives through a videogame motivational model. Paper presented at the annual meeting of the *American Educational Research Association*. Chicago, IL, April 9–13, 2007.

Sherry, J., & Pacheco, A. (2006). Matching computer game genres to educational outcomes. *The Electronic Journal of Communication*, 16(1&2). Retrieved June 2, 2014, from http://www.cios.org/EJCPUBLIC/016/1/01615.HTML

Sicart, M. (2008). Defining game mechanics. *Game Studies: The International Journal of Computer Game Research*, 8(2). Retrieved Jan 22, 2014, from http://gamestudies.org/0802/articles/sicart

Smith, P., & Ragan, T. (1993). *Instructional design*. New York, NY: Merrill.

Streibel, M. J. (1986). A critical analysis of the use of computers in education. *Educational Communications and Technology—A Journal of Theory, Research and Development*, 34(3), 137–161.

Trefry, S. (2010). *Casual game design: Designing for the gamer in all of us*. Burlington, MA: Morgan Kaufmann Publishers.

Turkle, S. (1995). *Life on the screen: Identity in the age of the Internet*. New York, NY: Simon and Schuster.

Vygotsky, L. S. (1978). *Mind in society: The development of higher psychological processes*. Boston, MA: Harvard University Press.

Wagner, R. K. (1987). Tacit knowledge in everyday intelligent behavior. *Journal of Personality and Social Psychology*, 52, 1236–1241.

Winn, W. (2002). Current trends in educational technology research: The study of learning environments. *Educational Psychology Review*, 14(3), 331–351.

8
Aesthetics, Inquiry and Research

The purpose of this chapter is to discuss modes of inquiry into game-based learning that present alternatives to science-based methods of inquiry: connoisseurship and criticism. This chapter begins with a discussion of connoisseurship. This section is followed by a discussion of educational criticism for game-based learning. The chapter concludes with a short discussion of qualitative criticism as a means of integrating arts-based and science-based modes of inquiry.

Connoisseurship and Game-based Learning

In *Paradigms Regained*, Denis Hlynka and John Belland (1991) challenged the prevailing quantitative and qualitative research paradigms commonly used in educational technology research and advocated for a third "critical" paradigm. The third paradigm they proposed was for the use of arts-based methods of inquiry for educational technology products and practices. Among the different art-based methods proposed are Elliot Eisner's (1998) educational *connoisseurship* and *educational criticism*. According to Belland (1991), the *connoisseurship model* is an effective means of "getting inside" of experiences. During the past decade, there has been a growing interest in game-based learning. While both qualitative and quantitative methodologies have been used, game-based learning environments are dynamic spaces constructed of multiple influences from the arts and sciences and, as such, can benefit not only from science-based methods of inquiry but also from arts-based methods. The purpose of this chapter is to discuss the value of cultivating connoisseurship in game-based learning and the application of educational criticism as a mode for critiquing and "getting inside" of game-based learning environments.

Science-based modes of inquiry are important and illuminating for inquiry about game-based learning; however, the foundation of digital games, like other forms of educational media (educational films and television), is that of media established primarily for the purposes of entertainment. With entertainment media along with the fine and performing arts, criticism is a means of evaluating, judging and validating works based on deep understanding. Hlynka and Belland (1991) argue that criticism offers a third paradigm or a "critical paradigm" not based on statistical-based methodologies (quantitative research) or anthropological

142 • Aesthetics, Inquiry and Research

or sociological models (qualitative research), but instead provides insight about the qualities and distinctions from those with experience and insight into a medium or process.

Belland (1991) proposed the use of connoisseurship as a means of reviewing instructional systems and instructional media without the need for elaborate mechanisms of qualitative or quantitative inquiry. Connoisseurship is, as Eisner (1998, p. 63) states, "the art of appreciation" and an "act of knowledgeable perception." Connoisseurs use their vast experiences to gauge and understand the fine distinctions in their field of knowledge. The connoisseur has the ability to relate new experiences with antecedent knowledge of the context and to understand different characteristics and distinctions. Developing connoisseurship would foster instructional/learning designers who have insight into the varied and interdisciplinary nature of game design and game-based learning.

According to Belland (1991), becoming a connoisseur in educational technology and media would require the development of fine discriminations, a hierarchal system of concepts, organizing principles to structure the relationships among concepts and, finally, strategies to focus on the salient aspects. In Belland's (1991) initial proposal about adopting connoisseurship, he provided an example of becoming a connoisseur of educational films. This would likely include study in filmmaking, film history and film criticism and involve watching classic entertainment films and classic educational and training films. Developing connoisseurship in educational films would be time-consuming and extensive; however, films are linear media. With some exceptions, they are typically one to three hours in duration. In contrast, digital games are interactive environments that are not always linear and require a much greater investment of time. A typical video game may take between one and 30 hours to complete, and other games—such as MMORPGs—may have no ending and require an investment of hundreds of hours. Is it realistic to foster connoisseurship in educational games and game-based learning? After all, games are not merely sensory experiences, they are interactive experiences. Yet, as games become more pervasive and available in many forms, they also become more integrated in our lives. Developing connoisseurship in game-based learning would certainly require an investment of time, yet fostering this investment in developing connoisseurs may result in creating the type of educational games and game-based learning that actually fulfills the promise of games and educational media.

Perceptual Discriminations

In Belland's proposal for becoming a connoisseur of educational technology, he advocates cultivating knowledge of (a) fine perceptual discriminations, (b) concepts with indeterminate limits, (c) hierarchies of concepts that delineate qualities in finer levels of distinction and (d) principles. Perceptual discriminations center around sensory experiences and the fine distinctions of how elements related to sensory experiences operate. Eisner (1998) maintains that there are distinctions

Aesthetics, Inquiry and Research • **143**

between fine characteristics of wine that a wine connoisseur may perceive that the novice might not notice. Belland (1991) uses the example of typefaces that are used in the design of print material. A novice may not understand the fine distinctions that a typeface such as *New Century Schoolbook* possesses or understand how the use of that typeface can convey a sense of permanence and authority to a reader. While Belland (1991) acknowledges that some sensory experiences may be beyond the capacity or sensory limits of some people, for most, discriminations can be fostered and developed. In Belland's example of typefaces, he proposes that a novice designer might sit with an expert as they discussed typefaces and, through peripheral participation, begin to develop knowledge of fine distinctions conveyed through the use of different typefaces. Belland further contends that instructional/learning designers need to move beyond the surface sensory experiences and examine differences among the fine distinctions, understand the subtleties and nuances, and understand how the work fits within the larger body of work.

Digital games are sensory experiences that may include visuals, music, interactive sound, audio dialogue, motion, animation and narrative, along with game mechanics. A connoisseur in game-based learning would need to understand the aesthetics of a game-based environment and how it supports the desired learning processes and goals. A connoisseur of educational games and game-based learning would first need a comprehensive knowledge of game genres. Digital games include a diverse group of genres. Different genres include different types of aesthetics, mechanics, dynamics and even cultures. There may be some commonalities between genres and even overlapping game mechanics, but there are also some very broad differences. In addition to knowing about different game genres, the connoisseur would need to have a thorough understanding of the types of game mechanics commonly used in different game genres and understand how these mechanics might foster various higher-order thinking skills. Game mechanics are the rules of the game and the types of interaction afforded and constrained by the rules. While a connoisseur would certainly have a comprehensive knowledge of game genres and the relationship between game mechanics, game-based learning is a broad term and is often used for more than just games. Game-based learning also encompasses environments that are not necessarily games but include game-like elements such as virtual world environments. A connoisseur would also have to have considerable experience with these environments to understand the nuances and fine distinctions in the affordances of the environments provided by different applications.

Principles

Belland advocates two main principles for developing connoisseurship: lifelong learning and courage of one's convictions. The connoisseur should continually learn and draw knowledge from research, theory, philosophy, criticism and experiences. This principle is certainly valuable for game-based learning. Game design

144 • Aesthetics, Inquiry and Research

is a field that appropriates, integrates and weaves together a wide array of the arts along with science-based disciplines. Game design encompasses many domains including programming, literature, psychology, fine art, graphic design, sound design and music. Developing connoisseurship in game-based learning would encompass diverse knowledge in how these are manifest in games, along with experience playing games of all sorts (both contemporary and those considered to be "classics"). The connoisseur would also have to develop knowledge and experience with educational games and game-based learning environments—both firsthand when possible and through research and reflection when the media is not available. Developing connoisseurship would require learning the history of games and game-based learning and an appreciation for the pioneers and trailblazers.

The second principle Belland advocates for connoisseurs is "courage of one's convictions." The connoisseur must believe that her/his experiences and judgments are valid, even when they conflict with others. The connoisseur's convictions are altered only based on new experiences and not due to persuasion or conflict with others. This is particularly important for developing connoisseurs in game-based learning. With media that historically has been designed primarily for male recreation, those who are outside will need to rely on their knowledge, experience and the courage of their convictions particularly to break with tradition in how games are discussed.

Strategies

Belland (1991) maintains that the intellectual strategies of the connoisseur are like problem-solving inasmuch as the connoisseur must remain open to new ideas and experiences while applying recollections of previous experiences. He further contends that the strategies employed by connoisseurs also differ from problem-solving because, with connoisseurship, the experience begs interpretation rather than being framed as a problem. According to Belland, connoisseurship strategies focus on:

1. Maintaining "extensive and intensive" involvement
2. Interrelating new experiences with previous experiences
3. Ensuring that critical dimensions have been observed and analyzed
4. Reflecting on new experiences in relation to previous experiences

Finally, Belland (1991) provided a list of actions to help foster the development of connoisseurs. I adapted his list for the purpose of developing connoisseurship in game-based learning (Dickey, 2012).[1]

1. Connoisseurs need to experience the "classic" works in the field of games and game-based learning.
2. Connoisseurs need to review and critique all forms of games and game-based learning environments.

3. Connoisseurs need to interact with a heterogeneous array of individuals who are in various stages of developing connoisseurship in the field.
4. Connoisseurs need to read critical literature in the field as well as artistic criticism published in popular online press.
5. Connoisseurs need to develop courage to hold and express unique observations and analyses and be able to interact with others based on them.
6. Professors of educational technologies/instructional designers will need to study the extent to which connoisseurship in game-based learning can be developed in order to prepare scholars.
7. Researchers will need to examine the extent to which connoisseurship in game-based learning will improve the gathering of data even under traditional paradigms.

The connoisseurship model would help to yield greater insight into the design and integration of game-based learning by encompassing insights, skills and techniques from artistic disciplines and by providing a new lens for looking at interactive media.

Educational Criticism

While connoisseurship is a relevant step for those involved in the design of game-based learning (and indeed any area of instructional/learning design), connoisseurship in itself, as Eisner notes, is primarily an internal act. Connoisseurship is of value for fostering and developing designers who are informed (Belland, 1991), but the purpose of connoisseurship is not to persuade or inform, but to appreciate and understand. In contrast, criticism is the "public face" of connoisseurship. Criticism has long been used in the arts and is, as Eisner (1998, p. 86) contends, "the art of disclosure." The purpose of a critic is to illuminate qualities of a piece of work (novel, film, painting, etc.) and to appraise. It is the public side of connoisseurship and as such is a form of inquiry that offers insight into game-based learning. Although most of Eisner's (1998) examples of the application of criticism center around classrooms and classroom-based practice, Belland, Duncan and Deckman (1991) argue that criticism holds much relevance for the field of instructional/learning design. At the time of Belland, Duncan and Deckman's (1991) discussion of the application of criticism as a means of assessing instructional design, much of the field centered on the design and development of media that borrowed and appropriated strategies from mainstream media (film, television, comics, etc.). These are fields in which criticism is common practice. Educational criticism is particularly applicable for game-based learning because it involves looking at the context of both an educational experience and methods or elements of a type of media (games) in which criticism is part of the wider discourse. Criticism is a common method for the review and appraisal of commercial games and, as such, criticism is part of the field. Criticism involves more than likes and dislikes about a performance, game, painting, etc.; it requires one

146 • Aesthetics, Inquiry and Research

to be a connoisseur and well versed in the qualities of the work and able to not only identify qualities and translate them into experiences for the reader, but also make judgments about work based on its antecedent and context. Critics must be conversant in past work and the context for the work in review and be not only conversant with the qualities, but also able to appraise, make judgments and justify those judgments through the qualities and the context of what is observed or experienced. Criticism also involves making vivid the recounting of a work or experience, of knowing what to illuminate and how to reconstruct the work or experience for a reader within a wider context of the field of the work.

According to Eisner (1998), educational criticism includes the four dimensions of *description, interpretation, evaluation* and *thematics*. Eisner contends that these dimensions are not a structure per se but rather should be viewed as a heuristic for constructing an educational critique, not as prescriptive rules or an outline. Descriptions create a public work of the experience that is being presented. The description needs to be vivid to allow the reader to vicariously see or experience the media and/or environment. To do this, critics must understand the qualities of the media or environment and the distinctions. To describe an environment or media, one must be able to make sense of the experience, provide a context and highlight qualities to recreate it for readers. The purpose is not merely to recount but to inform and help the reader's understanding. One of the key aspects of description is to provide a vivid account to enable the reader to understand the emotions or how it feels being in the setting. The critic must be selective in perception and disclosure. As Eisner (1998, p. 90) notes, "a good teacher knows what to neglect," and so must a critic. A description should provide an account that addresses and is attentive to the following:

- Qualities
- Context (antecedents)
- Vivid account
- Selective content
- Account of emotions

The second dimension in Eisner's (1998) heuristic is interpretation. Whereas the description provides the depiction, the interpretation provides the meaning behind the depiction. The critic provides an understanding of the meanings of the actions within the context of the setting. The interpretation might include theoretical ideas to account for the description, although, as Eisner warns, theories should be viewed as guides, not static procedures for predication. Eisner advocates using theory to "satisfy rationality, to deepen conversation, to raise fresh questions" (p. 95). The critics' justification for the interpretation is provided in the context of the description.

The third dimension of educational criticism is evaluation. Evaluation is used to determine the educational value of the experience described and interpreted. According to Eisner (1998), educational critics must also appraise the experience to determine if the experience is, as Dewey (1938/1998) characterizes, non-educational, miseducational or educational. According to Dewey (1938/1998), education is growth, and when there is no growth, there is no education. Miseducation is the condition when education is insufficient or without direction, in contrast to an educational experience that provides direction, challenge and balance for the learner. However, making those determinations requires the critic to make judgments, and judgments are based on a sense of purpose and ideal. In the case of education, values tend to shift based upon dominant epistemology, culture, politics and economics of the time. Eisner advocates not relying upon objective standards for basing judgment but instead employing criteria upon which to base evaluation ("the discussion of form in relation to matter" [Dewey, 1934, p. 322]).

The fourth dimension outlined by Eisner (1998) is thematics. Within every educational experience, there are features in common with other similar experiences (classrooms, schools, teachers, media, etc.). According to Eisner, individual instances can have significance for the grouping to which they belong. Eisner states, "The theme, embedded in the particular situation, extends beyond the situation itself" (1998, p. 103). To distinguish themes requires the critic to identify dominant elements and pervasive qualities that reoccur within the observation.

Educational criticism offers much relevance for the study of game-based learning as a method of inquiry to guide design, inquiry and practice. The critic must be knowledgeable and able to identify the relevant qualities and make judgments about experience based on extensive knowledge of content and context. This means the critic must be a connoisseur of different genres of games and the qualities that different genres may bring to the learning environment. The critic must be conversant with different examples and contexts of game-based learning and different aspects of game design. The critic must be able to vividly describe the experience as well as interpret the meaning behind the actions, design, context and practice. The critic must be able to appraise the game and/ or experience. With regards to a game or game-based experience, this would require "an intimate, well-informed, and insightful understanding of the technological medium itself and the effects if may have in human experience" (Belland, Duncan & Deckman, 1991, p. 153). As a method of inquiry, educational criticism provides a public forum for the media (artifact) or experience, as well as the public practice of disclosure that is innate to the act of criticism. The critic must both vividly describe the media and/or experience, as well as demonstrate in the interpretation and evaluation the trajectory of thought and insight of how s/he arrived at that position. Eisner (1998) and Belland, Duncan and Deckman (1991) argue that scientific inquiry is rarely public but is instead merely a report from the researcher.

Belland, Duncan and Deckman (1991) outline six areas in which educational criticism can contribute to the understanding of technological objects and their educational effect. Although they were discussing the technology and media of the early 1990s, these six areas are relevant to the study of game-based learning.

148 • Aesthetics, Inquiry and Research

The following includes each of the six contributions criticism offers to educational technology as outlined by Belland, Duncan and Deckman (1991).

1. Criticism could help explain a technological object or process in terms of the quality of the relationship between its content and its form.
2. Criticism could help explain a technological object or process in terms of the relationships among the constituent parts and the whole.
3. Criticism may provide insight into the unifying theme(s) and design(s) that help to hold the technological object or process together in all its richness and complexity.
4. Criticism may reveal the nature of the intimate experience a well-informed, sensitive and reflective individual has with the process or product of educational technology.
5. Criticism may reveal the grounds upon which interpretations and judgments of the processes and objects of the educational technology may rest, as well as the consequences the object and/or process may entail in human experience.
6. Criticism may serve to synthesize the knowledge derived from disparate research processes into more comprehensive theory.

Aesthetics in games and game-based environments impact experiences. The critic has an understanding of game aesthetics, mechanics and genres and a deep understanding of the relationship between these elements and human interaction. Games are the composite of different aesthetics and design, and the critic can help provide insight and understanding of the relationship of the parts to the whole. The critic can also provide insight into both design and practice in game-based learning. The critic has specialized understanding and rich experience with games, game aesthetics and mechanics, as well as educational practices of game-based learning and the wider discipline of education. The critic has insight into the impact and consequences of integrating game-based learning. Finally, the value of applying educational criticism as a method of inquiry for game-based learning is that it would add to understandings of the relationship between aesthetics and learning. Aesthetics are more than mere graphics, but are differing aesthetics of perspective, narrative, agent, environment and interaction. Educational criticism provides a means of getting inside the design and, as such, it should be part of the research continuum in learning design, particularly with regards to arts-based media.

As with all modes of inquiry, validity is of great importance. Eisner (1998) describes three ways in which educational criticism meets reasonable standards of credibility:

1. Structural corroboration: the triangulation of data and evidence to support judgments
2. Consensual validation: the extent to which there is consensus or agreement among other critics
3. Referential adequacy: the extent to which the critic's interpretations can be located and that the reader is able to follow the critic's reasoning about the qualities addressed

Eisner's educational criticism is an important paradigm for research about game-based learning. The four dimensions outlined by Eisner provide guidance on how to approach game-based learning in many forms (as media, as a classroom experience, as an informal educational activity, etc.). Criticism has long been part of the review process for the arts and popular media. Critique is common to reviews of popular games. Game-based learning can involve more than a game; it also encompasses the use of game-like elements for teaching and, in that case, educational criticism can help inform and provide insight about the application of the game-based learning experience. The four dimensions establish the critic's expertise and validity in accounts of using games and game-based elements for teaching and learning.

Qualitative Criticism

When offering an alternative paradigm of inquiry for consideration and extolling its strengths, one risks framing the new paradigm in opposition to existing paradigms. Connoisseurship and criticism provide an arts-based mode of inquiry that offers a means of gaining insight into aesthetics and experiences. Criticism provides the necessary component of evaluation that is missing in current research about educational games and game-based learning. Yet connoisseurship and criticism should not be considered in opposition to science-based methods of inquiry, but instead as part of a continuum of modes of inquiry. To that end, Swartz (1993) provides an insightful model of synthesizing criticism and qualitative research that he terms *qualitative criticism*. Qualitative criticism combines methods of qualitative research and criticism.

Qualitative research is typically used to explore a phenomenon or answer a question through the collection and analysis of non-statistical data. Qualitative researchers establish trustworthiness through prolonged and persistent engagement in the field and triangulation of data with other forms of data collection, including interviews, observations, documents and notes. Central to qualitative inquiry is time spent in the field and the role of the researcher as a participant in the construction of understandings. In contrast, the purpose of criticism is evaluation. However, in order to evaluate, the critic must also be a connoisseur. Becoming a connoisseur involves prolonged and persistent engagement to develop an in-depth understanding of the qualities, distinctions and antecedent knowledge of the context.

Central to qualitative research is the understanding that inquiry is value-bound and so is the researcher. According to Swartz (1993, p. 5), "a qualitative critic substitutes his or her connoisseurship and experience for prolonged and persistent engagement, and selects a specific event or object to critique instead of collecting a large array of data over time." Swartz argues that qualitative criticism includes the three qualities of criticism (description, interpretation and evaluation), yet also includes the qualities of qualitative inquiry, which address the "values, knowledge, and experience of the creator of the thing or act being evaluated" (Swartz, 1993, p. 5).

150 • Aesthetics, Inquiry and Research

Swartz maintains that to understand the subject (media or process) of criticism, it is judicious to inquire about the values, standards and experience of the creator/s. The benefits of the synthesis of qualitative methods and criticism are (a) the inclusion of evaluation and judgment that is not part of qualitative inquiry and (b) awareness of the intent of the creator of the thing or act being evaluated.

Conclusion

The purpose of this chapter is to examine connoisseurship and educational criticism as a means for critiquing and "getting inside" game-based learning environments. The connoisseurship model advocated by Belland (1991) provides an arts-based alternative to the existing science-based paradigms of qualitative and quantitative research methodologies; yet as Eisner (1998) acknowledges, connoisseurship is primarily an internal process. Connoisseurship and, in particular, the model adapted from Belland's work would provide guidance for fostering designers who are conversant in the many aspects of games and game-based learning. Educational criticism would help establish the expertise of reviewers to ensure that there is validity in both design and accounting of game-based learning.

Aesthetics is a broad and diverse term in game design, but it is a fundamentally important aspect of games that is greatly overlooked in discourse about game-based learning. Aesthetics are more than mere graphics; they are intertwined in all aspects of design. The aesthetics impact behavior and cognition and are the foundation of the experience. Connoisseurship and educational criticism provide guidance for understanding the differing aesthetics in games and game-based learning and how they shape experiences. Fostering connoisseurship and integrating educational criticism in game-based learning would certainly require an investment of time, yet this investment may result in creating the type of educational games and game-based learning experiences that fulfill the promise of games and learning.

Note

1. John Belland was my advisor, and I take the liberty of adapting his work because I believe he would have approved.

References

Belland, J.C. (1991). Developing connoisseurship in educational technology. In D. Hlynka & J.C. Belland (Eds.), *Paradigms regained: The uses of illuminative, semiotic and post-modern criticism as modes of inquiry in educational technology* (pp. 23–35). Englewood Cliffs, NJ: Educational Technology Publications.

Belland, J.C., Duncan, J.K., & Deckman, M. (1991). Criticism as methodology for research in educational technology. In D. Hlynka & J.C. Belland (Eds.), *Paradigms regained: The uses of illuminative, semiotic and post-modern criticism as modes of inquiry in educational technology* (pp. 151–166). Englewood Cliffs, NJ: Educational Technology Publications.

Dewey, J. (1934). *Art as experience.* New York, NY: The Berkley Publishing Group.

Dewey, J. (1938/1998). *Experience and education.* Indianapolis, IN: Kappa Delta Pi.
Dickey, M. D. (2012). Aesthetics and game-based learning: Applying John C. Belland's connoisseurship model as a mode of inquiry. In S. Fee & B. Belland (Eds.), *The role of criticism in understanding problem solving: Honoring the work of John C. Belland* (Explorations in the Learning Sciences, Instructional Systems and Performance Technologies) (pp. 101–114). New York, NY: Springer.
Eisner, E. W. (1998). *The enlightened eye: Qualitative inquiry and the enhancement of educational practice.* Upper Saddle River, NJ: Merrill.
Hlynka, D., & Belland, J. (1991). *Paradigms regained: The uses of illuminative, semiotic and post-modern criticism as modes of inquiry in educational technology.* Englewood Cliffs, NJ: Educational Technology Publications.
Swartz, J. D. (1993). A study combining criticism and qualitative research techniques for appraising classroom media. Paper presented at the *Annual Meeting of the American Educational Research Association,* Atlanta, GA, April 12–16.

Index

Page locators in *italics* indicate illustrations.

Abernathy, T. 68–9, 84
achievement 67
Achtman, R. L. 30
action games 28–31, 136–7
Active Worlds (virtual world) 104
Adams, C. 18–19, 33, 103, 118; *Fundamentals of Construction and Simulation Game Design* 31–2
Adams, D. M. 19
Adams, E. 9, 15–16, 29, 31, 43, 48, 68–9, 73, 103–6, 127–8, 135
ADVENT (game) 44
Adventure (game) 44
adventure games 13–20, 43–4, 59–60, 131–2
aesthetics, definitions 6–7
"Aesthetics of a Virtual World" (Gigliotti) 49–50
affective domain, the 82–4, *83*
Alice (game) 105
AlphaWorld (virtual world) 35
American McGee's 105
Amory, A. 18–19, 33
amusement parks 110–12, 120
anchored instruction 106
Anderson, L. W. 130
Ang, C. S. 26
animation 85, 93–5, 97–8
Annetta, L. 26
anticipation 96–7
Apnes, J. 44
appeal 98
appearance of characters 21–2, 87, 92–4, 100
arcade games 28, 41
archetypes 88–93, 99–100
architecture 109, 120–1
arcs 68–9, 97
Aristotle 4, 49
art, games as 7
Art as Experience (Dewey) 3
art design, aesthetics and 6–7
"art of disclosure" 145

arts-based methods 141
Asteroids (game) 28
Atkinson, R. K. 86
atmospherics 110
attitudes 83–4
attractiveness 93–4
attributes 21–2, 135
audio puzzles 15, 132
authoring tool kit 19
automatons 62
avatars 34–5, 47, 71, 90
Avery, T. 94
avoidance strategies 129

backgrounds: of action games 28; of adventure games 13–14; of MMORPGs 23–4; of RPGs 20; of simulations 31; of strategy games 32; virtual worlds 34–5
backstory 60–3, 76
Bailey, F. 113
balance 31
Baltra, A. 17
Barab, S. A. 113
Barthes, R. 57, 76n1; *An Introduction to the Structural Analysis of Narrative* 76n1
Bartle, R. 20, 44
Bates, J. 85, 94
Bavelier, D. 30
Baylor, A. L. 86
behaviors 84–5, 109–10
beliefs 48, 83
believable agents 85
Belland, J. 141–5, 147; *Paradigms Regained* 141
Bernstein, J. 68–9
Bers, M. 112–13
Bickmore, T. 85
Billinghurst, M. 85
blaxxun (virtual world) 35
Bloom, B. 9, 82–4, 126, 130
board games 41

153

154 • Index

body design 94
body language 45
bots 85
boundaries 115–16, 120
bounty quests 132–3
Braswell, R. 27
Brecht, B. 49–50
Brown, J. S. 107
Bruckman, A. 5, 71–2
Bruner, J. 57
Burgos, D. 19
BUTORSTAR (game) 27

cameras 15, 33, 42–3, 65–6
Campbell, J. 74; *The Hero with a Thousand Faces*
    63–4
Campbell, L. 85
Carbonaro, M. 27
Carnegie Mellon University 44
Carson, D. 110–11, 117–18; "Environmental
    Storytelling: Creating Immersive 3D Worlds
    Using Lessons Learned from the Theme Park
    Industry" 110
Case-based Learning 72
case studies 106
casinos 109, 120
Cassell, J. 85, 112–13
Catcher in the Rye, The (Salinger) 45
catharsis 49–50
cathedrals 108–9, 120
causal patterns 62
Cavallari, B. 17–18
challenges/mechanics in adventure games
    15–16, 18
Chang, K. 85
character-based narrative 59
character design 81–102; affective domain 82–4;
    development of 87–93; dialogue 98–9; for
    game-based learning 86–93; heuristic for
    99–100; overview 81–2; pedagogical agents
    84–7; visual representation 93–8
characteristics 17–18, 115
characterizing function 83
characters 87–93; in action games 28–9; in
    adventure games 14, 16, 19–20, 60; design
    of game-based 86; development and quests
    65–6; dialogue for 98–9; roles and functions
    of 75, 87–93, *90*; in RPGs 21–2; in simulation
    31; strategy games 32
Charitos, D. 114–17
chat worlds 34–5
checkpoint 29, 36n5
Chelburg, D. 113
Chen, H. P. 26
chess 125
"Chess as an Art Form" (Humble) 125
Childress, M. D. 27
choice 67
Civilization (game) 42
classroom-based practice 145

Classroom Multiplayer Presential Game
    (CMPG) 27
class selection in RPGs 21
Clodius, J. A. 71
clues for solving puzzles 15–16, 35–6n2
CMPG (Classroom Multiplayer Presential
    Game) 27
CMS (construction and management simulation
    games) 31
cognition, game mechanics and *130*
cognitive: apprenticeships 107; domains 82–5,
    130; overloads 26
Coleridge, S. T. 48
collaboration 20, 23–4, 27, 70–1
collective unconscious 88
Collins, A. 107
color selection 117–18
Colossal Cave Adventure, The (game) 13, 43–4
combination puzzles 15, 132
communal play 70
competition 13, 125–6
computers 19, 20
Computers as Theater (Laurel) 49
concepts 142
conditions of learning (Gagne) 106
conflicts 13, 19, 75, 93
connoisseurship and game-based learning
    141–6
construction and management simulation games
    (CMS) 31
construction mechanics 129
constructivism 128
consumer behavior 110
consummation 3
context 106
controls 46–50, *47*
conversational function 85
Cordova, D. L. 67
core game mechanics *129*
core mechanics 126–9
cosmetic attributes 135
Costikyan, G. 7
courage of one's convictions 143–4
Crawford, C. 7
creative thinking 4
critical paradigm 141–2
criticism, educational 141, 145–50
Crowther, W. 43–4
Csikszentmihalyi, M. 48
culminations 2, 61
curiosity 66
Curran, A. 50
Curtis, P.: *LambdaMOO* 34
cutscenes 60–1, 76

Daniels, F. 69
Dantas, A. 27
Darken, R. P. 113–14
Deckman, M. 145, 147
declarative knowledge 133–4

Index • 155

Dede, C. 5, 71
description 146
design: of adventure games 15–20; of agents 86; body 94; character 87–93; of educational material 51–2; emotional 84; face 93–4; guidelines 72–6; heuristics 74–5, 76n6; identification 33; interface 18; learning 4; of MMORPGs 23–4; narratives in game 57–8; socio-constructive 27; space 119–21; top-down 41; of virtual environments 112–16; visual 93–8, 116–18
Dewey, J. 1–4, 103, 106, 147; *Art as Experience* 3
Diablo (game) 65, 104
dialogue 15, 98–9, 131
dice 20
Dickey, M. D. 76n6, 113; "Engaging by Design" 51–2; "Game Design and Learning: A Conjectural Analysis of How Massively Multiple Online Role-Playing Games (MMORPGs) Foster Intrinsic Motivation" 132–4, *134*
diegetic immersion 48
dimensions 103–6, 119
direct control 16, 47
discriminations 143
Disney, Walt 94, 121n3
Disney theme parks 110–12
Doom (game) 42
Dormans, J. 127–8
Doswell, J. T. 85
Dot and The Line: A Romance in Lower Mathematics, The (animation) (Jones) 98
Duguid, P. 107
Duncan, J. K. 145, 147
Dungeon Master (game) 20
Dungeons and Dragons (game) 20, 70
Dye, M. W. G. 30
dynamic organization 4

edges 115–16
education: adventure games for 17–20; connoisseurship and 141; implications for 51–3, 70–1, 128–9; technology for 141; virtual environments and 112–13
educational criticism 145–50
educators, guidelines for 53
Eisner, E. W. 4, 141–2, 145–50
Elder Scrolls (game) 65
e-learning 27
elements 3, 114–15
Elias, V. L. 27
elimination mechanics 129
Ellis, S. 19
embodiment 46–50, 85
emergent culture 34
emotional content 6
Emotional Design (Norman) 84
emotional intelligence 84
emotioneering techniques 98

emotions: in adventure games 60; and character design 82–5; in design 84; Dewey on 2–3; dimensions of 105–6, 119; proximity and 71
empathy 85
endogenous fantasy 73
"Engaging by Design" (Dickey) 51–2
Entraining Effect 62
"Environmental Storytelling: Creating Immersive 3D Worlds Using Lessons Learned from the Theme Park Industry" (Carson) 110
environment design 103–24; dimensions 103–6; guidance 118–21; and instructional/learning relevance 106–7; and physical spaces 107–12; virtual 112–18
environments: in action games 28; and perspective 14–15, 20–1; virtual 35, 112–16
episodes 69
escort quest 133
ethical dimensions 105, 119
evaluation 146–7
EverQuest (game) 70
EverQuest2 (EQ2) (game) 26, 104
evocative places 109–10
exaggeration 97
exhibition design 108
exits 43
exogenous fantasy 73
experience design 107–8
experience points (XP) 22
experiences: defined 1; Dewey on 1–2, 4, 106; and games 1–11; sensory 142–3; value for learning 3
externalizing understanding 128

Fable (game) 65
face design 93–4
fantasy 19, 48, 66, 71, 73
FedEx quests 133
feelings *see* emotions
feng shui 114
Fernández-Manjón, B. 19, 27
Fernández-Vara, C. 19
Ferris Bueller's Day Off (film) 50
FH *(FORmosaHope)* (game) 26
films 142
first-person perspective 43
FitzGerald, P. T. 85
flow 2–3, 48, 114
follow-through action 97
FORmosaHope (FH) (game) 26
fourth wall 50
Franklin, T. 113
Freeman, D. 98–9
Freytag, G. 49
Fuentes-Fernández, R. 27
functional attributes 135
functions 73, 85, 87–93
Fundamentals of Construction and Simulation Game Design (Adams) 31–2

156 • Index

Gagne, R. 106
gambling behavior 109
game-based learning 5–6; activities 28; character design for 86–93; environments 103–18; goals of 69–70; guidance 53, 118–21; inquiry and research into 141–51; integrating narrative into 72–6
"Game Design and Learning: A Conjectural Analysis of How Massively Multiple Online Role-Playing Games (MMORPGs) Foster Intrinsic Motivation" (Dickey) 132–4, *134*
game genres 13–39; action games 28–31, 136–7; adventure games 13–20, 59–60; examples of 64–6; Massively Multiplayer Online Role-playing Games (MMORPGs) 23–8, 70; role-playing games (RPGs) 20–3, 26–8; simulations 31–2; strategy games 32–3; virtual worlds 34–5
Game Master (GM) 20
game mechanics 125–39; for adventure, MMORPGs, and action and casual games 131–7; aesthetics and 125–6; and cognition *130*; core 126–9; secondary 129–31
Game Object Model (GOM) 19
gameplay and mechanics 22, 29, 31–3
games: aesthetics in 6–7; conflict within 13; dimensions 103–6; endings of 23, 36n4; environment design dimensions 103–6; graphical 41–3; open-style 68; spaces 14–16; tabletop 20; text-based 43–5; time management of 13, 35n1; user-extensible 45
Gee, J.P. 5
gender 21, 136–7
genres *see* game genres
Gigliotti, C. 52–3; "Aesthetics of a Virtual World" 49–50
Gillen, J. 113
GM *(Game Master)* 20
Goal-based Scenarios 72
goals 15–18
god's-eye view 41
Gold, R. 26
GOM (Game Object Model) 19
Gooch, B. 26
Graesser, A. C. 86
Grand Theft Auto (game) 106
graphical environment 14
Green, C. S. 30
Green, R. 27
guidance: for character dialogue 98–9; for game-based learning design 118–21; for learner positioning 53; for narrative in game-based learning 72–6
Guide Wars (game) 70

Habitat (Lucasfilm) 34
Hamlet on the Holodeck (Murray) 48
Harris, P. 3
Harry Potter (series) 59

Hawpe, L. 62
health of characters 137
Heim, M. 114
Hendersen, D. 81–2, 84
herald, function of the 89
hero, role of the 88, 100n3
hero's journey 63–4, *65*
Hero with a Thousand Faces, The (Campbell) 63–4
heuristics: for character design 99–100; for educational design 127; Eisner's 146; for narrative design 74–5, 76n6
hidden objects 17, 35n1
Hlynka, Denis 141–2; *Paradigms Regained* 141
Humble, P. N. 125–6; "Chess as an Art Form" 125
Hunicke, R. 6
HyperCard 18, 33, 36n6

identification signs 115
illusion of life 94
immersion 7, 47–50, 87
information processing 30, 114
inquiry and research 141–51; connoisseurship and game-based learning 141–5; educational criticism 145–9; qualitative criticism 149–50
instructional/learning and environment design 106–7
intelligence, emotional 84
interactive fiction *see* adventure games
interactivity 7, 16–17, 58, 85
interfaces: action games 30; adventure games 16–17; MMORPGs 26; RPGs 23; simulation 32
interpretation 146
intersections 116, 121
Introduction to the Structural Analysis of Narrative, An (Barthes) 76n1
inventories: adventure games 16–17; manipulation 131; RPGs 22; strategy games 33
Isbister, K. 86–7, 93–4
isometric view 42
Iyengar, S. S. 67

Jang, Y. 26–7
jigsaw puzzles 15, 132
Johnston, L. 85, 93–4, 96, 98
Johnston, O. 93
Jonassen, D. H. 128
Jones, C. 94, 98; *Dot and The Line: A Romance in Lower Mathematics, The* (animation) 98
journeys 63–4
Ju, E. 18
judgments 147
Jung, C. G. 88, 91

Klettke, B. 86
knowledge, types of 133–4

Krathwohl, D. R. 130
Krumdieck, S. 27

LambdaMOO 34
landmarks 115, 120
language learning 26
Lasseter, J. 95–6, 98
Launching Effect 62
Laurel, B. 19, 49, 52–3, 91; *Computers as Theater* 49
learning: and action games 30–1; and adventure games 17–20; aesthetic experiences for 3–6; connoisseurship and game-based 141–5; lifelong 143–4; and role-playing games 26–8; simulations and strategy games 33–4; from virtual reality and virtual worlds 112–13
LeBlanc, M. 6
Leendertz, V. 19
Lepper, M. R. 67
Lester, J. C. 85
levels 22, 29, 67
Lien, C. J. 26
lifelong learning 143–4
lighting 111
literature, character roles in 87–93
lives of characters 28–9, 137
locations 13, 43
locks 15
long-form narrative 68, *69*
loots 22
Lu, Y. L. 26
Lucasfilm: *Habitat* 34
Lui, C. 113
Lynch, K. 115–17

MacNamara, A. 19
McQuiggan, S. W. 85
Mahmood, S. 26
Malcolm in the Middle (television show) 50
Malone, T. W. 17, 66–7
Manero, B. 19–20, 93
Marsh, T. 113–14
Martínez-Ortiz, I. 19
Massively Multiplayer Online Role-playing Games (MMORPGs) 23–8, 44–5, 132–4
Mathevet, R. 27
Max Payne (game) 46
Mayer, R. E. 19
Mayles, J. 113
mazes 15, 131–2
mechanics: in action games 29; in adventure games 15–16; collection 129; gameplay and 22; in strategy games 32
mechanics, dynamics and aesthetics (MDA) framework 6
Medal of Honor (game) 105
media 39, 55, 79, 102, 124
memory 81–2
mentor, role of 88–9

messenger quests 133
metacognitive knowledge 133, 135
meta-inferencing 67–8
"Method, The": Stanislavski, C. 19
Michotte, A. E. 62
Microsoft's User Research Group 81
Miller, C. H. 98
miseducation 147
Mitrovic, A. 85
MMORPGs (Massively Multiplayer Online Role-playing Games) 23–8, 44–5, 132–4
Moar, M. 113
MOOs (Multi-user Object-Oriented) 34, 43–4
MOOSE Crossing (text-based environment) 71–2
moral code 21
Moreno, K. N. 86
Moreno-Ger, P. 19, 27
Mortensen, T. E. 7
motion 94–5
motivation: and character design 93; and games 17; and problem-solving 61–2, 66–70
movement 94–5
mudders 34
Multi-user Domains (MUDs) 20
Multi-user Dungeons (MUDs) 20, 34, 43–4
Multi-user Object-Oriented (MOOs) 34, 43–4
Murray, J. 50; *Hamlet on the Holodeck* 48
museums 108–9, 119–20
Myers, D. 7
Myst (game) 14, 59

Naicker, K. 18–19, 33
Nancy Drew (game) 14, 46
narrative: action games 28; adventure games 14, 19, 59–60; environments 31–2, 110–12; in game-based learning 72–6; immersion 48; long-form 68; MMORPGs 23–5; questions for educators 53; RPGs 20–1; type of 73–4; virtual worlds 35
narrative design 57–79; description of 57–8; heuristics 75–6; integration guidelines 72–5; structure 58–72
narrator 45
Nass, C. 86
navigation 114–15
nested objects 19
networking 35, 84
Neverwinter Nights (platform) 27
Nibbaragandla, K. 86
nine old men 94
non-aesthetic experiences 2
non-player characters (NPCs) 14, 21
Norman, D. 84
Norrath (game) 104
notes taking 18
NPC (non-player characters) 14, 21
NUCLEO (e-learning framework) 27

158 • Index

objects 43; in adventure games 16; nested 19; in virtual spaces 114–15
obstacles 75–6
off-the-shelf games 5
OnLive! Traveler (virtual world) 35
Open Sims (virtual world) 104
open-style games 68
organizing function 83
Oughton, J. 83
overlapping action 97
Oz project 85

Pacheco, A. 126
Pac-Man (game) 28, 41
Palace, The (virtual world) 34–5
Papargyris, A. 26
paradigm, critical 141–2
Paradigms Regained (Belland and Hlynka) 141
PARC (Xerox Palo Alto Research Center) 34
Parisi, T. 34–5
Parrish, P. E. 3–4, 106
Parrish's principles 4
Passini, R. 115
paths for navigation 111, 116, 120
pedagogical agents 84–7, 93
perceptual discriminations 142–3
personality 87, 91–2
perspective: in action games 29; in adventure games 14–15; in MMORPGs 26; questions for educators 53; in RPGs 20–1, 23; in simulation 32; in strategy games 33 *see also* point of view (POV)
Pesce, M. 34–5
physical space design 119–21
Pierre, E. 83
platforms of adventure games 17
plausibility 62–3, 67
player perspective 41–55; educational implications of 51–3; embodiment 46–50; learning guidelines 53; narrative 45–6; positioning 41–5
players 21, 28
plot-based narrative 59
plot hooks 60
plot integration 76
point and click 14, 16, 47
point of view (POV) 41, 45–6, 53 *see also* perspective
Polkinghorne, D. E. 62
Pong (game) 41, 43
pose-to-pose action 97
positioning, player 41–6
Poulymenakou, A. 41
power-ups 137
Prensky, M. 5, 126
pre-rendered games 15
principles 142–4
problem-based learning 106
problems 18, 62–3, 66–70

procedural knowledge 133–5
programming skills 27
progressive mechanics 127–8
project-based learning 106
psychomotor domain 82–3
puzzles 131–2; environment 15, 132; inventory manipulation 15; solving 13; types of 15–16
pyramid of dramatic structure (Freytag) 49

Quake (game) 42
qualitative criticism 149–50
Quest for Independence (simulation) (Quinn) 33
quests: archetypes in 88–93; character development and 65–6; and character mechanics 132–4; collection 133; goodwill 133; in MMORPGs 23–5; and narrative structure 63, 74–5; in RPGs 21–2
"quick twitch" games 28
Quinn, C. N. 17–18, 33; *Quest for Independence* (simulation) 33

race mechanics 129
race selection 21, 117–18
Rankin, Y. 26
Raybourn, E. M.: *Simulation Experience Design Method* 33–4
reaction time 30
reader-response theory 48
realism 106
real-world settings 112
reassurance signs 115
receiving function 83
reflective design 84
replay-ability 21
research: action games 30–1; adventure games 17–20; character design 81–2; emotional proximity 71–2; inquiry and 141–51; pedagogical agents 84–6; qualitative 149–50; RPG/MMORPG 26–8; science-based 5, 141; strategy games 33–4; 3D design problems 113–14; virtual environments 112–13, 116; visual representation 93
Resnick, M. 71
resource management mechanics 129
resources 31–2
responding function 83
retail 109–10
rewards in RPGs 22
Rieber, L. P. 5, 73
Riner, R. D. 71
risk-taking 71
Riven 59
Robinson, J. A. 62
Rogers. S. 110–11, 117–18
role-playing games (RPGs) 71–2; for learning 26–8; and MMORPGs 20–3, 27–8; quests in 64–5; text-based 44–5
roles 46, 87–91

"Roles of Emotion in Believable Agents, The" (Bates) 85
rooms 13, 43
Rouse, R. 68–9, 84
rules 126–7
Ryu, J. 86
Ryu, S. 26–7

Sahimi, S. M. 86
Salinger, J. D.: *Catcher in the Rye, The* 45
Sancho, P. 27
scenario-based learning 106
scenarios 31
Schell, J. 15–16, 91
science-based inquiry 5, 141
scoring systems 137
secondary action 98
Second Life (virtual world) 27, 35, 104, 113
second-person POV 45
Sedano, C. I. 19
seeking mechanics 137
sensory experiences 142–3
settings 75, 104, 106–7, 112
shadow, function of the 89–90
shapeshifter 89
Sheldon, L. 50, 91
Shen, E. 86
Sherry, J. 126
showing rather than telling 98
Sibert, J. L. 113–14
side quests 67
side-scrollers 42
Sierra, J. L. 19
signs for wayfinding 115, 120
SimCity (game) 31, 42
Simpson, J. M. 27
Simulation Experience Design Method (Raybourn) 33–4
simulations 31–3
single-frame games 42
situated immersion 48
situated learning 107
slider puzzles 15, 132
slow In and out spacing 97
small quests 27, 65–6, 132–4, *134*
social interaction 14, 35, 44, 127
social play 23–4
Sony's Community Player (virtual world) 35
sorting mechanics 137
Space Invaders (game) 28, 106
spaces 43, 107–12, 119–21
spatial awareness 30, 114
squash and stretch 95–6
Squire, K. 5
staging 96–7
Stanislavski, C. 93; "The Method" 19
Steinkuehler, C. 26
still-frame design 42
storied spaces 108–9

stories 13, 19, 58–60, 69
storylines 20–1, 59 *see also* narrative
straight-ahead action 97
strategies: of connoisseur 144–5; design 60–1; games 32–4; immersion 48; knowledge 133, 135; narrative 68–70
structure: dramatic 49–50; Freytag's pyramid of *49*; and learning 18; narrative 58–72; story *59*
substructures 68
Super Mario Bros. (game) 42
suspension of disbelief 48
Sutinen, E. 19
Swartz, J. D. 149–50
Syberia (game) 46, 47, 60, 62–3

TACA SIM *(Travel Activity Constraint Adaptation Simulation)* (survey tool) 27
tactical immersion 48
tactical maneuvering mechanics 127–9
taxonomy, Bloom's 9, 82–4, 126, 130
Taylor, L. N. 47–8
technology 6, 141, 147–8
temporal dimensions 119
Tetris (game) 43
text-based environments 13–14
text-based games 43–5
texture 117–18
thematics 146–7
theme parks 110–12
There (virtual world) 35
third-person 42–3, 45–6
Thomas, F. 93–4, 96, 98
three-act story structure 58–63, *59*, 68
3D computer animation 94
3D virtual worlds 34, 113–14
threshold guardian, function of 89
thresholds 116, 120
time management 13, 35n1, 104–5
timing 96
TinyMUD 44
toggling 23, 26
Tomb Raider (Lara Croft) (game) 46, 59
top-down design 41
Towns, S. G. 85
traits and personalities 91–2
Travel Activity Constraint Adaptation Simulation (TACA SIM) (survey tool) 27
trickster 89
Trubshaw, R. 20, 44
2½D views 42
2D side-scroller 42
2D simulations 31–2, 34
typefaces 143

unity 3
University of Essex 44
University of Southern California 68
user-extensible systems 44–5

160 • Index

validity of criticism 148
values 83
Vertex project 113
Vilhjalmsson, H. 85
Villalta, M. 27
Vincent, J. 18–19, 33
Vinni, M. 19
violence 106
virtual realities (VRs) 84–5, 112–16
Virtual Reality Markup Language (VRML) 35
virtual spaces 34–5, 48–9, 85, 112–16
visceral design 84
visual design 93–6, 116–18
visual skills 30
Vogler, C. 63–4, 88–9, 91, 99–100

Wagner, C. 18
Wainess, R. 19
Walling, D. R. 3
Watcharasukarn, M. 27
wayfinding 114–15, 120–1

WebQuests 72
weenies 111, 121n3
Wilensky, U. 71
Wilson, B. G. 4
Wizard of Oz, The 74–5
Woods, D. 43–4
World of Warcraft (game) 70, 104
Worlds Chat (virtual world) 35
Worlds Inc. 35
Wright, P. 113–14

Xerox Palo Alto Research Center (PARC) 34
XP (experience points) 22

Yan, H. 85

Zadarh (game) 19
Zakharov, K. 85
Zaphiris, P. 26
Zork (game) 44
Zubek, R. 6

An environmentally friendly book printed and bound in England by www.printondemand-worldwide.com

This book is made of chain-of-custody materials; FSC materials for the cover and PEFC materials for the text pages.

#0077 - 050516 - C0 - 229/152/10 [12] - CB - 9780415720946